Games of Inheritance

Games of Inheritance

Kabbalah, Tradition, and Authorship in Jorge Luis Borges

YITZHAK LEWIS

Rutgers University Press

New Brunswick, Camden, and Newark, New Jersey

London and Oxford

Rutgers University Press is a department of Rutgers, The State University of New Jersey, one of the leading public research universities in the nation. By publishing worldwide, it furthers the University's mission of dedication to excellence in teaching, scholarship, research, and clinical care.

Library of Congress Cataloging-in-Publication Data

Names: Lewis, Yitzhak, 1981– author.
Title: Games of inheritance : Kabbalah, tradition, and authorship in Jorge Luis Borges / Yitzhak Lewis.
Description: New Brunswick : Rutgers University Press, 2025. | Includes bibliographical references and index.
Identifiers: LCCN 2024046781 | ISBN 9781978843950 (v. 1 ; paperback) | ISBN 9781978843967 (v. 1 ; hardcover) | ISBN 9781978843974 (epub)
Subjects: LCSH: Borges, Jorge Luis, 1899–1986—Criticism and interpretation. | Borges, Jorge Luis, 1899–1986—Knowledge—Judaism. | Cabala—History. | Judaism in literature. | Jews in literature.
Classification: LCC PQ7797.B635 Z773475 2025 | DDC 868/.6209—dc23/eng/20250101
LC record available at https://lccn.loc.gov/2024046781

A British Cataloging-in-Publication record for this book is available from the British Library.
Copyright © 2025 by Yitzhak Lewis

References to internet websites (URLs) were accurate at the time of writing. Neither the author nor Rutgers University Press is responsible for URLs that may have expired or changed since the manuscript was prepared.

♾ The paper used in this publication meets the requirements of the American National Standard for Information Sciences—Permanence of Paper for Printed Library Materials, ANSI Z39.48-1992.

rutgersuniversitypress.org

For Edna Aizenberg z"l (1945–2018)
In memoriam

Contents

Acknowledgments

The inception of this project was my doctoral dissertation. Although many years have passed, the insight of my mentors Graciela Montaldo, Gil Anidjar, Dan Miron, and Edna Aizenberg still accompanies my intellectual development. Early in the process, the guidance from Graciela Montaldo was instrumental in conceiving how this project would bring together Borges studies and Jewish studies. Gil Anidjar has supported me throughout the search for my own intellectual footing in academia and offered thoughtful feedback on a draft of this book. Dan Miron inspired my confidence that a study of Borges would be relevant to the field of Jewish literature. I have also benefited from the mentorship of Hannan Hever, who encouraged me to pursue the themes of Hasidism and Buber in Borges. I thank them all for their care and support.

Parts of this work have been presented at conferences of the American Comparative Literature Association and the Association for Jewish Studies. At these conferences, I met Michal Ben-Horin, whose feedback helped shape the presentation of this project. At these same conferences, I was also fortunate to meet Kitty Millet, whose scholarship and academic organizing in the fields of Jewish studies, comparative literature, and mysticism have offered me both intellectual inspiration and practical support. Shlomy Mualem, a fellow Borges reader, invited me to present my work on Borges and the Kabbalah at Bar Ilan University. Our conversations on the topic have been helpful in conceptualizing my approach to the topic. I thank Malachi Hacohen for the invitation to present this project at the North Carolina Jewish Studies Seminar and the participants of the seminar for their feedback.

Over the past decade, I have found a welcoming home for my scholarship at the Latin American Jewish Studies Association. I want to thank the LAJSA leadership Darrell Lockhart, Adriana Brodsky, Alan Astro, and Ariana

Huberman for their friendship and support. Through the association's conferences, I was fortunate to receive helpful feedback on parts of this work from Florinda Goldberg and Naomi Lindstrom. Ariana Huberman and Naomi Lindstrom also supported me in seeking funding to support the research and development of this project.

This book was written across four countries—Argentina, the United States, China, and Israel. I could not have collected some of the archival material for this work without the support of Maria Kodama. She generously allowed me to scan parts of Borges's personal library at the Fundación Internacional Jorge Luis Borges in Buenos Aires. I received support from the research support staff at the Biblioteca Nacional Argentina and the library staff at the Seminario Rabínico Latinoamericano in Buenos Aires as well. Thanks also to Magdalena La Porta and Leslie Daniel for supporting my research needs for this manuscript. Roberto Cataldo, a prominent bookseller in Montevideo, has generously provided me with scans of some pages from a first edition Borges book. The portraits of Borges featured on the cover of this book were done in 1988 by José de Jesús Martínez Álvarez. I thank him for generously granting permission to feature them here.

Parts of this book were written over the COVID-19 pandemic, during two years that I was locked out of my home in China. I thank the team of the Duke Office of DKU Relations that supported me during this COVID-19 exile in Durham. The final push to complete this book was made during the semester of sabbatical leave I received from Duke Kunshan University and final edits and indexing were made possible by the DKU Faculty Scholarship Grant. I thank the Faculty Development Committee, the Office of Faculty Affairs, and Vice Chancellor for Academic Affairs Scott MacEachern for their support in the completion of this book. Parts of this book were written during summers at the National Library of Israel, where I benefited from the encouragement, curiosity, and support of Zvi Leshem, director of the Gershom Scholem Collection.

At Rutgers University Press, my thanks to Carah Naseem for support in the publication process and to the readers who reviewed the manuscript and offered helpful feedback toward the final draft. I want to acknowledge my friend and editor Kali Handelman for her masterful assistance in the development and editing of this manuscript.

My discussion of Borges's exchange with the *Crisol* editors in chapter 4 and my reading of Veblen in chapter 5 were previously published in Yitzhak Lewis, "Modeling Marginality: Borges, Veblen, and the Argentine Writer." *Variaciones Borges* 44 (2017): 173–188. I thank the editors of *Variaciones Borges* for their permission to reprint excerpts of that text here.

In fall 2009, I had written a graduate school paper on Borges and, at the advice of Graciela Montaldo, I sent a copy to Edna Aizenberg to ask for her feedback. We met a week later in Butler Library at Columbia University. I was grateful for the time she spent reading my paper and filled with admiration for the depth and breadth of her scholarly reflections. Edna invited me into the Latin American Jewish Studies Association, generously offered her time and feedback, and served as the external reader on my dissertation committee. When she passed, her late husband Yehoshua Aizenberg very generously offered to pass on to me her Borges library. I felt that her personal copies of *Obras Completas* and other Borges books should remain as a family heirloom. But I did inherit many books from her scholarly collection in Borges studies. As I consulted these books while working on this manuscript, here and there a note in the margins would appear, speaking with that familiar combination of scholarly sternness and compassionate mentorship I first encountered as a graduate student fifteen years ago. This book would not be possible, this part of my scholarly journey would not be possible, without the time I was awarded with Edna Aizenberg. I dedicate this book to her memory.

And to my family, for their continued support, encouragement, and adventurous spirit, my thanks and love.

Games of Inheritance

Introduction

A Game of Inheritance

Jorge Luis Borges played many games with his readers. One of the best known is the game of creating and recreating his own precursors. This book is about Borges's creation of "the Judaic" as a central precursor to his literary and intellectual activity. We will track how this game was played over many decades of his career, and what was at stake—for him, for Argentine letters, perhaps even for world literature. Along the way, we will see "the Judaic" implicated in Borges's conceptualization and articulation of his views on literature: Who is an author? What is tradition? How does one write? In that sense, the Judaic is a consistent interest throughout this book, but it is not the subject of the book. This book is about the horizon of literature.

Decades before the academic study of his Jewish influences began, Borges himself entertained the idea of such inheritance. In his 1934 essay "Yo, Judío [I, a Jew]," he states: "Who has not, at one time or another, played with thoughts of his ancestors, with the prehistory of his flesh and blood? I have done so many times, and many times it has not displeased me to think of myself as Jewish."[1] Though in this same essay he admits not finding Jewish ancestry, he never stopped playing with the ancestral theme, in statements such as: "I may have Jewish ancestors, but I can't tell. My mother's name is Acevedo: Acevedo may be a name for a Portuguese Jew, but again, it may not."[2] These and similar statements have fueled decades of scholarship on Borges's Jewish connections, influences, and debts. As Lisa Block de Behar remarks: "The references multiplied by his poems, stories, articles, lectures and interviews are so frequent that this profusion is surprising in a writer who . . . does not vindicate the need to be Jewish to claim it—and one could think that the choices of this affective affinity [indicate] a departure from genetic or dogmatic fatality by pure attraction."[3]

The scholarly discussion of fatality and attraction may seem a sharp contrast to the playful tone of Borges's own statements. However, when read in the context of Borges's mid-twentieth-century opposition to xenophobic nationalism, Nazism, and Argentine populism, it is clear such statements express consequential positions well beyond his family tree or his literary debts. My first argument in this project, then, is that Borges does not so much incorporate Jewish textual traditions into his writing as he does imaginatively invent the Judaic as an idiosyncratic point of reference. Understanding what Borges perceives as Judaic is not a question of content but of context. This framing of Borges's game of Judaic inheritance should shift our focus away from questions of accuracy and understanding, toward an appreciation of the poetic utility of Borges's persistent reference to the Judaic. That shift, in turn, will provide a better understanding of the nuance of his views on the issues that most animate his oeuvre: authorship and writing, literature and tradition.

Borges saw this game of inheritance, playing with the prehistory of his blood, as part of a literary and cultural program whose primary focus was to identify a point of departure for Argentine letters. Broadening the frame of the familiar Borges and the Judaic theme will allow us to shift our reading of Borges from questions of influence toward questions of literary imagination and creative intellectual practice. This broader framework will also allow us to appreciate Borges's engagement with figures who were central not only to his intellectual world, but to his construction of the Judaic—T. S. Eliot, Thorstein Veblen, Eduardo Mallea, and Franz Kafka, to name a few—alongside familiar figures of the Judaic realm in Borges's work, such as Gershom Scholem and Martin Buber. Moving beyond the intellectual divisions that previous scholarly focus on the Judaic has asserted in Borges studies, this project appreciates both the key role that the invented realm of the Judaic plays in Borges's thought, and the fact that in important ways this realm is poetically and intellectually produced by his expressed views on the most consequential questions of his time, about nationalism and literature, empire and postcolonialism, populism and aesthetics.

To be sure, Borges's games of inheritance are not limited to the Judaic. Ricardo Piglia has analyzed Borges's self-fashioning more generally, along two complementary lines of lineage, familial and literary.[4] In Piglia's view, Borges constructs the fiction of his own origins as a double lineage: the family and the library. Through these two lines, Borges defined his place within Argentine society and within the field of literature, respectively.

Borges creates his place in Argentine society by presenting his familial ties to the earliest years of the Argentine colonies and the Argentine Republic. He emphasizes his maternal Iberian lineage and the participation of his family members in familiar episodes of Argentine history, such as in the 1929 poem about his grandfather, "Isidoro Acevedo."[5] At the same time, Borges also emphasizes his literary lineage by referring to his British grandmother Frances Anne (Fanny) Haslam and his early childhood encounter with the British literary tradition.[6] Piglia focuses on the coarticulation of familial and literary lineage in creating the authorial persona of Borges. The best expression of this is perhaps in Borges's "Autobiographical Essay."[7] Piglia's analysis highlights the ideological dimension of this "fiction of origins," as he states: "The coherence of this construction is such that we should not see it as a secret that the critic needs to decipher, but the visible signs of an ideological interpretation that Borges himself offers in order to define at one and the same time his location within society and his relation to literature."[8]

I follow Piglia in reading Borges as a consciously self-fashioned author. What I add here is that Borges's Iberian family and British library serve to locate him *within* national and literary lineages. There is another dimension to this game of inheritance, one that is central to Borges's self-positioning in terms of both these lineages, and which positions him as an *exception* to both—the inheritance of the Judaic. The jocular intimations of possible Jewish heritage cited above, alongside allusions to Jewish sources that populate many of his texts, serve to dislocate him from the construction of his place within a narrow delimitation of familial and literary lines. When, in his famous lecture "The Argentine Writer and Tradition," for example, Borges speaks against narrow understandings of the scope of Argentine national literature, he invokes the Judaic to make his point.

The duplicity of this game of inheritance, at once locating and dislocating Borges from his Argentine setting, should be read in the simultaneity with which it occurs in his writing. As Beatriz Sarlo observes, "neither of these two lineages can be completely repressed or abolished; neither should be emphasized to the point of obliterating the other. Their coexistence results, however, not in any classical symmetry but in conflict."[9] Borges's Jewish family and his Jewish bookshelf are as formative of his authorial persona as are his Iberian family and his British bookshelf. And both these games of inheritance form part of a larger question regarding Borges's location, between local or national literature and world literature. This game of Judaic inheritance underwrites some of the more productive episodes in the intellectual conflict that Sarlo signals, between Borges's Argentine location and his view toward a world literature. From his position in mid-century Argentina, Borges wonders how far writing might take someone from their time, their place, their ideological environment, their tradition or lack thereof. And all this, like viewing the Aleph under a staircase, without leaving Buenos Aires. How does the author effectuate such departure and how might writing take him beyond the horizon of contemporary literature?

The Judaic

This book enters into the problematic of Borges's self-positioning as an author, and his reflections on the role and activity of the author, via one of his most emblematic literary stylizations—the Judaic. My goal is not to argue that Borges is invested in something he identifies as Judaic. That argument has been made and elaborated by several notable scholars whose work will be cited throughout this book (including my teacher, Edna Aizenberg). The argument I seek to build in this book is not about the *existence* of this affinity, but about the *utility* of this affinity—on both the political and aesthetic level—in the context of World War II and Borges's anti-Nazi polemics, and in the context of the Argentine literary debates Borges engaged in. Most of all, I will deconstruct the utility of the Judaic as it relates to the aesthetics of Borges's texts and his self-reflections on questions regarding authorship and literature.

It is important to note at the outset that "the Judaic" is an abstraction, a construct that aims at totalizing an object of study out of a wide variety of references and allusions that Borges makes—with implications for Latin American literary studies more broadly. The Judaic refers to something that Borges may or may not know much about, but which he projects onto his local context and concerns. The term relates to the way authors imagine themselves as maintaining a conversation with Jewish textual and intellectual traditions, regardless of the "real" existence of such a conversation. This object is by definition fictional and idiosyncratic, or, for my present purposes, literary and Borgesian.

Borges is not unique in this regard among Latin American authors. There is a rich body of scholarship on the role of the figure of the Jew in Latin American culture and literature going back to the earliest days of European presence in Latin America. Dalia Wassner, for example, identifies "a transatlantic, multigenerational literary conversation whereby questions of imperial, regional or national identity are tied to the presence—be it theoretical or physical—of the Jew within society."[10] Erin Graff Zivin has framed the same topic through her discussion of the Jew as a signifier in Latin American culture and literature in her book *The Wandering Signifier: Rhetoric of Jewishness in the Latin American Imaginary*.[11] This is the existing scholarly context for reading the engagement with Jewish textual traditions and intellectual histories as part of broader Latin American concerns.

The present book takes a more pointed aim at Borges's literary and intellectual activity within this context. Mariano Siskind, in his book *Cosmopolitan*

Desires: Global Modernity and World Literature in Latin America, argues that for Borges and other Latin American authors, "'elsewhere' . . . this signifier of exteriority was a blank screen upon which cosmopolitan writers projected their aesthetic desires and their longing to participate in the actualization of modernity."[12] My aim is to elucidate the Judaic as a central component of Borges's cosmopolitan projections and analyze its function in generating the Borgesian world of letters. Beyond the discursive construction of a cosmopolitan literary horizon by Borges and his contemporaries, we must pay further attention to the poetics, by which Borges rejects the local aspects of Argentine literature, and the utility of the Judaic in such rejections. The manner and articulation of these rejections are instructive in appreciating the role of the Judaic as a formative if elusive component of these projections.

This claim can be illustrated by examining one of the earliest bibliographic references Borges offers for his knowledge of the Judaic. In his early essay "A History of Angels [Historia de los ángeles]" (published in his 1926 collection of essays *El tamaño de mi esperanza*[13]), Borges already lists two sources: "Dr. Erich Bischoff, in his German book entitled *The Elements of the Kabbalah*, published in Berlin in 1920, enumerates the ten *sefiroth*, or eternal emanations of divinity. . . . Stehelin, in his *Rabbinical Literature*, links the first ten letters of the *aleph-beth*, or alphabet of the Hebrews, to these ten lofty worlds."[14]

John Peter Stehelin's *Rabbinical Literature* (1732) is in fact a translation of a work by antisemitic German orientalist Johann Andreas Eisenmenger, *Entdecktes Judentum* (Judaism Uncovered) (1700).[15] The book was a major work of Christian polemic against the Jews of his day. This fact did not escape Stehelin, who, on the first page of the preface to his translation, notes: "The opposition the Jews among us, or some of them, have made to the Undertaking, must needs be pretty well known in Town since they published in the *Daily Courant*, a long and very free Letter against it."[16] Borges did not in fact know either of these books; as he admits in a 1971 interview, he took the reference to Stehelin from the appendix to Henry Wadsworth Longfellow's English version of *The Divine Comedy*, and it is Longfellow's error attributing the book to Stehelin rather than Eisenmenger.[17]

These bibliographic incidentals help make a point I have already begun to introduce. When it comes to his Judaic sources, Borges is little concerned with questions of accuracy. Just as a misattributed reference to Stehelin is presented as a source on Kabbalah, so too does Borges mention Scholem as his authority on Kabbalah while repeating arguments he read in other books, some of which Scholem would himself reject.[18] It is telling that the pseudepigraphic nature of the *Zohar* is what earns it a place alongside *Don Quixote* in Borges's self-fashioned library of precursors.[19] Borges's effort to represent the Judaic as a central influence on his writing also glosses over other debates in his present moment, such as those between Scholem and Buber.[20] Borges continuously represents these two as his major sources on Kabbalah, Hasidism, and Jewish tradition, even as he borrows from a broad array of undisclosed writings on these topics. He does so in order to stake a claim in his present Argentine setting, not in any Jewish historical setting. When Aizenberg describes Borges as "a latter day incarnation of Hebraists," we should understand this also in the sense that, like the early modern Hebraists, representing the Judaic as his precursor is part of Borges's claim to an authority and an authenticity in his own present.[21] In this present, the accuracy of this Judaic is always bracketed by the literary authority he derives from alluding to it.[22]

Throughout the book I refer to the Judaic as a "web of allusions." This phrasing too is meant to draw attention away from a sense of accuracy in Borges's reference to the Judaic and toward an understanding of the effect that repeated mentions of Judaic themes has on his readers and, by extension, on his own authorial persona. In 1961, reflecting on his work to date, Borges proposes an orientation toward his writing that is illuminating with regard to the Judaic as well. He writes: "Croce held that art is expression; to this exigency, or to a deformation of this exigency, we owe the worst literature of our time. . . . Sometimes, I, too, sought expression. I know now that my gods grant me no more than allusion or mention."[23] The self-conscious utility of the Judaic as allusive, rather than expressive, will be a recurring theme in the following pages.

This should also assuage any concerns that my preoccupation with Borges's self-fashioned authorial persona is an effort to revive "the author" from its famed death in the last century.[24] It is not my intention to recover an authorial intention within the texts we will read in this book. Rather, it is my intention to show that the literary stylizations that support the many varied and divergent readings Borges has received were themselves intentional, to the extent that Borges develops this "allusion or mention" into a poetics. In that sense, we might locate Borges alongside his mid-century contemporaries in foreclosing the search for authorial intention, not by arguing against it in literary theoretical terms (as did thinkers from William K. Wimsatt and M. C. Beardsley to Roland Barthes) but by his investment in a poetics that would support and indeed encourage his readers to pursue further and different interpretations with every reading.[25]

Borges will persistently draw his readers' attention to the fact that what they will make of these texts is out of his hands. The analogy he offers is to the divine author of scripture, a figure he wishes to approximate, who expresses no claim or desire to control the interpretation of that text. Borges's divine author leaves the infinite interpretability of scripture to the Kabbalists. To the extent that this argument may be paraphrased in terms of debates regarding the death of the author, Borges's Divinity is adjacent to Barthes's "scriptor," who puts words on a page in a way radically detached from the meaning they will acquire by the activity of their reader. In Barthes's argument, the scriptor too has an allusive, rather than expressive, function: "the scriptor no longer bears within him passions, humours, feelings, impressions, but rather this immense dictionary from which he draws a writing that can know no halt."[26] My argument is that Borges makes a conscious effort to approximate the infinite interpretability of scripture on the poetic level and, concomitantly, to develop an authorial persona akin to the scriptor. In his 1932 essay "A Vindication of the Kabbalah," Borges calls this the intellectual author approximating divinity and he finds his ideal reader, the true author of textual meaning, in the figure of the Kabbalist.

From Kabbalah to Tradition (the Structure of the Argument)

This book is primarily concerned with Borges's evolving understanding of authorship, and the role and activity of the author. Within this, the Judaic occupies a central place in the articulation of his views on authorship. However, this is not a book about Kabbalah or about Jewish tradition, it is about Borges's lifelong effort to engage questions regarding authorship and literature, in part through reference to the Judaic. Kabbalah and tradition name this problematic of writing and authorship for Borges. As the arc and structure of the argument will show, Borges changed and refined his views on these questions over his career and this is also expressed in the ways his focus on and allusion to the Judaic change over time. In his earlier writing the Kabbalah is a central touchpoint for articulating his concept of "the intellectual author" and a key component of his anti-Nazi polemics. This will be the topic in the first part of this book.

Following World War II, Borges's increased engagement with questions of postcolonial tradition and national literature drew him away from his anti-Nazi activity and focused his attention on postwar Argentine nationalism. In this context, the Kabbalah loses its centrality in the articulation of his views on authorship and literature and his engagement with the Judaic is refocused on questions of tradition. The second part of this book will discuss the entanglement of the concepts of literary tradition, Jewish tradition, and national tradition in Borges's postwar thought and writing.

The two most emblematic texts to deal with the problematic at the heart of the book's first two parts are, respectively, "A Vindication of the Kabbalah" (1932) and "The Argentine Writer and Tradition" (1951). Within them, the centrality of the Kabbalah and Jewish tradition, respectively, cannot be overstated. Along with these two terms and texts (Kabbalah and tradition), we will also encounter two of Borges's precursors: Gershom Scholem and Martin Buber. Scholem's role in Borges's writing will be discussed in the part on Kabbalah. Buber's central role in Borges's thought about these same questions will only become evident in the third part of the book, when we deal with Borges's most explicit postwar metaphor for authorship. However, a warning is due for the reader: Scholem and Buber are Borgesian precursors. The former does not exist as such until after Borges proclaims him to be, while the latter remains a hidden precursor that emerges only via Borges's discussion of Kafka's precursors. The book is thus divided into three parts, dealing with Kabbalah, tradition, and authorship, respectively. These are shown to be integral to Borges's thought, while also demonstrating that the Judaic element in his writing is not a stable object of knowledge or reference, but rather an intellectual and poetic idiosyncrasy.[27]

Reading Borges's engagement with the question of authorship, and the role of the Judaic within it, will proceed in a generally chronological manner. Although this may blur some of the coherence in Borges's positions, it will serve well to highlight the evolving nature of Borges's thought and the ways in which his engagement with the Judaic also evolves in the context of his changing local preoccupations. Part I will deal with Borges's writing published before the end of the 1940s, covering his early years, World War II, and its aftermath. Part II will pick up in 1949 and continue through to the 1970s, covering the emergence of postwar questions about postcolonial tradition and literature, his trips to the State of Israel, and his encounters with Scholem. Part III will interject the reading of an overlapping moment in Borges's writing, from the late 1940s to the late 1950s, and will analyze the evolution of Borges's metaphor for authorship as his thinking progressed from the World War II era to the postwar moment.

The academic interest in Borges's Jewish affinities has been most pronounced in the study of Borges and the Kabbalah. Engagement with the Kabbalah can be traced back to Borges's earliest texts. Before encountering Scholem for the first time, Borges was already deeply invested in the Kabbalah as a metaphor for authorship and, moreover, had developed a Kabbalistic image of the author that served very explicitly to polemicize against Nazism in Argentina in the 1930s and 1940s. The first part of the book discusses this nuanced relation between authorship and political ideology in Borges's work and demonstrates the centrality of the Kabbalah to the development of Borges's concept of authorship. In this part, I unsettle the assumption that Scholem was Borges's guide to the Kabbalah through close readings and intellectual historical analysis of Borges's early activity. I also argue that Borges's understanding of the Kabbalah cannot be fully appreciated outside of his engagement with World War II ideologies.

Chapter 1 introduces the background and intellectual history of studying Borges and the Kabbalah and presents the intellectual biographies of Scholem and Borges as parallel lines that meet only when they encounter each other in 1969 in Jerusalem. In chapter 2, I read Borges's early reference to the Kabbalah in his essay "A Vindication of the Kabbalah" (1932). The chapter discusses the model for the author–reader relations that Borges finds appealing in the Kabbalah. This is demonstrated in a reading of Borges's story "Tlön, Uqbar, Orbis Tertius" (1940). The chapter ends with a discussion of Borges's 1944 essay "A Comment on August 23, 1944," which demonstrates the echoes of his views on Kabbalah in his anti-Nazi polemics. Chapter 3 turns to Borges's postwar activity, reading "The God's Script" (1949) as Borges's effort to retell Plato's parable of the cave, demonstrating how he recreates the relation between the divine author and the Kabbalist reader in his own writing. The part concludes by returning to the intellectual history of Borges's encounter with Scholem, arguing that, while Scholem had no significant intellectual influence on Borges's understanding of Kabbalah, their encounter had a significant influence on Borges's readers and the Kabbalistic reception of his writing.

Creating a tradition and writing within a tradition are questions that come to the fore in Borges's thought following World War II, and in step with general postcolonial intellectual developments. While these questions are not considered through allusion to Kabbalah, Borges sees the Jews as having a unique relation to them. This view is an outgrowth of his views on the Kabbalah as a genre that attempts to subsume the individual's lived experiences as part of a tradition and, in so doing, creates and recreates that same tradition. However, in calling Borges a "postcolonial precursor," scholars such as Aizenberg have not given due consideration to important postwar shifts, not in Borges's preoccupations, but in his representational and allusive strategies.[28] The second part of this book will track the evolution of his Judaic web of allusions from the Kabbalah to notions of tradition, focusing on the postwar Argentine debates about national literature and literary tradition, in which Borges was a major participant.

The three chapters in this part read Borges's engagement with three conceptions of tradition. Chapter 4 discusses the role of T. S. Eliot—especially his essay "Tradition and the Individual Talent" (1917)—in Borges's understanding of literary tradition after World War II and the development of his thoughts on the theme of postcolonial authorship. Chapter 5 is focused on the role of Thorstein Veblen—especially his essay "The Intellectual Pre-Eminence of Jews in Modern Europe" (1919)—in Borges's understanding of Jewish tradition and the adjustments Borges made to this understanding, beginning in the aftermath of World War II and continuing into the 1970s. Chapter 6 reads Borges's engagement with Israeli literature, and in particular S. Y. Agnon, in order to arrive at a more nuanced understanding of the intellectual debates Borges maintained with Argentine nationalists about literature and "local color" in those same years.

The third part of the book brings the argument full circle to Borges's earliest years in Geneva and his first encounter with Kabbalah, Kafka, and Buber, and tracks an alternative literary history of his engagement with Jewish tradition from Buber onward. After reviewing Borges's thought on tradition in the previous chapters, we will see more clearly the imprint of Buber on Borges's thought about authorship. The importance of Buber to Borges's post–World War II thought would not be fully legible without the discussion in the previous part. And only once we discuss Borges's relationship to Buber can we have a full view of his own notion of tradition, adding a layer to the depth of his investment in the Judaic. Chapter 7 analyzes Borges's engagement with the works of Kafka and Buber as two figures central to his reflections on authorship. The chapter reads his well-known essay "Kafka and His Precursors" (1952) as part of a larger group of texts from the late 1940s to the late 1950s, in which Borges engages the work of Buber. The role of Buber's writing in Borges's articulation of "precursors" as a form of self-created tradition is then read in two of Borges's poems from this period, "Chess" (1960) and "The Golem" (1958). Chapter 7 is thus presented as a separate part for the way it returns to an important source of Borges's Judaic imagination that, while predating the discussion in the previous chapters, only comes to light following the analysis of Kabbalah and tradition that has been offered thus far.

Methodological Notes

Over the past two decades, publications of Borges's drafts and marginalia, alongside existing publications of his lectures and interviews, have made it possible to depict a richer literary history of Borges's writings.[29] These publications all make it possible to contextualize the moments of inception, publication, editing, and re-editing within Borges's own intellectual development. Throughout this book I make reference to Borges's notes in the back pages of the books he read. In many of his books, Borges would write his name and the date and location he acquired the volume. These materials allow us to date his encounter with various texts that influenced his thinking and writing, as I do when I recreate the timeline of Borges's encounter with Scholem in chapter 2. It also allows us to identify connections between texts that do not betray their affiliation with an idea or common influence, as is the case with the role of Buber in Borges's writing, which I discuss in chapter 7.

And yet with all these recent publications, the archive is in limbo! A few years ago, I was able to do archival work at the Fundación Internacional Jorge Luis Borges, which houses Borges's estate, and collect valuable materials for this project. Borges's widow, Maria Kodama, graciously granted me access to some of his personal volumes, including books by Scholem and Buber. When I asked to take photos of the material, she would question me as to the significance of the material and the intended use of the images. Based on my replies she was sometimes very forthcoming, asking the foundation's secretary to prepare high-resolution scans for me, and at other times she would refuse my request. Other materials that would shed further light on the history of Borges's evolving concerns remain inaccessible. Ms. Kodama passed away in March 2023 leaving no will and only recently has the management of the estate passed to her nephews. As of this date, the estate has begun offering limited guided tours but is not yet accessible for research. It remains unclear who may grant me permission to publish the scans I possess. These events have left Borges scholars at a loss. I refer to the scans in my possession on several occasions in this book and I will find a way in the future to share this material more fully. All translations of this and other material are my own, unless otherwise indicated.

The attention this project pays to the evolution of Borges's thought and expression highlights the way this book departs from previous and prevailing scholarship on Borges and the Judaic as well. Since the 1970s, research on Borges and the Kabbalah has developed into a rich field that has illuminated many aspects of Borges's writing. However, studies in this field tend to take Borges's oeuvre as a coherent whole and juxtapose it with the vast body of textual traditions known as the Kabbalah. Borges's writing, or literature, nouns that are used to rarify and totalize an object of critical utility, is analyzed for its similarities and differences with the equally rarified and totalized object of the Kabbalah. The result is insightful readings of Borges's stories that shed light on the relations between literature and mysticism, literary-philosophical Idealism, and Kabbalistic theosophy. Examples of this range from the early 1970s with the work of Jaime Alazraki and Saul Sosnowski to recent works by Shlomy Mualem.[30]

The insights these scholars and others offer us about literature and mysticism, about reading and misreading in literary traditions, are invaluable to our appreciation of modern literature and of Borges as a unified concept. But not of Borges the human aspiring to approximate the God of the Kabbalists. They sometimes lose sight of Borges the author, who did not deliver his body of work to humankind all at once the way the God of the Kabbalists did. He toiled away at it over many decades, writing, revising, editing, publishing, and republishing. And along the way he sometimes changed his focus or changed his mind. In fact, one of Borges's persistent efforts is to problematize our ability to totalize any object of "writing" or "literature." As he puts it in his story "The God's Script"—"Shadows or simulacra of . . . all a language can embrace are the poor and ambitious human words, *all, world, universe.*"[31]

It is through the question of authorship that the present book enters the conversation. Borges worked to produce a body of text that would be legible through similar assumptions as the Kabbalists made in approaching Scripture (the topic of chapter 3) or as Agnon made in approaching tradition (the topic of chapter 6). In fact, he is very open about his desire to be read in similar ways. Many groundbreaking studies of his writing were produced by adopting this imperative to read as a Kabbalist. But how did Borges signal to his readers his desire to be read in this way? My effort here is to deconstruct the critical edifice of Borges and the Judaic, to highlight central points along the way that contributed to its construction and canonization, and to highlight Borges's own very active involvement in the development of a readerly attitude toward his writing. Along the way, we will track the evolution of themes, ideas, and metaphors as they take shape. What we will find is that the writerly edifice of Borges's Judaic imaginary is in fact the ballast of greater and more pressing questions for Borges, about authorship and the horizon of literature.

Part 1

Kabbalah

1

Kabbalistic Stories

INTERVIEWER: Have you tried to make your own stories Kabbalistic?
BORGES: Yes, sometimes I have.

—Interview exchange quoted in Christ, "Jorge Luis Borges, The Art of Fiction No. 39," 161.

Borges's engagement with the Kabbalah is a notable feature in his construction of a Judaic web of allusions and of his literary project more generally.[1] The interview exchange cited above has framed scholarship on this engagement for decades. Scholars have debated whether and to what extent his stories can be regarded as Kabbalistic stories and this has been a productive question whether one's interest is in "the Jewish Borges," in a broader appreciation of his literary art, or even in the contemporary relevance of Kabbalah to literary studies. The question emerged in the early 1970s, when the adjective Kabbalistic was first appended to various aspects of Borges's style.[2] Yet what precisely is intended by this adjective remains only loosely defined.[3] Jaime Alazraki, a groundbreaking scholar of Borges and the Kabbalah, describes his stories thus: "Behind his transparent texts there lies a stylistic intricacy, a certain Kabbalistic texture."[4] He adds that it is possible to identify "in his stories a Kabbalistic aura"[5] and, in an article titled "Kabbalistic Traits in Borges' Narrative," Alazraki states: "One of the wonders of Borges' art is precisely that Kabbalistic feature apparent in many of his narrative texts."[6] Saul Sosnowski, another scholar forging a path into this field in the early 1970s, focused on the Kabbalah's attitude toward language. He qualifies Alazraki's broad statements by suggesting that while "it is an undeniable fact that Borges uses Kabbalistic motifs," nevertheless, Borges "does not write historical manuals nor Kabbalistic texts."[7] For Sosnowski, Borges's texts "contain Kabbalistic elements," and it is "the task of the literary critic to study these motifs in their fictional context."[8]

The question of whether the use of "Kabbalistic motifs" makes a text Kabbalistic, or how many "Kabbalistic elements" it takes to create a "Kabbalistic texture," is a secondary issue. The first thing to note is that the adjective Kabbalistic is never—in any of the research on Borges and the Kabbalah—defined or explained in any significant way. As Sosnowski notes, studies attributing this appellation to Borges's stories are nonetheless conducted within the discipline of literary studies. The engagement of Borges's readers with questions in the field of Jewish mysticism is thus understandably limited. For the most part, the term is taken to have a commonsensical meaning, which is almost exclusively borrowed from Gershom Scholem.[9] Furthermore, a closer look at some of the stories taken up by readers of Borges and the Kabbalah reveals that there is an uncritical slippage between Kabbalah and mysticism. Elements of mysticism that are only loosely related to Jewish traditions are nonetheless interpreted through the lens of Kabbalistic stories. A clear example of this slippage can be found in readings of Borges's 1949 story "The God's Script."[10] The first-person account of a mystical experience composed of allusions to Eastern and Mesoamerican mystical traditions is nonetheless read as a "Kabbalistic quest."[11]

On the other hand, denying the proliferation of allusions to major texts and figures of the Kabbalah in the writings of Borges would be equally misleading.[12] Not only do his texts repeatedly refer to terms and symbols such as the ten *sefirot* or the Golem, but also to specific books of Kabbalah, such as *Sefer Yetzirah* and the *Zohar*. How are we to read these references, giving them the attention they merit as persistent components of Borges's stories, while keeping in view their deployment, which, as Sosnowski has noted, is neither mystical nor scholarly? Scholars have already formulated this question more generally with regard to Borges's interest in esotericism. Didier T. Jaén, for example, dismisses the "suspicion that the profusion of allusions to esoteric and metaphysical doctrines in Borges conveys some philosophical or mystical meaning. . . . Why, then, so many allusions to esoteric texts? [Jaén asks, replying that] Borges repeatedly stresses that his interest in such doctrines was mainly aesthetic."[13] We should follow Jaén in focusing on the aesthetic rather than the esoteric. At the same time, the strokes that would paint Borges's allusions to Kabbalah as part of a more general interest in esoteric traditions are too broad.

Several factors would justify a narrower focus on the Kabbalah in Borges's work. One is the recurring reference he makes to the Kabbalah in discussions of authorship, which thematically distinguishes the Kabbalah from other esoteric traditions in Borges's writing. Another factor is the entanglement between Borges's relation to the Kabbalah and his relation to prominent twentieth-century scholar of Kabbalah Gershom Scholem, an entanglement that exists both in Borges's own writing and in scholarship. Complicating this further, as Edna Aizenberg notes, is Borges's own very clear "desire to be considered as an author influenced by . . . the Kabbalah."[14] A reader of Borges and the Kabbalah must forge an interpretative path between Borges's self-presentation, Scholem's looming presence over the field, and the concrete examples of allusions to Kabbalah in Borges's texts. It is thus necessary to review the methodological implications of focusing on the Kabbalah in Borges's writing and attempt to deconstruct the entanglement between Borges and Scholem before we can move on to an analysis of Borges's allusions to the Kabbalah.

Kabbalistic Methodologies

Beyond the lack of clarity in the denotation of a genre or style of writing, the label "Kabbalistic stories" has had profound methodological implications for the study of Borges's writing. Calling his writings Kabbalistic locates them within a discursive field, the limits of which are presumed at the outset rather than investigated. A mere allusion to something related to Kabbalah suffices to activate this definition. And this definition is taken as an answer to questions regarding aesthetic decisions made by the writer. Alazraki's first example of what "generates in [Borges's] stories a Kabbalistic aura whose source goes far beyond a fortuitous familiarity with the Kabbalah" is the mention of various sources relating to Kabbalah and Hasidism in Borges's stories.[15] First among these sources is *Borges's own* "A Vindication of the Kabbalah," which the narrator places on the bookshelf of Doctor Marcel Yarmolinsky, the first character to be assassinated in the story "Death and the Compass."[16] For Alazraki, the identification of these stories as Kabbalistic begins with their allusion to the role of Kabbalah in Borges's writings. Alazraki illustrates a general problem, in which privileging the Kabbalah as an interpretive lens draws first and foremost on the autoreferential tendency of Borges, who inserts his own titles on the Kabbalah into his stories.

A related methodological problem concerning this adjective, already alluded to, is that scholars of Borges and the Kabbalah are deeply indebted to Gershom Scholem for their definition of the Kabbalah, but rarely make this explicit in any way. Before we move on to discussing the possible effects Scholem may have had on the writing of Borges's stories, we must pause to note the effects Scholem has had on the literary scholars reading Borges's texts. This will help us avoid mistaken assumptions and methodological limitations that an overemphasis on Scholem's role in Borges's stories has long been imposing on our ability to read Borges's narratives. For many of Borges's readers cited above, a familiarity with Scholem precedes their scholarship on Borges, intellectually if not historically. In contradistinction to these readers, Scholem's role in mediating Borges's own interest in and knowledge of the Kabbalah was limited.

If Borges's array of Kabbalistic characters and concepts reads like a table of contents for some imaginary volume on "Major Trends in Scholem's Writings on Jewish Mysticism," it is a result of the interpretability of his stories and the academic orientation of his readers—not a result of influence by Scholem, and certainly not evidence of bibliographic familiarity with Scholem's work. "Selection and abbreviation themselves constitute a kind of commentary," Scholem states in the first pages of *Major Trends in Jewish Mysticism*.[17] And indeed, Scholem's scholarship has been markedly and enthusiastically embraced in commentary on Borges's engagement with the Kabbalah.

How then might we read this persistent reference to Scholem by Borges's readers? Starting in the 1960s, Scholem was a conscious selection whose name Borges used to underscore allusions to the Kabbalah in his own work. Thus, for Borges's readers Scholem became one of Borges's more identifiable precursors. Borges creating his own precursors should not surprise us. Though his success at creating them as precursors amazes, confuses, and delights his readers.

Does it matter that Scholem does not stand out among Borges's library of Kabbalah scholarship, if they both refer to the same Kabbalistic bibliography? What might appear to be bibliographic incidentals become interpretive considerations when we recall that scholars who have written on Borges and Kabbalah have relied on Scholem to authorize their definition and delimitation of what they understand the Kabbalah to be. At least as much as Borges invited this by creating Scholem as his precursor.[18] Though this certainly does not detract from the exceptional quality of the analysis, such reliance on Scholem does suggest a possible substitution of "Kabbalah" for what might more accurately be named "Scholem." What is thus presented as a clear indication of Kabbalistic influences on Borges—"Borges utilizes Kabbalistic notions, employs exegetical elements, and cites names and texts that directly refer to this theme"[19]—is in fact only the demonstration of a correlation (bibliographic and thematic) between Borges's self-fashioned precursor on the Kabbalah and his readers' source of authority on the topic. Most scholarship on Borges and the Kabbalah is written by scholars who (like Borges himself) have knowledge of Kabbalah that goes well beyond the couple of Scholem books that Borges read. But the reliance on Scholem that these same scholars exhibit, in bibliographic citation and in the identification of themes, suggests that for them, as for Borges, Scholem serves to authorize their knowledge of the Kabbalah. This mirroring of Scholem's function as a rhetorical invocation of authority is a central aspect of the methodological problem at hand.

Alazraki ultimately admits that his preexisting familiarity with the Kabbalah, which he studied with Scholem a decade before he began work on Borges and the Kabbalah, showed him a way to read Borges. As he reflects about his own interpretation of Borges's stories, collected in his book *Borges and the Kabbalah*: "It will be too prolix to justify whatever Kabbalistic premise was at work in each of the chapters of this volume. What truly matters, I feel, is that aspects of Borges' work . . . are dealt with as layers of a text constantly seeking to be unraveled."[20] How can we recognize the difference between the Kabbalistic premises at work in the literary critic's analysis and those at work in Borges's literary expression?

This problem is compounded by the fact that for Borges, as for the academic study of Kabbalah, mysticism and its phenomena are encountered as themes. Or what Scholem, more interested in intellectual history than in literary poetics, has called "trends." In relying on academic studies for their knowledge, Kabbalah is mediated in important ways, for Borges and his readers alike, by the academic lens. This certainly predetermines the conditions under which Borges and his readers acquired their knowledge. Mediated by academic study, key elements of Kabbalah, such as ecstatic experience and a functional (if not metaphysical) distinction between exoteric and esoteric knowledge—two examples that feature extensively in Borges's handling of Kabbalistic themes[21]—are entirely absent from an encounter with the academic study of Kabbalah. After all, none of the scholars on the topic are themselves Kabbalists. They do not instruct their readers in the attainment of ecstatic experiences, nor do their texts maintain a functional distinction between exoteric and esoteric knowledge. They certainly report these to be key elements of Kabbalah, but the academic lens blurs the possibility of clearly distinguishing between the key elements of Kabbalah and the key terms in the investigation of Kabbalah. That is, the lived experiences and concerns of Kabbalists become themes in the writing of Kabbalistic studies.[22]

This creates a further set of interpretive limitations that result from relying on Scholem for a definition of the Kabbalah. Scholem's understanding of Kabbalah is historiographical and his investigation is oriented toward identifying trends within the intellectual-historical transformations of the Kabbalah. He espouses a dialectical model of intellectual development that takes place within a defined social-psychological context, and these developments usually occur in an effort to escape from history.[23] Scholem does not develop tools for reading the aesthetic or poetic dimensions of the Kabbalah. Using Scholem's work as a frame of reference for Borges and the Kabbalah is helpful for thematic and philological reconstruction of the sources he used but—in line with Scholem's own attitude toward Kabbalistic texts—it stops short of asking aesthetic questions about the literary nature of these Kabbalistic stories. In that sense, a reliance on Scholem serves only to perpetuate the deferral of questions regarding Borges's own intellectual and poetic relations to the Kabbalah.

In an illustrative article on the topic, in which Borges is presented as greatly "indebted to Kabbalistic conceptions," this debt soon turns out to be "regardless of the accuracy of his understanding of its doctrine."[24] Throughout the article, reference to Kabbalah is qualified by the phrase "as understood by Borges."[25] This qualified notion of influence is symptomatic of Alazraki as well, for whom, as we have seen, reference to Kabbalah is sufficient proof of influence. How are we to understand this debt to conceptions, regardless of any accuracy in understanding them, and which might only exist in as far as it was understood by Borges himself to exist? One suggestion has been that "[Borges's] art is Kabbalistic in a sense defined by Borges himself in his essay 'A Vindication of the Kabbalah.'"[26] There is a questionable tautology produced here: we recognize Borges's writing to be Kabbalistic because it is Kabbalistic in the sense Borges himself means when he says his writing is Kabbalistic. I would like to avoid such tautology in exploring what an interest in Kabbalah might mean in the context of Borges's writing.

A further observation is that in all of the research on Borges and the Kabbalah the standard of proof that is the indication of influence—what above I have proposed to call correlation—involves a comparison between a story by Borges and a doctrinal text of Kabbalah, which is usually available to the researcher in fragments, predetermined by Scholem's choice of citations.[27] Demonstrating that in stories such as "The God's Script" or "The Aleph" Borges speaks of ecstatic revelation the same way Moses Cordovero or Abraham Abulafia do, substitutes for the aesthetic effect of Borges's persistent reference to the Kabbalah a claim to some Kabbalistic influence, the nature of which remains unarticulated, not for esoteric reasons but precisely because it is taken to exist "regardless of the accuracy of [Borges's] understanding of its doctrine."[28]

As Alazraki has already stated, Borges developed his own idiosyncratic understanding of Kabbalah. In this context, it is important to emphasize that disagreement with Scholem is not the same as a misunderstanding of Kabbalah. For example, Scholem is consistent in his view that "Kabbalistic speculation[s] are in the last resort ways of escaping from history rather than instruments of historical understanding."[29] As we will see when we read "A Comment on August 23, 1944," Borges could not disagree more.[30] "It is important to outline fields: Borges is not a philosopher, nor a theologian, nor a cabalist, nor an historian: He is a maker of fictions," states Sosnowski.[31] Though perhaps such a demarcation is too decided for the continual blurring of fields and genres that Borges offers, what this important outline should suggest is that, in our attempt to offer the proper regard to Borges's understanding, we would do well to shift our focus from the Kabbalah—as an object that can be accurately (or inaccurately) understood—to the ways in which reference to this object generates poetic effects and authorizes Borges's position as an author.

In order to avoid these same limitations and inconsistencies in our present study of Kabbalah in Borges's writing, I suggest we begin by contextualizing the scholarly interest in Borges's Kabbalistic stories. In a somewhat Borgesian twist, it was only after two encounters between Scholem and Borges in Jerusalem (in 1969 and 1971) that scholars began to take a more pointed interest in the Kabbalah in Borges's writing. Aside from one French article published pseudonymously in 1964 in the context of Borges's French reception, which pointed to Borges's interest in the Kabbalah, no other scholarly work was done on this question until the early 1970s.[32] To summarize the point before we pass to a discussion of Scholem: Borges scholars have been as much under Scholem's influence as they claimed Borges was, when they transcribed his interest in Kabbalah into a debt to Scholem. Discussing the Jewish imaginaries in Borges's fiction, Evelyn Fishburn goes as far as to state that "each of [Borges's stories with a Jewish connection] is connected with one or other aspect of Kabbalah."[33] Considering the centrality of references to the Kabbalah in the way Borges stylizes the Judaic element in his fictions, it is necessary to explore the role of these references as a literary element.

Before we can do this, however, we must address the truism prevailing in Borges studies, that Scholem was Borges's guide to the Kabbalah. Scholem does not stand out in Borges's library of Kabbalah studies and, in fact, was first encountered by Borges only after several of his canonical collections had already been published. This fact suggests to us a way forward in the study of Borges, the Kabbalah, and Scholem. First, we must recreate the timeline of Borges's engagement with the Kabbalah, and position Scholem along this literary-historical trajectory. Second, we need to elaborate a methodology for reading Borges's engagement with the Kabbalah that is apace with this trajectory and does not anachronistically project Scholem's influence into Borges's earlier writings. Third, given the scant mention of Scholem in Borges's stories, we need to rethink the literary utility of Borges's allusions not only to the Kabbalah, but to Scholem himself. I propose that references to Scholem should not be read as indicating an intellectual influence but rather as themselves a self-presentation that Borges creates in an effort to mark the Kabbalah as a literary precursor. In so doing, my effort ultimately will be to replace the literary-historical questions of influence with literary-aesthetic questions.

Encountering Scholem

To engage the question of Scholem's role in Borges's relation to the Kabbalah, I would like to begin by dispelling two generally held views. The first is that Scholem was Borges's guide to the Kabbalah. This view is unfounded. Only recently, with expanded access to Borges's drafts, notes, and personal volumes, has it become possible to reconstruct a timeline of his encounter with Scholem.[34] Until recently, evidence for Borges's familiarity with Scholem has been circumstantial or interpretatively produced.[35] In fact, Borges read many books about the Kabbalah and Scholem does not stand out among them as mediating Borges's knowledge of the Kabbalah in any unique way. It is hard to see what grounds scholars have found for this assumption, beyond their own dependence on Scholem discussed previously.

The second widely held view, which follows upon the former, is that Borges's stories, by weaving the web of allusions to Kabbalah mentioned previously, demonstrate a grasp of Scholem's insights and engage with Scholem's scholarship. This latter view assumes that Borges was engaged not only with the Kabbalah as a literary theme, but with Scholem's academic view of the Kabbalah. As we will see when we read his essay "A Vindication of the Kabbalah," Borges did not change his views on the Kabbalah even after he read the opposite in Scholem. But more to the point, there is no indication that Borges had an interest in the scholarly differences between Scholem, Buber, Bischoff, and others he read on the topic. Yet these two perceptions feed each other, creating the impression of a strong intellectual link between Borges and Scholem.[36]

While Borges does mention Scholem in some of his lectures, and makes (limited) reference to his scholarship, Borges's stories do not explicitly engage Scholem's work on the Kabbalah. Nor does Scholem's presentation of the Kabbalah stand out in his stories any more than do the other sources he consulted about the subject. This is true for Borges's canonical collections *Discusión* (1932), *Ficciones* (1944), *El Aleph* (1949), and *Otras Inquisiciones* (1952), and it is doubtful Scholem had any greater influence on his later stories as well.[37] However, Scholem does play a key role in framing Borges's literature for a world readership—a role he is assigned by Borges himself.

In understanding the relation between Scholem and Borges, what I would like to emphasize is that the two men led parallel existences for most of their lives. Scholem and Borges were born less than two years apart—late 1897 and mid-1899, respectively—and their intellectual development follows similar contours of twentieth-century history. They both spent their youth in Europe—Borges moved from Argentina to Geneva with his family in 1914 and Scholem was born in Berlin—and both lived through World War I on the same continent. Most importantly for the parallels between them, they both developed their interest in the Kabbalah around the same years, at the end of World

War I. Scholem developed an academic interest in Kabbalah while in graduate school. Borges (an autodidact) developed his literary interest in the Kabbalah through the character of the Golem in Gustav Meyrink's popular novel *Der Golem* (1915) and the academic works of German orientalist and religion scholar Erich Bischoff, in particular his two volumes *Die Elemente der Kabbalah* (1913).[38] Around this same period, both were also influenced by Martin Buber—Scholem interacted with Buber as a member of Jung Judah in Berlin and Borges read many of Buber's publications from those years.[39] Scholem and Borges both left Europe in the early 1920s and moved to the cities that would be their homes for the rest of their respective careers—Scholem to Jerusalem and Borges back to his childhood Buenos Aires.

Also noteworthy is the fact that both developed their early interest in Kabbalah in the context of a prevailing attitude that was dismissive of the Kabbalah as a valuable object of academic study or worthy of literary engagement. In this context, both engage in an effort to "vindicate" the Kabbalah. Scholem pushes back against Jewish Enlightenment notions that dismiss the Kabbalah as an outmoded, antirational element of Judaism that is of no interest to modern Jewish studies.[40] Likewise, Borges frames his earliest engagement as apologetics in his 1932 essay "A Vindication of the Kabbalah."[41] What I want to emphasize here is that Borges's interest in the Kabbalah was not inspired by Scholem, but by some of the sources and circumstances that inspired Scholem's own interest in the Kabbalah. Drawing this parallel demonstrates the similarity but also the distance between the two.

Borges continued his interest in the Kabbalah his entire life, reading many books on the topic, including Christian Ginsburg's *The Kabbalah* (1920), Joshua Trachtenberg's *Jewish Magic and Superstition* (1939), Scholem's *Major Trends in Jewish Mysticism* (1941), and Macgregor Mathers's *The Kabbalah Unveiled* (1957), as well as many books by Buber.[42] During the 1920s and 1930s, he published many poems, essays, and stories in many publications in Argentina, several of which make reference to the Kabbalah. Those same years span Scholem's completion of his doctoral dissertation (1922) and extend to the publishing of his seminal essay "Redemption through Sin" (1937).[43] The year 1941 marks another significant milestone along the intellectual timelines of both Scholem and Borges. This was the year in which each of them published what would be their first canonical work. Scholem published his *Major Trends in Jewish Mysticism* and Borges published *The Garden of Forking Paths*.[44] These works would earn their authors world renown in their respective fields and would drive their international careers over the next two decades.

By the time he published *The Garden of Forking Paths*, Borges had already incorporated reference to the Kabbalah in several of his works. The earliest mention appears in his 1926 essay "A History of Angels," where he mentions the books by Bischoff and Stehelin and discusses the symbolism of the letter *aleph*.[45]

In 1932 he published the well-known essay "A Vindication of the Kabbalah," and in 1934, in his polemical text "I, a Jew," he takes pride in his intellectual affinity for the Kabbalah.[46] These references all clearly predate Scholem's own major publications. Last, in 1944 Borges published his collection *Ficciones* that included stories such as "Death and the Compass," which makes extensive reference to figures and concepts of Jewish mysticism (including bibliographic allusions to Buber's writings) but does not mention Scholem.

Only in 1946 does Scholem's name begin to appear in Borges's marginalia. That year, Borges left references to Scholem's *Major Trends in Jewish Mysticism* in the back pages of his copies of Bischoff's *Die Elemente der Kabbalah* and Buber's *Vom Geist des Judentums*.[47] The following year, in 1947, he left a reference to the same book by Scholem in the back pages of his copy of Buber's *Tales of the Hasidim*.[48] That same year, Borges read Nachum Glatzer's book *In Time and Eternity: A Jewish Reader* (1946), which he mentions in his essay "On Chesterton" of the same year.[49]

In June 1951, Borges was invited to speak at the twenty-five-year anniversary celebration of the Sociedad Hebraica Argentina.[50] In his address he lists the many Jewish texts he is familiar with, including "the books by Scholem."[51] It is curious that Borges mentions "books" in the plural. As of 1951, Scholem had only published two books Borges knew of, *Major Trends in Jewish Mysticism* (1941) and *Zohar: The Book of Splendor* (1949). Borges had already referred to the *Zohar* twice in texts published in 1947 (predating Scholem's book) and cites his source as Glatzer's book *In Time and Eternity*.[52] At any rate, since first encountering Scholem around 1946, this is the first public proclamation of Borges's own familiarity with Scholem's work.

In those same years, Borges made repeated reference to the Kabbalah in his stories. A well-known example is the story "The Aleph," published in his 1949 collection of the same title. Similarly, in his book of essays *Otras Inquisiciones* (1952) Borges makes reference to Kabbalah (as well as to Buber, Kafka, and other figures that existed in Scholem's orbit). In this regard, it is notable that while Borges mentions other authors such as Buber and Glatzer in texts he was writing around the time he read them, Scholem is absent from all of Borges's collections into the mid-1950s. While the Kabbalah was clearly a field of interest and a developing web of literary allusions in Borges's oeuvre, Scholem's name makes absolutely no appearances in it.

Another place to look for Scholem in Borges's writing would be their shared interest in the figure of the Golem. Borges had read about the Golem in studies of Kabbalah and recalls enjoying the aforementioned novel by Meyrink. He first begins to cite primary sources in connection with this Kabbalistic topic only in the mid-1950s. The earliest examples of this appear in two coedited anthologies that Borges published in those years, where he quotes excerpts from the Babylonian Talmud. This primary source appears in the entries "Un Golem" in the anthology *Cuentos breves y extraordinarios* (1955) and "The Golem" in *Manual de zoología fantástica* (1957).[53] Both of these offer an extensive quote (translated, Borges knew no Hebrew or Aramaic) discussing the mythical character of the Golem taken from the Babylonian Talmud (Tractate Sanhedrin 65b). There is no mention of Scholem in either of these works. This exact rabbinic source was referenced and quoted in Scholem's earliest work on the Golem, first published in 1954.[54] However, Borges was already familiar with this passage from the book *Hebraic Literature: Translations from the Talmud, Midrashim and Kabbala*, which he read in 1945 and in which the very first note he made in the back pages is to this paragraph of the Talmud.[55]

The pattern that emerges from these early encounters and overlaps is that Scholem seems to repeat what Borges already knows about these topics. Borges's marginalia seem to plug Scholem into what he already knows from previous sources on the Kabbalah, while his references to Kabbalah in his stories and essays of the same years continue to favor those same previous sources over the later-encountered work by Scholem. This is true whether Borges's familiarity with Scholem is confirmed—as in the case of the references to Scholem in the back pages of Buber and Bischoff—or whether it is unconfirmed—as in the case of possible familiarity with Scholem's work on the *Zohar* or the Golem. One explanation for the absence of Scholem from Borges's canonical texts is that, whenever encountered, Scholem seems only to recap what Borges already discovered in other sources—all of which he references in his writing. When we add to this that Borges often cites his source, as the many references in his canonical texts demonstrate, we must conclude that the absence of Scholem from these texts attests to a lack of direct engagement with his work. Only around the time of their encounter in Jerusalem did Borges begin to value Scholem over other sources on the Kabbalah. This shift will become evident in interviews Borges gave in the early 1970s.

Given the above timeline, and the pattern that emerges, we must now try to identify the moment at which Borges first engages with Scholem in his own writing. The first time Scholem's name appears in Borges's writing is in 1958 when, in his poem "The Golem," Borges rhymes the words "golem" and "Scholem" twice.[56] Here is the first such couplet:

> The Kabbalist who officiated the numen
> To the vast creature gave the nickname Golem
> These truths are conveyed by Scholem
> In a learned passage of his volume.[57]

How are we to read this tongue-in-cheek reference to Scholem in the context of Borges's decades-long engagement with the Kabbalah? Scholarly opinions have been inconsistent on this matter. Alazraki states that "Borges' debt to Scholem is acknowledged in [this] couplet from his poem," asserting that the poem's referenced "volume" refers to *Major Trends in Jewish Mysticism*, "undoubtedly the most authoritative work on the subject and a model of scholarship."[58] And yet this "debt" is imperceptible in our readings of Borges's most canonical texts, many of which predate Scholem's own work, and none of which make reference to Scholem.

Alazraki indicates another inconsistency, pointing out that while he himself asserts the poem's reference is to *Major Trends in Jewish Mysticism*, Scholem's book "hardly devotes a few lines to the question of the golem."[59] In fact, the only mention of the Golem in *Major Trends in Jewish Mysticism* is contained in a single passage.[60] The information Borges's poem presents about the Golem is more consistent with what Borges read in Meyrink's novel, Alazraki concludes. Years later in his "Autobiographical Essay," Borges would admit Scholem was a "name I had twice used as the only possible rhyming word in a poem of my own on the Golem."[61] An entertaining literary confabulation perhaps, but certainly not an acknowledgment of debt.

Since the Golem is indeed merely a passing mention in *Major Trends in Jewish Mysticism*, another possibility may be that Borges's poem is referring to Scholem's well-known chapter about the Golem in *On the Kabbalah and Its Symbolism*. This book was not published until 1960 in German and 1965 in English. However, the chapter about the Golem is based on a lecture that Scholem delivered at the 1953 Eranos conference in Switzerland. The lecture was printed in the conference proceedings the following year. It is possible that Borges had read Scholem's paper about the Golem in the Eranos conference proceedings of 1953.[62] This lecture became the chapter about the Golem in *On the Kabbalah and Its Symbolism*. If this is the case, then the confabulation in the poem does not relate to the source of Borges's knowledge of the Golem, but rather to the attribution of this knowledge to "his volume."

Scholem himself had read this poem in the mid-1960s.[63] When he met Borges for the first time in 1969, and with the knowledge of Borges's interest in the Golem, he gave Borges a copy of *On the Kabbalah and Its Symbolism*.[64] Borges retuned to Argentina with the book and proceeded to thoroughly annotate the chapter on the Golem, and only the chapter on the Golem. This suggests perhaps that he was not familiar with this publication earlier.

Either way, Borges has certainly taken poetic license in this poem and my intention is not to reduce this poem to its bibliographic incidentals. Rather, I want to use this poem and its confabulation to indicate two conclusions. First, we can now estimate that it was at some moment around 1958 that Scholem is drawn into Borges's web of allusions to the Kabbalah and, by extension, into Borges's intellectual engagement with the Kabbalah, whether this is in response to Scholem's Eranos lecture about the Golem or not. Second, Borges's references to Scholem are not bibliographically motivated. Any attempt to read such references in terms of "citation" or "debt" will lead to inconsistencies. Rather, Borges's references to Scholem are poetically motivated. Their proliferation in interviews and lectures in the 1960s and onward established Scholem as a Borgesian precursor for a particular stylistic and poetic goal Borges had in mind. In fact, he clearly states this poetic goal in his well-known essay "A Vindication of the Kabbalah," published in 1932, long before Scholem arrived on the scene. In the following chapter, we will turn our attention to understanding what Borges perceives himself as doing when he inserts such references into his stories, and how he represents those poetics in his own reflections on writing.

2

The Ideal Author

Borges's two collections, *Ficciones* (1944) and *El Aleph* (1949), mark the stabilization, if not canonization, of his narrative voice. These collections include several stories with reference to the Kabbalah. Some are more obvious, like the visions of the *ein sof* (the infinite divine) in "The Aleph" or the mention of books such as *Sefer Yezirah*, *Biography of the Baal Shem*, and *History of the Hasidic Sect* in "Death and the Compass" and "The Secret Miracle." Some have required more interpretive work to appreciate, such as the person behind the veil in "The Approach to al Mu'tasim," or the Golem-like creation in "The Circular Ruins." As noted, much has been written about these Kabbalistic stories in Borges's oeuvre and the bibliography of the present study refers to many of these fine publications.

What interests me here is not so much the identification of these themes. I would like rather to ask about Borges's self-reflection on the use of these themes. It is doubtful that mentions of a vision of the *ein sof*, or the creation of a Golem, are connected to any mystical practices Borges might have taken up as a result of reading Erich Bischoff, Martin Buber, or, later, Gershom Scholem. And it is equally unlikely that in spite of his external appearance as an Argentine intellectual Borges was in fact secretly a charismatic mystic (despite some suggestion to the contrary).[1] What is clear is that he makes use of these allusions to weave the fictions he is renowned for. How, then, does Borges see the place of these allusions in his own writing? If we are able to pursue this question while avoiding the methodological pitfalls outlined in the previous chapter, the answer will lead to the heart of Borges's idiosyncratic take, not only on the Kabbalah, but on the Judaic more generally.

The understanding of Kabbalah as a mode of reading and interpretation was introduced in Borges studies by Jaime Alazraki and Saul Sosnowski in the early 1970s. This view was soon to be promoted by both Harold Bloom and George Steiner in their respective 1975 books. In his book *After Babel*, Steiner sees Borges as a modern-day Kabbalist, while Bloom understood the Kabbalah more generally as a mode of creative misreading in his book *Kabbalah and Criticism*.[2] In his later work, Alazraki references Bloom as encapsulating his own attitude toward Borges: "The pathways charted by Bloom in his book, *Kabbalah and Criticism*, lead Borges to similar conclusions regarding the nature of the literary act."[3] Edna Aizenberg, reversing (or correcting) the temporal logic, argues that it was Borges who inspired the literary-theoretical understanding of Jewish textual traditions in Bloom, Geoffrey Hartman, and others.[4] Borges "anticipated and inspired one of the principal currents of contemporary criticism, a Hebraist current that presumes to find a paradigm . . . in Jewish hermeneutics."[5] Following Aizenberg, it seems to me that one notable consequence of this intellectual relation outlined by Alazraki and Aizenberg—between Borges and his readers, and between Borges and a contemporary theory of reading—is the uncritical melding of Borges-as-author with Borges-as-reader, and Borges-as-reader with Borges-readers. This slippage has led scholarship away from questions about Borges's own perception of his role and activity as author. Yet Borges's expressed attitude toward the Kabbalah should trouble this uncritical overlap.

Throughout his career, Borges relied on allusions to the Judaic as a way of expressing his thoughts on the problematic of authorship. What is introduced in this context as "the Kabbalah" in his early writings develops over the decades into a fuller expression of his thoughts on authorship, growing at once more integral and more idiosyncratic as time goes by. As we turn our attention to the earliest mentions of the Kabbalah in Borges's writing, we should bear in mind this intellectual and poetic trajectory that the current study aims to track. If we see Borges depart from what we (and indeed he himself) may know about the Kabbalah, it will be toward an expansion of the Judaic into a powerful encapsulation of the problematic of authorship. Furthermore, developments in his thought should be read contextually, and always in relation to his contemporary social moment. This is how we will read his turn from discussing Kabbalah to discussing Jewish tradition and, presently, this is how we will read his turn from understanding the Kabbalah as a mode of reading to seeing the Kabbalah as a paradigm for writing. We must track the origins of the perspectival shift Borges signals in his own discussions of the Kabbalah, away from questions of reading and interpretation and toward questions of authorship. In so doing, we will shift attention to the central role of the Kabbalah, not in the interpretive work of the scholar but in Borges's self-reflections as an author, and highlight the way reference to the

Kabbalah helps Borges articulate his notion of authorship already in the early years of his career.

A Vindication of the Author

Self-reflection on the literary use of the Kabbalah was present in Borges's writing during the same years in which he composed his fictions. While its literary utility as a poetic element is evident in *Ficciones* (1944) and *El Aleph* (1949), the Kabbalah is also a persistent reference in Borges's essays on literature. One of the preoccupations in his equally renowned collections of essays *Discusión* (1932) and *Otras Inquisiciones* (1952) is with the role and activity of the author.[6] Here too Borges will refer to ideas he sees expressed in his readings on the Kabbalah. What I would like to highlight here is that Borges uses the Kabbalah both aesthetically to stylize his narrative fictions, and intellectually in his essays reflecting on his role and position as the narrator of fictions. This utility of the Kabbalah in formulating thoughts on intellectual questions of writing and authorship is evident in his discussions of the Kabbalah as early as his essay "Una vindicación de la Cábala [A Vindication of the Kabbalah]" published in *Discusión* (1932).[7]

This 1932 essay was the first of two texts Borges devoted to discussion of the Kabbalah. They were published almost five decades apart, "A Vindication of the Kabbalah" in 1932 and his lecture "The Kabbalah" in 1977.[8] What is pertinent to my argument is that, already in 1932, well before Scholem's major works had been published, Borges identified the Kabbalah's relevance for explaining his own activities as an author. Several decades later, Scholem's works would come to expand and reinforce this relevance.

It is certainly true that Borges identifies in Kabbalistic interpretive practices what Alazraki calls "possible alternatives to the reading of a text."[9] But these alternatives are only the "technical side of Kabbalism."[10] They are operations limited to the extraction—through endless interpretation—of a plurality of meanings from the perfect text that is the Bible. Ingenious as they may have been, Borges is not as concerned with the Kabbalists and their operations as might first appear. What interests Borges is what the applicability of such technical operations implies about the authorship of the text. He already signals as much in the opening lines of "A Vindication of the Kabbalah," where he introduces his interest in the theme (as is often the case in his essays) rather disingenuously.

> Neither the first time it has been attempted, nor the last time it will fail, this [vindication] is distinguished by two facts. One is my almost complete ignorance of the Hebrew language; the other, my desire to defend *not the doctrine* but rather the hermeneutical or cryptographic *procedures* that lead to

it. These procedures, as is well known, include the vertical reading of sacred texts, the reading referred to as boustrophedon (one line from left to right, the following line from right to left), the methodical substitution of certain letters of the alphabet for others, the sum of the numerical value of the letters, etc. To ridicule such operations is simple; I prefer to attempt to understand them.[11]

Among the procedures Borges enumerates are "the methodical substitution of certain letters of the alphabet for others, the sum of the numerical value of the letters, etc."[12] It is clear why, to some researchers, such procedures have implied an interest in "alternatives to reading." However, this opening paragraph is somewhat misleading. "According to Gershom Scholem," explains Alazraki, "none of these techniques of mystical exegesis can be called Kabbalistic in the strict sense of the word," implying that Borges's vindication might not actually be concerned with the Kabbalah at all, but rather with a set of technical procedures.[13] Of course, Borges could not have known this in 1932, well before he would have read these lines in Scholem.

Borges's focus on "procedures" becomes all the more central to understanding his intellectual engagement with the Kabbalah (and his relationship with Scholem) when we note that the opening lines of the essay cited above are the opening lines from the second (1957) edition of this essay, which has since been the version to appear in all reprints and collections, and which any reader looking up this essay will encounter.[14] Noting that the opening paragraph of this essay in the first (1932) edition was slightly, but importantly, different than what was just cited only adds to the curious nature of Borges's opening statement. Here is how Borges introduces his interests in the first (1932) version of this essay.

> Neither the first time it has been attempted, nor the last time it will fail, this [vindication] is distinguished by two facts. One is my splendid innocence of the sacred language; another is the attenuating circumstance that I do not want to vindicate the doctrine, *nor its mechanism*, but rather the general principle they postulate. . . . The Kabbalah, it is known, is the infinite interpretation of Scripture, through the permutation of letters, the calculation of their numerical value, observed inconsistencies, the decomposition of words in sentences, skipping [words] as one reads or [reading words] vertically, and other formal rules. To mock *this methodical trifle* is a paltry occupation. I prefer to attempt to understand it.[15]

In this first version, Borges states that he does not want to vindicate the doctrine, *nor the mechanism* of the Kabbalah—which he refers to as "methodical trifle."[16] Although he enumerates several such trifles, what he proposes is to understand the general principle, the postulate of the Kabbalah. Here is the short passage from Scholem (referenced by Alazraki) about these interpretive practices:

> Certain techniques of mystical speculation which are popularly supposed to represent the heart and core of Kabbalism, such as Gematria, i.e. the calculation of the numerical value of Hebrew words and the search for connections with other words or phrases of equal value; Notarikon, or interpretation of the letters of a word as abbreviations of whole sentences; and Temurah, or interchange of letters according to certain systematic rules. As a matter of historical fact, none of these techniques of mystical exegesis can be called Kabbalistic in the strict sense of the word.[17]

To Alazraki's point, it seems Borges focused his essay on those reading practices that cannot be called "Kabbalistic in the strict sense of the word" rather deliberately. Borges would have encountered these lines in Scholem ten years before the second edition of this essay, and yet he revised the opening paragraph so it would state an interest in precisely those "trifling" techniques rather than the "general principle" of the Kabbalah. That is, familiarity with Scholem notwithstanding, Borges doubles down on his statement, asserting that it is not the doctrine of the Kabbalah (Scholem's intellectual purview) that he wishes to vindicate, but rather the hermeneutical procedures. This revision demonstrates that Borges is not taking his cues from Scholem, at least not in the way previous scholars have presented it (as a debt). Following this understanding, we must now address the broader question: What, then, is at stake in this revision?

What is an Author?

Between the self-irony and the list of odd hermeneutical procedures, one change to the opening paragraph is easily glossed over. In 1957, Borges states quite clearly his "desire to defend not the doctrine but rather the hermeneutical or cryptographic procedures *that lead to it*."[18] The question is: hermeneutical procedures that lead to a doctrine? Clearly, the odd interpretive practices Borges calls "hermeneutical procedures" are the *result* of a doctrine regarding the sacred origin of the text. The infinite interpretability of Scripture, which would be the justification for developing such cryptographic procedures, is concluded from the doctrine that sees in Scripture "an absolute text, where the collaboration of chance is calculated at zero."[19] That is, believing the Bible to be perfectly and absolutely interpretable leads to developing these alternative techniques of reading. It is the doctrine that leads to and authorizes the "procedures," based on what in 1932 Borges terms "the general principle they postulate."[20]

In the 1957 edition, Borges seems to have flipped the causal relations between interpretation and doctrine, identifying the procedure as that which leads to the doctrine, and not the reverse. Borges suggests the doctrine of a sacred text is not the basis justifying the Kabbalists' odd interpretive procedures. This doctrine is rather a result of the success (perhaps unexpected) of these procedures at generating a multiplicity of meaning in the text. This is not a surprising editorial revision, at least not when we realize that this change only enhances the departure that follows Borges's initial statement of interest (in both editions), and that guides the essay toward its concern with conceptions of authorship rather than procedures of readership. In typical fashion, Borges rather casually glosses over what will be a central point of his essay—the reversal of this causal logic. That is, Borges will maintain that the fact that interpreting the Bible through such alternative techniques is able to yield meaning leads to the conclusion that it is a perfect text.

To make sense of this reversal, we might note that this early essay already marks an understanding of Kabbalah that will shape Borges's future reading of Scholem and remains consistent in his lifelong interest in the Kabbalah. The Kabbalah suggests to Borges a powerful conceptualization of the perspective of a narrator (rather than an interpreter), and this perspective is unaltered by Borges's encounter with Scholem. When Borges refers to the Kabbalah (and later to Scholem), we should be attuned to the way he uses such reference to express his interest not in questions of interpretation but in the implications of authorship. Returning to the 1932 essay, I want to keep tracking the perspective shift from reader to author.

A second departure from Borges's stated intention in the opening paragraph of "A Vindication of the Kabbalah" comes when, having declared his interest in method rather than doctrine, for the rest of the essay he proceeds to consider only the doctrine of a perfect book and never again mentions any interpretive technique. "Thus one may justify the dogma," he concludes after some discussion.[21] After stating his justification of the dogma of a perfect book, he moves on to a discussion of its exemplary narrative. "A general census of the publications of the Holy Spirit," Borges writes, are "modestly calculated at a hundred and some; but the one that interests me now is *Genesis*: the subject matter of the Kabbalah."[22] The Kabbalists took the entire Bible, many texts of the Talmud, and even other Kabbalistic writings as their subject matter, and Borges was surely aware of the Kabbalah's varied subject matter, having read Bischoff and others. Yet this generalization about the Kabbalah should not surprise us. After all, Borges is not a historian nor a researcher of the Kabbalah. What he signals here is his narratological preoccupation, that what he has in mind when he speaks of the dogma of a "perfect book" or an "absolute text" is a narrative, a story. What better example of this than the biblical story of Genesis, the text of which, the Kabbalists believed, was itself the story narrated by divinity in order to bring the world into existence. A story about how a story created the world, which turns out to be that selfsame story—it hardly gets more Borgesian than that.

"The Kabbalists believed . . . in the divinity of that *story*, in its deliberate writing by an infinite intelligence. The consequences of such an assumption are many."[23] One such consequence, we might suspect, is the development of cryptographic procedures. Borges seemingly admits this, the gloss in his opening paragraph notwithstanding—it is the doctrine that leads to the interpretive practices. Yet this is of no concern to Borges, who will in fact, in a final departure, insist on the implications of his original statement—procedures lead to doctrine. I would like to explain this duplicitous statement regarding the causal relation between interpretation and doctrine as part of Borges's effort in this essay to shift the perspective from the reader, interpreter—that is, the Kabbalist—to the writer, to the Holy Spirit as an author. From the perspective of the Kabbalists, the doctrine of a sacred text leads to their hermeneutical procedures. But from the perspective of the divinity who conceded and descended (as Borges will put it) into human writing, it is the procedures that lead to divinity's successful manifestation in the world, exhibited through the multiplicity of meaning in the text. Thus, the consequences Borges speaks of do not relate to the practice of reading so much as they do to an understanding of the various (human) practices of narrating. It is the idea of an infinite intelligence narrating a story that appeals to Borges.

Borges provides three examples of human writing in order to explain (vindicate) what he is drawn to in the Kabbalah. First, the journalistic text, as an example of prosaic writing, is very little concerned with form. What it seeks to communicate is its content. Its form is therefore subject to arbitrary results. For in such prosaic texts, "the length and sound of the paragraphs are necessarily accidental. The contrary occurs in poetry, whose usual law is the subjection of meaning to euphonic needs."[24] Poetry, as the opposite example, is primarily concerned with form. Its content is therefore subject to arbitrary results. Borges introduces this distinction between poetry and prose, not to delve into their subtle differences but simply to disqualify the activities of the poet and the journalist as paradigms for writing. Neither poet nor journalist defines the kind of authorship Borges is attracted to, and which Kabbalistic doctrine identifies in the stories of Genesis. Precisely because the collaboration of chance in their composition is measurable, they do not lend themselves to the techniques of infinite interpretation. The applicability of these techniques, we will recall, leads to the doctrine of infinite interpretability.

This doctrine has direct narratological implications for Borges, who comes here to his most striking suggestion in this essay. "Let us consider a third writer: the intellectual. In his handling of prose . . . or of verse, he has certainly not eliminated chance, but he has denied it as much as possible, and restricted its incalculable compliance. He remotely approximates the Lord, for Whom the vague concept of chance holds no meaning."[25] Borges's vindication of the Kabbalah is the vindication of a doctrine that privileges God-as-storyteller and provides a model for the intellectual narrator to aspire toward. "Let us imagine now this astral intelligence, dedicated to manifesting itself . . . in written words,"[26] proposes Borges, ambiguously omitting the subject of "this intelligence." In this analogy Borges is not the Kabbalist, who must develop alternatives to reading in order to plumb the meaning of a perfect text. *He is its author.*[27]

Already in this early essay, with its early references to Kabbalah, it is the role of the intellectual author that Borges is concerned with. A role that, through the writing of stories, desires to approximate "the Lord, the perfected God of the theologians, Who sees all at once . . . not only all the events of this replete world but also those that would take place if even the most evanescent—or impossible—of them should change."[28] In his divine approximation, the intellectual narrator explores alternatives to "this world" through speculation on, and narration of, its evanescent or impossible variations.

It may be true, as Alazraki suggests, that "Borges challenges the reader to activate all his resources, to become himself a Kabbalist," so to speak.[29] But this is only a further indication of Borges's difference from the Kabbalists. For Borges, the adjective Kabbalistic is far more importantly a modifier of the authorial function than of any mechanism of analysis. In this important sense, Borges wants to be understood as a divine narrator rather than a Kabbalistic interpreter. And identifying his texts as Kabbalistic stories should indicate that his readers encounter in them a strong suggestive sense, which Borges creates through the web of allusions at his disposal, suggesting that there are multiple and hidden meanings in his writings. This has been the inclination among the finest scholars of Borges and the Kabbalah, including Edna Aizenberg in this Borgesian pseudepigrapha:

> Hermeneutically and cryptographically, I will let my readers follow the revelations lying in wait in the opening and final paragraphs of "Tlön, Uqbar, Orbis Tertius." . . . I will also encourage them to observe the mechanisms of infinite purposes of the *ab aeterno* Library-Universe of "La biblioteca de Babel." . . . I will suggest that they notice the infallible variations of the archetypal Hebrew signs of the combinatory *Sefer Yetsirah*, translated into German by Jaromir Hladík in "The Secret Miracle." . . . And I will encourage them to note the superimpositions of light reflected from the YHVH, the Tetragrammaton [in "Death and the Compass"].[30]

As a divine narrator, Borges invites his readers to be Kabbalists, or at least to read like a Kabbalist. Most importantly, however, his success at eliciting this engagement from his readers vindicates his own approximation of the divinity-as-author through his role as an intellectual narrator. And yet, in this essay Borges offers no clear statement of what it means for an author to approximate the Lord. Creating a fictional narrative world, as rich as it may be, seems to fall short. After all, the God of the Kabbalists did not create a fictional world but narrated "this replete world" into existence. Having demonstrated Borges's reliance on the Kabbalah in order to articulate his perception of the author in this early essay, we must also attempt to read this same expression in Borges's narrative texts. We will turn now to examples of such stories by Borges that both express this view of the author and strive to exemplify it through the intellectual narrator's storytelling. Our challenge will be to assume the role of the reader-as-Kabbalist without losing sight of Borges-as-(divine)-author.

Another Creation Story

Readers familiar with Borges may already sense that I am leading the discussion toward a story in which "this replete world," our world, is narrated into existence. The story "Tlön, Uqbar, Orbis Tertius" is one of Borges's most famous. In it, a secret cabal (I use this word very deliberately) conspires to narrate a world into existence. A terrible, unsustainable world, a world that turns out to be Borges's own world under Nazism.

There are many excellent readings of this story as a commentary on Nazism at the time.[31] Borges himself makes this clear to his readers as well. In the postscript he draws direct connections between the world that was created first in the imagination of a "shadowy man of genius" and then, through its narration in encyclopedias, invaded reality and overtook it.[32] What I want to highlight are two ways that this 1940 story echoes Borges's thoughts about God-the-narrator, already expressed in his 1932 essay on the Kabbalah that we have just read.

In the creation of Tlön, Borges exhibits what for an intellectual historian (such as Scholem) would be uncritical slippage between Gnosticism, metaphysics, and Kabbalah. At one moment, the heresiarchs of Tlön are Gnostics—"The text of the encyclopedia ran: For one of those gnostics, the visible universe was an illusion or, more precisely, a sophism."[33] At another moment, they are metaphysicians—"The metaphysicians of Tlön seek not truth, or even plausibility—they seek to amaze, astound. In their view, metaphysics is a branch of fantastic literature."[34] And at yet another moment, they are students of the Kabbalah—"A secret benevolent society . . . was born; its mission: to invent a country. In its vague initial program, there figured 'hermetic studies,' philanthropy, and the Kabbalah."[35]

As discussed in the previous chapter, when confronted with such expressions in Borges's work, rather than ask about the accuracy of his understanding, we must ask about the literary and representational value of such confluence of terms. In the case of the creators of Tlön, this slippage serves to characterize their activity precisely in the terms of the intellectual author Borges conceived of in 1932. Furthermore, in the world of Tlön, Gnosticism, metaphysics, and Kabbalah are all recast as representational strategies employed in the production of a story that will become reality.

Thus, the Gnostic heresiarch believes that while the visible world may exist, it is misleading to ask questions about this reality. "The world" is a sophism. The true question is about the story that created it. Similarly, the metaphysicians of Tlön, in speculating on what lies beyond the visible physical world, do not understand themselves as philosophers but as authors of fantastic literature, as narrators who seek to astound their readers. Finally, the idea that Kabbalah studies should be included in the program for inventing a country is recast in all its hubris by the main financier of the endeavor: "The reclusive millionaire Ezra Buckley...laughed at the modesty of the project. He told the man that in America it was nonsense to invent a country—what they ought to do was invention a planet.... Buckley did not believe in God, yet he wanted to prove to the nonexistent God that mortal men are able to conceive and shape a world."[36]

The Kabbalah serves as a touchpoint for representing the extent of the cabal's project, and hubris, by framing their efforts as a competition with God precisely in the realm in which Borges's intellectual narrator seeks to approximate divinity. If in "A Vindication of the Kabbalah" Borges conceives of the intellectual author as one who is seeking the power to create worlds, in "Tlön, Uqbar, Orbis Tertius" he casts the activity of world creation as dangerous and corruptible.

While the fictional authors in the story of Tlön are competing with God for the power of world-narrating, Borges, the "real" author of the story, is also attempting to approximate divinity in his activity as narrator. The framing of the story follows Borges's own elaboration of divinity in 1932, as what the author aspires toward. Recall Borges's description of the intellectual author. "He remotely approximates...the perfect God of the theologians, Who sees all at once...not only all the events of this replete world but also those that would take place if even the most evanescent—or impossible—of them should change."[37] Borges, the author of Tlön, constructs his story through a thought experiment on this (our) world and what "would take place if even the most evanescent... should change."[38] Thus, "the intent to set forth a world that is not too incompatible with the real world" is an intent Borges shares with the cabal of Tlön.[39]

What is the minor variation Borges introduces in order to create Tlön? Tlön is the narrative exploration of a world that would emerge if, in our own world, the "idealists" were to win the philosophical debate against the "empiricists." This is how Borges frames the comparison between Earth and Tlön: "Hume declared for all time that while Berkeley's arguments admit not the slightest refutation, they inspire not the slightest conviction. This pronouncement is entirely true with respect to the earth, entirely false with respect to Tlön. The nations of that planet are, congenitally, idealist.[40] Their language and those things derived from their language—religion, literature, metaphysics—presuppose idealism."[41]

Much of the story follows this thought experiment as Borges himself explores alternatives to "this world" through speculation on and narration of this seemingly impossible variation. What would the world be like if its inhabitants, rather than believe it is real and observable, thought it was a figment or projection of their own inner experiences? Anyone and everyone would be narrating their own world into existence. Narrating into existence a world that accords more with their desires than the empirical one that surrounds them. This, in fact, is the alluring power of Tlön: "Almost immediately, reality ceded at more than one point. The truth is, it wanted to cede. Ten years ago, any symmetry, any system with an appearance of order—dialectical materialism, anti-Semitism, Nazism—could spellbind and hypnotize mankind. How could it not submit to Tlön, to the vast and minutely detailed evidence of an orderly planet?"[42]

Idealism is the guiding logic of Nazism, suggests Borges, and the world is being made to correspond to the Nazi experience of it. The idea that the narration of a world could bring about its emergence into reality echoes Borges's account of the Genesis creation story mentioned in "A Vindication of the Kabbalah." Tlön is Borges's Genesis story, a story about how a story by a "shadowy man of genius" created our world. As Evelyn Fishburn suggests, "eventually, we may think of the story as being not so much about a world that has become permeated by idealism, but as being itself an illustration or embodiment of this idea, the experience of this, its dominant conceit."[43] If in Tlön the world does not exist outside of one's experience of it, the story "Tlön, Uqbar, Orbis Tertius" narrates this world-as-experience into existence, in the sense that it creates (or seeks to create) this experience in its readers, as "its dominant conceit." A story about how a story created our experience of the world, which turns out to be that selfsame story.[44] "That was the first intrusion of the fantastic world of Tlön into the real world."[45]

This story is an impressive demonstration of Borges's approximation of God-as-author, not in metaphysical or mystical terms, but in literary creative terms. Borges is drawn to the Kabbalah for its power in articulating the role of the author as literary-world-creator. The difference between Borges and Tlön is also a matter of esotericism. While Borges declares his desire to approximate the Lord, and defines such efforts in literary terms, the "man of genius" creating Tlön does so in the shadows, in secret societies and cabals. The story of Tlön is the story of a conspiracy.

Cabal and Complot

Before proceeding to the next text, I would like to take a detour to consider the literary role conspiracy plays in Borges and its relation to the ideal reader, whom we have seen conceived of as a Kabbalist in "A Vindication of the Kabbalah." The reader as a Kabbalist and the reader as a conspiracy theorist share a search for the concealed meaning of the text or the world. However, the Kabbalist as an ideal reader does not present Borges with the possibilities of political intervention that were becoming so urgent in the late 1930s and into the 1940s. In that sense, while Borges may be approximating divinity in his story of Tlön, the political force of his intervention into the cultural realities of Argentina in 1940 is expressed by the markedly conspiratorial depiction of literary world creation.

While the creators of Tlön are represented through allusion to the Kabbalah and divinity-as-author, the implied reader of the story is not placed in the shoes of a Kabbalist searching for traces of divinity in the world. Rather, they see the story through the eyes of a conspiracy theorist who slowly uncovers the truth about the Tlönian cabal. In this sense, the story does not only echo Borges's existing views on the Kabbalah but also marks a development in his thought about authorship. This development can be seen most clearly in the emergence of an overlap between the Kabbalist and the conspiracy theorist introduced in "Tlön, Uqbar, Orbis Tertius," an overlap that will continue to inform some of his most notable anti-Nazi activities in the 1940s.

In his essay "Teoría del complot," Ricardo Piglia reads conspiracy as a node that politicizes literature (in Borges and in Argentine literature more broadly).[46] He understands complot as the "other plot" that accompanies the fictional plot, and that reveals its underlying political subject. The assumption is that politics is not fictional, and that literature inevitably alludes to it and is informed by it. Following the above reading of "Tlön, Uqbar, Orbis Tertius" and its overlap with the theme of Kabbalah, I would like to consider the opposite possibility in Borges's writing, namely, that complot is a node that serves to fictionalize politics. That is, that Borges reads the conspiracies of politics as revealing the underlying literary nature of the political order. If the previous story was about an external conspiracy that invades the world, the next text—"A Comment on August 23, 1944"[47]—will introduce conspiracy as the center of political activity and historical causality. My reading of the overlap between Kabbalah and complot, and by extension literature and politics, will thus depart from Piglia's reading in the following two senses.

First, I do not want to search for explicit or obvious examples of conspiracy that have formal functions within a story, such as "Tlön, Uqbar, Orbis Tertius." Piglia also cites "The Theme of the Traitor and the Hero" and "The Lottery in Babylon" as further examples, but all these are stories that explicitly deal with conspiracy as their subject matter. I would like instead to pay attention to more successful conspiracies. That is, narratives in which the complot remains unresolved (as in "Emma Zunz") or misidentified (as in "The Man on the Threshold"), perhaps even requires a conspiracy theorist to identify it.[48] If, as Piglia suggests, Borges is trying to articulate the link between literature and politics through the notion of complot, we must assume literature to be as devious and dissimulating as politics. We must identify in Borges's writing not only the ways in which fictional narratives serve a political purpose, but the ways in which politics is secretly a literary endeavor.

Second, Piglia's discussion assumes that politics (via the state and the economy) function in a conspiratorial manner to influence the political subject. He is thus focused on "constructing a complot against the complot" as the individual's strategy of combating this overarching conspiracy.[49] As we have seen in the story of Tlön, it is equally possible, perhaps even a defining characteristic of "the world" for Borges, that it in turn is oblivious to the invisible forces that structure its destiny. The possibility of seeing reality itself both as the product of a world-making narrative and at the same time as the product of a political conspiracy draws our attention to the overlap between fiction and politics. This possibility is also recognized by Alberto Moreiras, who seeks to delimit the conceptual threat of such overlap, lest "conspiracy would seem exhaustively to coincide with the universe."[50]

I follow Moreiras in that I do not read Borges as producing a world—fictional or otherwise, infinitely interpretable or otherwise—that is coterminous with conspiracy. The conspiracy theorist is committed to a notion of reality as fixed, hidden yet knowable, and, most importantly, not produced by the author's activity. The author, always suspected of a cover-up by the conspiracy theorist, dissimulates the world. For the Kabbalist as for Borges, the author creates the world. For the conspiracy theorist as reader, the logic of the visible world is essentially political. For the Kabbalist, as Borges's ideal reader, the visible world is at its most fundamental level a fictional narrative. As Moreiras writes: "There is a crucial difference, repeatedly exposed in Borges's texts . . . between what can be derived from understanding the possibility of conspiracy and understanding that understanding the possibility of conspiracy is a fundamental act of poetic freedom that presupposes—necessarily—the possibility of nonconspiracy, of the finitude of conspiracy."[51]

We turn now to Borges's essay "A Comment on August 23, 1944" to offer an example that demonstrates such an act of poetic freedom by Borges.[52] My broader intention is to further demonstrate the overlap of literature and politics that develops in Borges's writing as a response to Nazism in Argentina and the ways in which this grows out of his existing interest in the Kabbalah. The ideal reader as a conspiracy theorist gained traction in Borges's writing during World War II and is perhaps most clearly expressed in "A Comment on August 23, 1944." Following the war, his depiction of the ideal reader returned to its original Kabbalistic orientation, as we will see subsequently when we read "The God's Script."

A Comment on Literature and Conspiracy

On August 23, 1944, a coup overthrew the government of Romania (one of Hitler's most loyal allies) and the country immediately surrendered to the Russian forces. A few days later the Allied forces liberated Paris. These events marked the beginning of the end for Hitler's ambitious military campaign. The liberation of Paris was welcome news in Argentina. In Buenos Aires and across the country, spontaneous celebrations broke out. People flooded the monument in Plaza Francia, placed flowers at the base of the monument, and held a celebratory vigil. This spontaneous celebration was repeated the following day. A multitude crowded Plaza Francia, placed more flowers, and remained in the plaza for hours celebrating the news.

Tracking the focus of reporting in the major daily paper *La Nación* over these few days will give us a sense of the magnitude and spontaneity of this public celebration. On the morning of August 23, *La Nación* was still reporting yesterday's news of the Allies advancing toward Paris from the southeast, including maps of the frontlines.[53] On the morning of August 24, the front page declared "Paris was liberated by French troops from within and the uprising of its population. Then a division entered."[54] One of the many stories on the front page was titled "Buenos Aires marked with joy the recovery of the French capital."[55] On the second page of the paper were pictures of celebrations in Uruguay, including a picture of Uruguayan president Juan José de Amézaga at a vigil in Montevideo. Only on page 8 does the paper report that "many vigils were improvised in the city [of Buenos Aires]" and that similar celebrations broke out in Tucumán, Mendoza, Córdoba, and other cities across Argentina.[56] Page 9 included a picture of the public singing "La Marseillaise" in front of the monument of San Martín in Plaza San Martín, Buenos Aires.

The order of reporting reflects the general attitude toward the war in Argentina. News of the war was central, followed by the international reactions to the Allies' success, and only then was the domestic response presented. However, the celebratory vigils continued and even intensified on the following day. On August 25, *La Nación* dedicated the front page to the noteworthy domestic responses to the liberation of Paris. The headline read "An imposing and fervent multitude paid highest homage to France," and a side story on the same page reported "the immense crowd remained in the plaza for many hours" accompanied by a large image of the multitudes gathered at Plaza Francia for the second day in a row.[57] Viewing the front page of *La Nación* on August 25, 1944, one might have imagined that Argentina had not actually been neutral all these warring years but in fact supportive of the Allies all along. It seems that it took the editorial board of *La Nación* a day to adjust their reporting to the public sentiment that was playing out in Argentina.

La Nación was not the only one surprised by the magnitude of public outbursts of joy. Borges had spent the war polemicizing against Argentine sympathizers of Nazism in lectures and articles, across many platforms. After so many years fighting the ideological and cultural influence of Nazi Germany in Argentina, the public joy he witnessed was surprising, confusing, and ripe for commentary. Two months later Borges published his "A Comment on August 23, 1944."[58] To make sense of Borges's surprise, and his remarks about the Argentine response to the liberation of Paris, it is worth reviewing some of his most combative essays of the previous years. The continuities and breaks between this 1944 essay and his previous wartime essays will help us focus our reading on the core of Borges's comments.

Borges had been polemicizing against Nazism since the mid-1930s on the pages of publications that varied from the literary journal *Sur* to the women's magazine *El Hogar*. His rhetorical efforts had two foci. The first was to undermine Nazi ideology (including Aryan supremacy, antisemitism, and xenophobia). He did this by arguing against the propaganda points that were filtering into Argentine public discourse and by highlighting the inconsistency or absurdity of the claims made by supporters of Germany. The second rhetorical focus in Borges's polemics was to develop the character of the Germanophile as the stereotype of a local supporter of Nazism, and then to ridicule this character.

These two rhetorical strategies are mixed in all his anti-Nazi polemics. For example, in his 1939 text "An Essay on Neutrality" he writes:[59]

> It is easy to prove that an immediate (and even instantaneous) effect of this much-desired war has been the extinction or abolishment of all intellectual processes. . . . I am thinking of the charlatans and apologists that indefatigable fate obliges me to encounter on the streets and in the houses of Buenos Aires.
>
> . . .
>
> It is possible that a German defeat might be the ruin of Germany; it is indisputable that its victory would debase and destroy the world. I am not referring to the imaginary danger of a South American colonial adventure; I am thinking of those native imitators, those homespun *Übermenschen* that inexorable chance would bring down upon us.[60]

This essay expresses the mix of disdain and fear Borges exhibited toward the local supporters of Nazism who, he suspected, were all too eager to imitate the Nazi atrocities they supported in Europe on the soil of their native Argentina. In another celebrated essay, published in 1940 and titled "Definition of a Germanophile," Borges ridicules the character as much as the worldview of the local supporters of Hitler, and expresses his exasperation with this group.[61]

I will reconstruct, reducing it to its essentials, a conversation I have had with
many Germanophiles—something in which I swear never to involve myself
again, for the time granted to mortals is not infinite and the fruit of these
discussions is vain.

. . .

The discussion becomes impossible because the offenses I ascribe to Hitler are,
for him, wonders and virtues.

. . .

[The Germanophile] is, thanks to a poverty of imagination, a man who believes
that the future cannot be different from the present, and that Germany, till
now victorious, cannot lose. He is the cunning man who longs to be on the
winning side.[62]

In December 1941, with wartime tensions building further as Japan entered
the war, Borges published an essay titled "1941."[63] Here too Borges expresses
disdain and fear toward the Germanophiles, mixed with efforts to illustrate
the intellectual inconsistency of their position. This latter intellectual effort is
dripping with sarcasm. Borges has forsworn those frustrating conversations
with the Germanophiles and has by now apparently given up hope of changing their mind. A new accusation appears here for the first time as well—their
narrative is banal.

The notion of an atrocious *complot* by Germany to conquer and oppress all
the countries of the atlas is (I rush to admit) irrevocably banal. It seems an
invention of Maurice Leblanc.[64] . . . Unfortunately, reality lacks literary
scruples. All liberties are permitted, even a coincidence with Maurice Leblanc.

. . .

Yesterday the Germanophiles swore that the maligned Hitler did not even
dream of attacking this continent; now they justify and praise his latest
hostility . . . who knows what celebrations they will unleash the day our cities
and shores are razed. It is childish to be impatient; Hitler's charity is ecumeni-
cal; in short (if the traitors and Jews don't disrupt him) we will enjoy all the
benefits of torture, sodomy, rape, and mass executions.[65]

This latest excerpt demonstrates well Borges's view of the danger that the
Germanophiles pose to Argentina. It also bitterly depicts them celebrating
the imaginary invasion of Argentina by Nazi forces. So, in August of 1944
Borges is genuinely surprised by "the puzzling and flagrant enthusiasm of
many who were supporters of Hitler."[66] Borges did not expect to see these same
people celebrating not the invasion of Argentina by Germany but the liberation of Paris by the Allies. Is this an ideological reversal or further proof of

their inconsistency, Borges wonders, reflecting: "I realized immediately that it was useless to ask those people themselves. They are fickle, and by behaving incoherently they are no longer aware that incoherence need be justified. . . . I also reflected that any other uncertainty was preferable to the uncertainty of a dialogue with these siblings of chaos, exonerated from honor and piety by the infinite repetition of the interesting formula *I am Argentine*."[67]

Even the surprising participation of Borges's familiar Germanophiles in the vigils celebrating the liberation of Paris was not enough to convince him that a conversation with this group will be any different than it was in 1940 when he swore never to engage them again. Borges also takes aim here at contemporary public intellectual Eduardo Mallea, who in 1937 coined the term *argentinidad* (Argentineity). This term of nationalist essentialism, in Borges's criticism, fueled the xenophobia and anti-immigrant sentiment of many Germanophiles.[68] At any rate, not wishing to engage and having something more imaginative in mind, Borges will go about explaining the surprising reaction of the Germanophiles in his own way. Along the way, Borges will also revisit his earlier anti-Germanophile rhetoric cited above in an effort to write not the reversal but the continuation of his previous essays.

Stating his desire to explain the events of August 23, 1944, Borges admits that "many will accuse me of trying to explain a fantastic event. Still, it happened, and thousands of persons in Buenos Aires can bear witness."[69] Either the widespread celebration of the liberation of Paris happened (and was witnessed) or it was a fantastic event. The initial dichotomy Borges sets up is between fantasy and reality. Next, he will begin to dismantle it. "Men have very little knowledge of the real motives of their conduct," Borges observes, thus disqualifying the Germanophiles not only for their inconsistency, but also for their unreliability as narrators of their own motives.[70] And yet in the context of an initial dichotomy between reality and fantasy, we might note that it is the real motives of their conduct that they have little knowledge of. There are perhaps other more fantastic motives yet to be discovered.

What motivation could they have that is not "real"? This is Borges's next proposal, that they are motivated not by the reality of Hitler's defeat, but by the symbolic value of the event. "Perhaps, I said to myself, the magic of the symbols Paris and liberation is so powerful that Hitler's partisans have forgotten that the defeat of his forces is the meaning of those symbols."[71] Here the dichotomy between symbol and reality seems too strict for the explanation Borges is after. He may not be searching for the real motives of their actions, but he is not satisfied with its exclusion either. "Wearily, I chose to imagine that the probable explanation for this conundrum was their fear, their inconstancy, and their mere adherence to reality."[72] The adherence proposed is the

Germanophiles' in the sense that this new hypothesis would suggest they simply reaffirm reality, however it unfolds. But it is also the adherence of Borges's own hypothesis, which seeks an explanation for the conundrum merely in the realm of reality.

Any reader of Borges knows he cannot end his essay here. The subsequent rejection of this adherence should be understood along the lines of both these hypotheses as well. For his understanding of the Germanophiles' behavior, Borges will continue the essay with a proposal that dissolves the distinction between reality and unreality. For our own interpretive approach to the text, lest it seem that by virtue of a detailed contextualization our own critical view is guilty of "mere adherence to reality," I refer to the insight offered by Annick Louis in an eponymously titled article: "Restoring the context of the production of Borges' stories does not mean inscribing the story with a documentary value but rather reevaluating what a (any) fiction tells us about Fiction and its uses in a given context."[73] The question is not in what way the context explains the text of this essay, but what the fictional nature of the way Borges resolves his opening question can teach us about fiction and its relation to reality.

"Several nights later," Borges reports, "I was enlightened by a book and a memory."[74] These come to unsettle the persistent dichotomy between reality and fantasy. In the book, Borges reads "that the horror of hell is its irreality."[75] The possibility of conceiving something—a space, an explanation, a motivation—that is beyond the dichotomy of reality and fantasy is enlightening to Borges, though it is hellish at the same time. (Herbert Ash, one of the members of Tlön's cabal, "was afflicted with irreality" as well.[76])

Daniel Balderston has focused his approach to reading Borges on this term—irreality. "Borges," writes Balderston, "for many readers and critics, means 'irrealidad,' and the adjectives that have been created from the surname seem to refer to the unreal, the fictive, even the fictive to the second or third degree."[77] Balderston's effort is "to reconsider the question of the relation of Borges' fictions to realities beyond the text" and, in so doing, he introduces possibilities for reading the connections between history, literature, and politics, in Borges's work.[78] I follow Balderston in my efforts to read Borges through a thick contextualization of his work. But at the same time, I also see Balderston reproducing the dichotomy between real (historical, political) and unreal (fiction, narrative) through his interpretive effort to read across what divides these realms. In Balderston's words: "Borges, reader of Schopenhauer, James, Valéry, and Russell, is clearly in sympathy with these rather skeptical approaches to matters of historical fact and (like them) values history for its pragmatic worth. Historical situations are useful to him in a special sense, though: they are linked to prior and subsequent situations, and notions of historical causality (however dubious in philosophical terms) imply narrative plots."[79]

I believe Borges complicates the relation between history and literature, reality and fantasy, politics and narrative—in short between reality and unreality—to such an extent that his "irreality" should not be read as a difference of degree but of kind. Thus, I would go (what I see as) one step further than Balderston and add that notions of historical causality imply narrative *complots*. A plot line that accompanies reality but is not real, and yet it is so closely related to reality that it is not strictly speaking unreal either—it is "irreal."

This is the point where Borges's comments about the Germanophiles' behavior in August 1944 will repeat his previous essays as well. "The notion of an atrocious *complot* by Germany to conquer and oppress all the countries of the atlas is (I rush to admit) irrevocably banal," he had stated in 1941; "unfortunately, reality lacks literary scruples."[80] The complot was banal precisely because it was too real. However, while reality may lack literary scruples, irreality does not. The new complot that Borges will propose in 1944 is certainly less real, and less banal. He continues from the book to the memory.

> The memory was the day that had been the exact and hateful opposite of
> August 23, 1944: June 14, 1940. A certain Germanophile, whose name I do
> not wish to remember, came to my house that day. Standing in the doorway,
> he announced the dreadful news: the Nazi armies had occupied Paris. I felt
> a confusion of sadness, disgust, malaise. Then it occurred to me that his insolent
> joy did not explain the stentorian voice or the abrupt proclamation. He added
> that the German troops would soon be in London. Any opposition was useless,
> nothing could prevent their victory. That was when I knew that he, too, was
> terrified.[81]

In Borges's account, the memory of June 14, 1940, is opposed to his present day in several senses. In historical terms, the opposition is between the occupation and the liberation of Paris. But there is also an opposition between the Germanophiles' behavior. If in 1944 he is unexpectedly celebrating the defeat of Germany, in 1940 he was surprisingly terrified at the prospect of Germany's success. This repeated inconsistency should not surprise us when we recall what Borges thinks of the Germanophiles. However, if we follow Balderston's insight (and our own addition to it), we may consider that "historical situations [for Borges] are linked to prior and subsequent situations, and notions of historical causality (however dubious in philosophical terms) imply narrative [*complots*]."[82] The historical opposition of these dates, together with the repetition of the Germanophiles' unexpected behavior, imply a narrative complot that, the reader discovers, it is the purpose of Borges's 1944 essay to expose. To do so, it will first be necessary to move the discussion into the realm of irreality. "To be a Nazi (to play the energetic barbarian, Viking, Tartar, sixteenth-century conquistador, gaucho, or Indian) is, after all, mentally and morally impossible. Nazism suffers from irreality, like Erigena's hell. It is uninhabitable; men can only die for it, lie for it, wound and kill for it. No one, in the intimate depths of his being, can wish it to triumph."[83]

The Germanophiles' behavior on both dates recalled by Borges demonstrates that they do not wish Nazism to triumph. They are stuck in a reality in which they continue to play a fictional role. A hell-born Don Quixote, Nazism suffers from irreality as though an actor playing the barbarian, Viking, or any other paradigmatic "bad guy" wandered off stage but could not shake off their roleplay. It is an audacious depiction of Nazism, and within this irreality the complot is exposed.[84] "I shall risk this conjecture:" Borges continues, *Hitler wants to be defeated*. Hitler is blindly collaborating with the inevitable armies that will annihilate him, as the metal vultures and the dragon (which must have known that they were monsters) collaborated, mysteriously, with Hercules."[85]

What a grand conspiracy! This is certainly less banal than the complot Borges originally ascribed to the Germanophiles in "1941." Hitler, knowing full well he is the bad guy in this narrative, has been planning to lose the war all along. He is in fact collaborating with the Allied forces, the other actors in his story. That is what the role prescribes. Borges exposes that the complot all along has not been to hide Hitler's defeat, but to hide his awareness of the complot itself. That is, to hide the *irreality* of his historical existence.

In this audacious article, Borges reimagines Hitler's bunker as the den of a global complot. And by exposing it, reveals the underlying literary logic that drives the political reality. The political confrontation is never merely that, it is always also a plot of collaboration, of a joint effort to narrate, an outcome of literary world creation. Hitler and the Allies, like Hercules and the monsters he slays, are intertwined in the overlap of plot and complot to the point that literature and politics are indistinguishable. Borges the conspiracy theorist reveals to his readers the manifestation of the story in reality, the manifestation of the story *as* reality. The overlap between the conspiracy theorist, as the role Borges assumes in this essay, and the Kabbalist, as depicted by Borges in "A Vindication of the Kabbalah," can now be further clarified as well.

Sosnowski states that, "while the Kabbalist risks his immortality with each linguistic transformation, Borges only entertains multiple variables whose basic purpose is to rejoice in the creative act that begins and ends in the writing of fiction. While the Kabbalist seeks an elusive opening in the mysterious lines of the Sacred Language, Borges reduces theology and metaphysics to a game."[86] To the extent that we recognize an overlap between the Kabbalist and the conspiracy theorist—an overlap that we have introduced in our reading of "Tlön, Uqbar, Orbis Tertius"—it becomes clear that Borges certainly sees literature as more than a game. For Borges, the creative act of writing fiction risks not his immortality but his mortality.

Reading "A Comment on August 23, 1944" in the context of Borges's articulation of authorship, and as a suggestion about the power of literature, casts the power of the literary creative act in a new light. It may be the case that Sosnowski, following Scholem, took the Kabbalists too seriously, denying them a joy in their creative act, a playfulness that Bloom and Steiner would later propose. But it is certainly the case that we should not take Borges too lightly. "A Comment on August 23, 1944" suggests that Borges sees the literary act as enormously consequential. Sosnowski is here working within assumptions about Borges as an apolitical author, which in the context of Borges and the Kabbalah are supported by Scholem's view of the Kabbalah as apolitical or escapist. Such assumptions have already been challenged by later generations of Kabbalah scholars, as well as by Borges scholars such as Balderston cited above.[87]

Methodologically, then, this suggests to us the false identity unintentionally and perhaps overzealously promoted by scholars of Borges and the Kabbalah (a consequence of taking Scholem's particular view of Kabbalah for a general definition of the Kabbalah) between Kabbalistic stories and escapist or apolitical stories. Interpretively, texts such as "A Comment on August 23, 1944" compel us to rethink Borges's position regarding the perceived relation between literature and politics, and the significance of his term "irreality." In the next chapter, we will read the story "The God's Script" and examine the way that previous readers have considered the mystic protagonist as an escapist, precisely because of an overcommitment to the lens of Borges and the Kabbalah.

The Ideal Reader

In the years immediately following World War II, the problem of authorship emerged with renewed vigor. In the same years that Theodor Adorno proclaimed, "to write poetry after Auschwitz is barbaric," Borges too was working through the question of writing in a postwar context and continued engaging the Kabbalah in his stories and essays as his thought continued to develop.[1] His book *El Aleph* (1949) is the poetic high point of this postwar engagement—including such stories as the eponymous "The Aleph" and "The God's Script"—and is perhaps the last prominent example of Kabbalistic allusions in his narrative fictions.[2] That very same year, Borges would begin turning his discussion to Jewish tradition as a way of articulating his developing thoughts on authorship. Presently, we will focus on the development that Borges's allusion to Kabbalah undergoes, from the previous example we read of his 1940 story "Tlön, Uqbar, Orbis Tertius" to his 1949 story "The God's Script."

The story "The God's Script" is perhaps the most explicit example of mysticism in Borges's oeuvre since it narrates the story of a mystic (Tzinacán) that includes a first-person account of his *unio mystica*, the ecstatic experience of union with divinity.[3] Jaime Alazraki and Saul Sosnowski both read this story as Kabbalistic, as they focus on Tzinacán's experience of *unio mystica*. The narrator is very explicit about this as well, putting these words in Tzinacán's mouth: "Then there occurred what I cannot forget nor communicate. There occurred the union with the divinity, with the universe."[4] However, it must be noted at the outset that experiences of mystical union between the mystic and God do not play a major role in Kabbalah and, in fact, Gershom Scholem himself questions the significance of this phenomenon in the study of

Kabbalah, writing: "To the general history of religion this fundamental experience is known under the name of *unio mystica*, or mystical union with God. The term, however, has no particular significance. Numerous mystics, Jews as well as non-Jews, have by no means represented the essence of their ecstatic experience . . . as a union with God."[5]

Nor is the Hebrew term *devekuth* a proxy for such union since its meaning is broader than *unio mystica*, claims Scholem.[6] Whether Borges had noted these lines in Scholem before drafting the story in 1949 is immaterial. His earlier readings on the Kabbalah, such as Erich Bischoff and Gustav Meyrink, do not discuss mystical union as a central component of Kabbalah either.[7] We must conclude that Borges's knowledge of *unio mystica* was taken from elsewhere and that reading this episode as Kabbalistic demonstrates a slippage between Kabbalah and a more general knowledge of mysticism.

An alternate source may be Christian mysticism, which ascribes a more central role to experiences of mystical union.[8] This is also suggested by Alazraki in discussing the core idea of "The God's Script," a secret writing that God has hidden in the world. Alazraki begins by referencing the appearance of this theme in the Kabbalah, citing Scholem's *On the Kabbalah and its Symbolism*—a book that did not exist in 1949.[9] Next Alazraki proposes Christianity as a source for this plot element, stating in passing that "the tradition of a magical and divine script that Borges recreates in his tale is also a Christian motif."[10] It is certainly the case that the Kabbalah, as well as the academic studies of Kabbalah that Borges was familiar with, discuss ideas of the all-powerful names of God (such as the Tetragrammaton that appears in "Death and the Compass") and the secret power of the Hebrew language (that is implied in *Sefer Yetzirah* and the Kabbalists' reading of the Genesis creation myth). But, by his own admission, Borges first encountered the nucleus of these ideas in Meyrink's novel *Der Golem* (1915), before reading their details in Bischoff or Scholem. In fact, the lack of Kabbalistic details surrounding the magic incantation Tzinacán is searching for would suggest that, while Borges may have initially encountered the idea in Kabbalah, the details of this particular story are drawn from other sources.[11]

This becomes clear when turning from the general frame of a quest for the language of God to the details of Tzinacán's search. The myth of a God hiding a specific secret formula (rather than the whole world being made of God's language), the symbolism of the pyramid, the jaguar and the tiger (which Borges uses interchangeably in this story[12]), the iconic structure of nested dreams that Borges returns to in several stories—these building blocks of the narrative are taken from elsewhere.[13] To borrow Borges's words, "the concrete enigma" of Tzinacán's search is less Kabbalistic than "the generic enigma of a sentence written by God" may initially imply.[14]

This is further evident through the analysis of Tzinacán's first-person account of his ecstatic experience. The bulk of the analysis Alazraki proposes relates to the Hindu sources that Borges draws upon to crate Tzinacán's mystical vision. Barely a page discussing Kabbalistic sources about mystical union and divine script is followed by four pages of detailed analysis, which include matching excerpts from the *Bhagavad Gita* with the content of Tzinacán's vision. And yet Alazraki's conclusion, and indeed the title of the analysis, is not that this story is Hindu but that it is Kabbalistic.

Sosnowski, in comparison, does not search for specific Kabbalistic sources of Tzinacán's story. He proposes to analyze the story with a focus on the search for the language of God, identifying an extensive analogy between Tzinacán and the Kabbalists. "By comparing Tzinacán's journey with the mystics' path, we shall attempt to clarify the meaning of his search for an all-powerful formula and the effects of this search upon him. We shall also demonstrate that the steps that he must trace in order to arrive at the Divine Light are *structurally analogous* to the prerequisites acknowledged by the Kabbalists."[15]

I would add to this observation that the Kabbalah is one element among several that structure Tzinacán's predicament, and that there is no significant influence of Kabbalah on the central episode of the story—his experience of *unio mystica*. An overlooked Kabbalistic element that we do find in this story is the echo of Borges's own "A Vindication of the Kabbalah." As I proceed to highlight the way this earlier essay underwrites Borges's treatment of the divine text and its reader, I would like to offer a reinterpretation of Alazraki's perceived relation between Borges and the Kabbalah. Let us recall that the first item mentioned by Alazraki in his "scrutiny of Borges' Kabbalah library" was this very same 1932 essay by Borges himself.[16] And that we have made it our goal to avoid the methodological tautology implied by his statement that Borges's "art is Kabbalistic in a sense defined by Borges himself in his essay 'A Vindication of the Kabbalah.'"[17]

In the epilogue to his book *El Aleph* (1949), the book containing this story, Borges comments: "The God's Script has been generously judged; the jaguar obligated me to put in the mouth of a 'magician of the pyramid of Qaholom' arguments of a Kabbalist or a theologian."[18] Sosnowski understands this as an admission that Tzinacán is on a "Kabbalistic quest."[19] But this too is further complicated by the fact that, as we will see presently, Tzinacán is repeating what Borges himself presents as Kabbalistic in "A Vindication of the Kabbalah." Do we consider Tzinacán a Kabbalist for repeating what Borges claimed the Kabbalah was about in 1932? The need to avoid such methodological tautology is clear here.

I propose instead to consider Tzinacán as an expression of Borges's search for a conceptualization of the ideal reader. As such, to the extent that his path is analogous to the Kabbalists, as Sosnowski has suggested above, it is because

Borges saw in the Kabbalists the model of an ideal reader. And to the extent that Tzinacán's deity is analogous to the God of the Kabbalists through an investment in writing, this would further lead me to propose that we should read this Mesoamerican deity as an articulation of Borges's own desired position as an author, which he saw reflected in the God of the Kabbalists and is now representing in the God of Tzinacán.

More significant than the influence of Kabbalah in Tzinacán's story, then, is what it shares with "A Vindication of the Kabbalah"—as indeed with much of Borges's appreciation of the Kabbalah—a preoccupation with the roles of author and reader. If we will find echoes of "A Vindication of the Kabbalah" in "The God's Script," this will not be a sign of Kabbalistic influence on the story. Rather, it will point to Borges's effort to express similar concerns in both these texts—his effort to characterize the ideal reader and the intellectual author. We should thus read this story along the lines of exploring the two perspectives developed in that earlier essay—the reader (Kabbalist) and the author (God)—and understand this story as narrating Tzinacán's process of becoming the ideal reader of a perfect text. Last, we should avoid reading this story as Kabbalistic in any way that would oblige us to ask questions about accuracy and influence on the one hand, or fall into methodological tautology on the other.

To trace the narrative of Tzinacán's transformation into the ideal reader of a perfect text, we must go back to the beginning of the story where the reader is first introduced to Tzinacán the prisoner. Before we can discuss the transformation he undergoes, and appreciate what he transforms into, we must begin with a discussion of what he transforms out of.

Borges's Parable of the Cave

The staging of Tzinacán's story repeats Plato's well-known "Parable of the Cave" from Book VII of *The Republic*.[20] Like the people in Plato's parable, Tzinacán is a prisoner in a dark cave. There is only one opening and the light pouring through it is obscured. For Plato's prisoners there is hope, in the form of the philosopher who has seen the light of day and will return to release them, guiding their vision from the shadows on the cave wall to the sunlit reality outside it. Plato refers to the cave dwellers in the third person and narrates the process of freeing one man who would return to free the others. There is no account of how the first person to escape the cave did so. Nor is this the point of the parable. It is focused on the possibility of, and resistance to, being rescued from the cave.

No one is coming for Tzinacán. He must free himself from his imprisonment and Borges narrates this effort in the first person, in Tzinacán's own voice. Yet he is not alone. He shares the cell with a jaguar, pacing on the other side of a wall and a window of bars. "At the shadowless hour . . . the light breaks into the vault; at that instant I can see the jaguar."[21] The only reality for Tzinacán is a daily game of light and shadows. Nicolás Emilio Alvarez focuses our attention on this fact, observing that "Tzinacán, like the prisoners of the platonic myth, remains incarcerated in darkness and immobile and only able to know the world of appearances."[22] Is it conceivable that Plato's prisoners, who cannot turn their heads away from the shadows, could free themselves through contemplation on the nature of shadows themselves? This is the point at which Borges's reimagining of the parable breaks with Plato, for this is precisely what Borges will have Tzinacán attempt. Not through philosophical reasoning, but through mystical speculation and experience.

This path begins with a recollection that will shift Tzinacán's focus away from the shadows. He remembers that his God is a writer. "The god foresaw that at the end of time there would be devastation and ruin, and on the first day of Creation he wrote a magical sentence with the power to ward off those evils. He wrote it so that it would reach the most distant generations and to ensure that *chance would not touch it*. No one knows in what characters it is written nor where it is written, but it is certain that it exists as a secret and that *a chosen one shall read it*."[23]

What characterizes the text written by Tzinacán's God is the same thing that characterized the perfect text written by the God of the Kabbalists in "A Vindication of the Kabbalah." Borges here repeats his idea that what defines God's writing is that nothing in it is given to chance. For divinity, mysticism is a question of writing, of manifesting itself in the world through written words. Tzinacán's deity, like the God of the theologians, has produced the same kind of text that Borges's intellectual writer aspired to in 1932—"an absolute text, where the collaboration of chance is calculated at zero."[24]

While for the deity mysticism is a question of writing, for Tzinacán (as for the Kabbalists) mysticism is a question of reading. Tzinacán's salvation, it seems, will depend on his ability to read the writing of the God. First, however, he must locate it. Here there is an important difference Sosnowski will point out: "The Kabbalist's design is not exploratory. He believes in an omnipotent God who has manifested His being and His will in the sacred letters of the Torah. He does not have to search for God's script."[25] And yet, the ease with which the Kabbalists access Scripture means they can be fully focused on mysticism as a question of reading. They do not have to ask themselves the question that Borges has been concerned with since 1932, and which he puts in the mouth of Tzinacán: "What type of sentence (I asked myself) will an absolute mind construct?"[26] For Borges, as for Tzinacán, mysticism begins with a question about writing.

Tzinacán understands that the first step to his liberation is not the question "how does the mystic read?" but rather "how does divinity write?" His self-release from the cave begins with a shift in perspective to ask about divinity as a writer. After that, he will figure out how to read. Borges introduces here a similar shift as he did in "A Vindication of the Kabbalah," from the Kabbalist as reader of a perfect text to God as author of a perfect text. "The conception alone of such a document is a greater wonder than those recorded in its pages," Borges concludes at the end of "A Vindication of the Kabbalah."[27] And Tzinacán, as though he had read those very same lines himself, continues the same shift in perspective: "Gradually, the concrete enigma I labored at disturbed me less than the generic enigma of a sentence written by a god."[28] He is moving from the concrete question of hermeneutical procedures to the generic question of divine authorship, the genre of God's writing. Sosnowski too notices this perspectival shift from reader to writer that Borges suggests in the story. "In order to discover the formula, [Tzinacán] considers it proper to attempt to think like the god himself."[29] Thus Tzinacán narrates:

> I considered that even in the human languages there is no proposition that does not imply the entire universe. . . . I considered that in the language of a god every word would enunciate that infinite concatenation of facts, and not in an implicit but in an explicit manner, and not progressively but instantaneously. In time, the notion of a divine sentence seemed puerile or blasphemous. A god, I reflected, ought to utter only a single word and in that word absolute fullness. No word uttered by him can be inferior to the universe or less than the sum total of time. Shadows or simulacra of that single word equivalent to a language and to all a language can embrace are the poor and ambitious human words, *all, world, universe.*[30]

The divine writer should not need more than a single word to manifest themselves in the world. But such fullness of meaning would be inaccessible to humans. It is the human reader that requires more words—in Tzinacán's case it will turn out to be fourteen words—in order to make sense of God's writing. Human language contains simulacra, shadows of that perfect word. By contemplating God-the-author, Tzinacán develops a kind of mystical panecastic thinking whereby everything is implied in everything ("there is no proposition that does not imply the entire universe"[31]), and through which humans can liberate themselves.[32] Tzinacán finally conceives his challenge not in terms of seeing more but in terms of how one reads what one sees. In so doing, Borges's story will recast the mystic's experience as the reader's experience, and Tzinacán as the ideal reader.

Returning to the analogy between Tzinacán's prison and Plato's cave, the shadows that delude Tzinacán are not those of real things passing on the cave wall before his eyes. The simulacrum that deludes him is language itself. Human words are the shadows he is forced to stare at, simulacra of the "absolute fullness" of meaning. Sosnowski suggests that with this insight, "Tzinacán has reached the limits of rational thought. The final step will have to be reached by magical means. No logical formula can bring forth what defies all rational and human patterns."[33] Yet Tzinacán's impasse is not ontological, between this world and the nonhuman or divine world. It is an impasse implied by representation, reflection, what Plato calls shadows and Borges here repeats as "simulacra." For Borges as for Plato, the limit is epistemological, and it can be transcended through a process of liberation. Borges and Plato agree that the question is not if but how.

This contemplation on the nature of divine language, narrated here as contemplation on God-as-author, leads to Tzinacán's mystical experience, narrated in the first person and explicitly referred to as "union with divinity."[34] Tzinacán has an ecstatic noetic experience—"O bliss of understanding"—granting him complete knowledge of everything, "and, understanding all, I was able also to understand the script of the tiger."[35] Passing through the "generic enigma" of a God's script, Tzinacán emerges back into the "concrete enigma" of becoming the ideal reader, that "chosen one [who] shall read it."[36] The possibility of liberation, of enlightenment, of reading God's writing, is also what should inform our understanding of the ending.

Having deciphered the God's script on the jaguar's skin, Tzinacán decides not to utter the magical incantation and accepts his place in the prison. "But I know I shall never say those words, because I no longer remember Tzinacán."[37] One cannot recognize the simulacra and go on insisting they themselves are not merely such a shadow. For Tzinacán, self-liberation takes the form of self-effacement, as he states: "May the mystery lettered on the tigers die with me. Whoever has seen the universe . . . cannot think in terms of one man, of that man's trivial fortunes or misfortunes, though he be that very man. . . . This is why I do not pronounce the formula, why, lying here in the darkness, I let the days obliterate me."[38]

While Tzinacán never escapes the confines of the prison, this ending is nonetheless fully consistent with Borges's recasting of Plato's parable. The prison and the cave are themselves illusory proxies for the simulacrum of language. This is where our reading departs most fully from previous readings. Sosnowski sees the ending as a failure of liberation. "'The God's Script' is the testimony of Tzinacán's successful search for Divinity and his ultimate refusal to enter into a non-human world."[39] Sosnowski thus creates an analogy between the Kabbalist and Plato's philosopher, in contradistinction to Tzinacán: "Here again we must stress differences—the Kabbalist's search does not end with his personal achievement. The successful voyage allows but one attitude: the seer will return to his people in order to broaden their sights, to serve as their teacher and divine messenger. Tzinacán's attitude is radically different."[40]

Sosnowski would read the ending as Tzinacán's choice between achieving liberation at the cost of annihilating his selfhood, or preservation of the self even at the cost of perpetual imprisonment. "He has to decide between two worlds. To pronounce the formula will lead to infinite power. . . . Not to pronounce the formula will perpetuate his imprisonment."[41] For Sosnowski, Tzinacán's choice not to pronounce the formula that would make him all powerful shows his egotistical preference for the self-security of the cave, while the Kabbalist would choose the altruistic duty of the philosopher.

However, for us, it is the question of reading that has come to define his entrapment in the prison. Following our reading of "A Vindication of the Kabbalah," and in line with the perspectival shift we have signaled, we must highlight that this ending has different significance for the reader and the author. Tzinacán-the-(ideal)-reader has interpreted the spots of the jaguar, he has identified it as a text composed by an infinite intelligence, considered its permutations, appreciated its revelations lying in wait. If procedures lead to doctrine, it is the successful interpretation of the jaguar's spots as infinitely meaningful that has led to (or corroborated) the dogma, according to which the jaguar is an attribute of the god, and its spots are the writing of the god. Tzinacán emerges as the ideal reader, as one who consecrates the divinity of the text by means of his interpretive activity. As the ideal reader, he must stop short of proving his to be the one true interpretation, the all-powerful invocation of absolute meaning. The ideal reader cannot foreclose the space in which God's writing is infinitely interpretable.

Further following the perspectival shift initiated in "A Vindication of the Kabbalah," we must also consider the significance of this ending for God-as-author. Recall that, from the perspective of divinity, the successful application of "procedures" to Scripture leads to divinity's manifestation in the created world. God-as-author does not need Tzinacán to pronounce the formula, only to interpret it, in order to manifest divinity in the world. The perfect text that Borges conceived of in 1932 is not manifest in its fullness of meaning but rather in its infinite interpretability. Through his allusions to Kabbalah, in both essays and stories, Borges examines the roles of reader and writer. This story is a good illustration of Borges's preoccupation with this question. While interpretations of the story have focused on the mystical experience of Tzinacán, we have focused on the questions Borges raises, through Tzinacán, about the possibility of approximating divinity-as-author. But how does one approximate a divinity that writes magical incantations on the skin of a jaguar or tiger?

"No logical formula can bring forth what defies all rational and human patterns," Sosnowski has stated.[42] If we have debated this statement from the perspective of the reader, "A Vindication of the Kabbalah" would encourage us to consider it from the perspective of the author as well. We must conclude that for Borges-as-(divine)-author such a formula does exist. Literature itself defies and undermines rational and human patterns. Just as the story of Genesis was the story that God narrated in order to create the world, so too there may be a text about the discovery of a secret writing by the god that is itself the selfsame script. Perhaps this divine script even carries the title "The God's Script." Borges titles his story with the very title of the text that Tzinacán himself is after. This story has put its readers in the shoes of Tzinacán, of the Kabbalists, of the ideal reader. Perhaps we too have already pronounced the god's script. To read the ending through the lens of Borges and the Kabbalah is to ask, finally, not whether Tzinacán has been freed, but whether Borges has approximated the god that printed the jaguar's spots.

The Narrator and the Kabbalist

We have seen the selective reception of Scholem's work and the late addition of his scholarship to Borges's web of allusions. We must now ask more directly: what role, if any, did Scholem play in Borges's writing? Scholem had very little to do with the narration of Borges's stories, but a great deal to do with the reception of Borges's stories as Kabbalistic. In fact, it was Borges himself who developed Scholem into a precursor and first suggested this connection between himself and Scholem. One important and telling moment in Borges's intervention into the Kabbalistic reception of his own work occurred in a July 1966 interview with Ronald Christ. Here is the exchange.

> INTERVIEWER: What about the Kabbalah? When did you first get interested in that?
> BORGES: I think it was through De Quincey, through his idea that the whole world was a set of symbols, or that everything meant something else. . . . When I lived in Geneva . . .
> INTERVIEWER: Have you tried to make your own stories Kabbalistic?
> BORGES: Yes, sometimes I have.

It seems the interviewer is familiar with the essay "A Vindication of the Kabbalah" and is expecting a reply in line with Borges's interest in hermeneutical and cryptographic procedures. Perhaps he is even expecting Borges to confess having concealed meanings in his stories, which must be deciphered using "Kabbalistic interpretations." He thus follows up.

> INTERVIEWER: Using traditional Kabbalistic interpretations?
> BORGES: No. I read a book called *Major Trends in Jewish Mysticism.*

Borges's answer seems to catch the interviewer by surprise. To the date of the interview, this book had not been mentioned in any of Borges's writing. The only allusion it seems to have received was in the reference to Scholem and "his volume" in the aforementioned 1958 poem "The Golem." The interviewer thus seeks confirmation.

> INTERVIEWER: The one by Scholem?
> BORGES: Yes, by Scholem and another book by Trachtenberg on Jewish superstitions. Then I have read all the books of the Kabbalah I have found and all the articles in the encyclopedias and so on. But I have no Hebrew whatever. I may have Jewish ancestors, but I can't tell. My mother's name is Acevedo: Acevedo may be a name for a Portuguese Jew, but again, it may not.[43]

Borges changes the topic, and the interviewer never follows up about this new information. It has been fifteen years since Borges told the crowd at the twenty-five-year anniversary celebration of the Sociedad Hebraica Argentina that he read "the books by Scholem." The interviewer was certainly not familiar with those remarks, and neither were contemporary Borges readers. While the reference to "his volume" in the 1958 poem indicated to Borges's readers that he was familiar with Scholem's writing, this is the most public statement of familiarity to date, and the first to acknowledge the book by name, *Major Trends in Jewish Mysticism*. Twenty years after referencing this book in his marginalia, Borges names it explicitly. Beyond reconstructing a timeline of his encounter with Scholem, however, the most interesting aspect of this statement for our discussion is Borges's suggestion that reading Scholem has somehow made his own stories Kabbalistic. What stories is he referring to and how does reading Scholem make them Kabbalistic?

Borges's answer is not satisfactory with regard to his canonical collections of stories in *Ficciones* (1944) and *El Aleph* (1949). Many of these stories were written before Scholem published *Major Trends in Jewish Mysticism*, or before any documentation of Borges's familiarity with it. Furthermore, even after its publication, while Borges mentions many other sources on the Kabbalah in his stories, reference to Scholem is markedly absent. As of the date of the interview, Borges had not published any other collection of stories since the 1949 publication of *El Aleph*. Nor is Borges's reply satisfactory with regard to the stories he was working on in those years and that would be published in his 1970 collection *El informe de Brodie*.[44] These stories contain no mention or allusion to Scholem either.

This is not the case for interviews and lectures Borges gave over the years. Beginning with this mention of *Major Trend in Jewish Mysticism* in the 1966 interview, Scholem's name became a staple of Borges's self-presentation and reflection upon his own work and literature more generally. In October 1966, just a few months after the interview, Borges wrote a letter to former Israeli Prime Minister David Ben Gurion. In it he introduces himself to Ben Gurion thus: "I have studied with singular dedication the mind of Spinoza, I have learned German through the works of Heine, I have attempted to penetrate through the pages of Buber and of Scholem the unfathomable world of the Kabbalah and the Hasidim."[45] The correspondence initiated with Ben Gurion resulted in an invitation for Borges to visit the State of Israel.

The following year, in his 1967 collection *The Book of Imaginary Beings*, Borges mentions Scholem for the second time in his writing. Describing the imaginary being of "the double" he writes: "For the Jews, on the other hand, the apparition of the Double was not foreshadowing of death, but rather a proof that the person to whom it appeared had achieved the rank of prophet. This is the explanation offered by Gershom Scholem.[46] A tradition included in the Talmud tells the story of a man, searching for God, who met himself."[47] This mention did not receive much more attention than the one nearly a decade earlier in Borges's 1958 poem "The Golem." In fact, although Borges had been mentioning the Kabbalah since his 1926 "A History of Angels," it was not until he met Scholem in person that his professional readers began paying critical attention to this fact.

During his first visit to Israel in 1969, Borges had the opportunity to meet Scholem in person in Jerusalem. They met again in 1971, when Borges retuned to Israel to receive the Jerusalem Prize, a biennial literary award. News of their meeting spread rapidly, giving rise to a rather sudden and very focused interest in Borges and the Kabbalah. In fact, the first two articles introducing this important theme to Borges scholarship, published by Alazraki in 1971 and 1972, frame their argument by referring to the above-quoted reply in the 1966 interview—"Yes, sometimes I have."[48] In the introduction to the 1988 book collecting his work on Borges and the Kabbalah, Alazraki recalls that it was a 1969 conversation he had with Borges, about the latter's recent trip to Israel, that sparked the idea for a study of Borges and the Kabbalah. "We talked about his visit and his memorable encounter with Gershom Scholem. While I was a student at the Hebrew University of Jerusalem [writes Alazraki] I attended Scholem's course on Jewish Mysticism."[49]

By 1969, Alazraki had written two books about Borges and knew very well that Borges had been mentioning the Kabbalah since the mid-1920s. And yet, in his own account, it is not the repeated mention of the *Zohar* or the *sefirot* that were the inspiration for his major contribution to the field of Borges studies. It was Alazraki's shared familiarity with Scholem (a commonality Borges certainly knew nothing of when he wrote his Kabbalistic stories) that serves as the conduit for the development of this new direction in Borges scholarship. Borges himself continued to fuel this interest by repeatedly mentioning Scholem in interviews and lectures. Through ongoing reference to Scholem, Borges contributed to the reception of his own stories as Kabbalistic.

The next available example of this is a lecture on the Kabbalah that he gave in 1970 at the Sociedad Hebraica Argentina and that was published posthumously by Alazraki as "The Kabbalah."[50] Having returned from his first trip to Israel the year before, Scholem now plays a major role in his exposition of the Kabbalah and is directly invoked by Borges to authorize his own knowledge of the subject. In this lecture he begins by repeating the argument from "A Vindication of the Kabbalah," discussing his desire to justify the method employed by the Kabbalists, and repeats the same examples of *boustrophedon* and *gematria*. He also repeats the three models of authorship, disqualifying prose and poetry before turning to the third option. "Let us now imagine an infinite intelligence that condescends to literature: such would be the case of the Holy Scripture . . . if an infinite intelligence dictates a text, we can safely assume that in this text nothing has been left to chance, everything has a meaning."[51]

Two expansions to "A Vindication of the Kabbalah" should be noted. The first is Borges's explicit presentation of a question about the relation between doctrine and procedure. The second is the explicit invocation of Scholem to authorize his own views on the Kabbalah: "The Kabbalists thought that their doctrines of Gnostic or Neoplatonic origins were already in Scripture. I have discussed this question with Scholem who, perhaps through sheer courtesy, approved this conjecture that the doctrine preceded the method."[52]

Borges cites Scholem directly to authorize his knowledge of the Kabbalah and, specifically, his impression that for the Kabbalists the doctrine preceded what in 1932 he termed cryptographic procedures. Recall, however, that the 1957 revision to the 1932 text of "A Vindication of the Kabbalah" was precisely to insist that the method preceded the doctrine, that cryptographic procedures lead to the doctrine. Here, Borges is using Scholem's approval to confirm his appreciation of the Kabbalists' perspective. But Borges still insists on the other perspective as well, that of the author. He immediately continues: "Yet, once the doctrine was accepted, it either led to mystical experiences or, conversely, these mystical experiences led to the formulation of the doctrine. The method was adopted so that the doctrine would remain within the confines of Jewish tradition. Let us now examine the doctrine."[53]

Borges goes on to explain the radical nature of the idea of God-as-author, of a divinity "that condescends to literature."[54] For Borges, the Kabbalah cannot be neatly, conceptually separated into doctrines, methods, "trends." It is the confluence that creates the object he is most drawn to—the perfect text. Scholem's academic lens is focused on developments and changes of doctrines within their social and intellectual histories, on what he calls "trends." He is not concerned with the question of whether Scripture is actually a perfect text, or if such perfection can be defined in terms of the relation of chance to meaning, let alone whether such a text can be reproduced by the intellectual author.

And yet, their differences notwithstanding, Borges will continue to draw his authority from Scholem and his work, even as he expands on it with insights and conclusions not contained therein, even as Scholem stands at the end of many decades of study and as a consolidation of Borges's lifelong interest in the Kabbalah. He thus brings his lecture to a close by stating: "The book I would like to recommend to you again and again is Gershom Scholem's *Major Trends in Jewish Mysticism*. This is the clearest work I have read on the subject."[55] As this lecture demonstrates, a central component of Borges's own intellectual interest in the Kabbalah is his understanding of divine authorship, an understanding that maintains strong affinity with his idiosyncratic perception of the Kabbalah.

The following year, in 1971, Borges gave interviews to Alazraki and Sosnowski, who were both trailblazing the research on Borges and the Kabbalah. Some of the interview comments Borges made repeat themselves, but there are a few noteworthy exchanges that took place and that give us a window into Borges's evolving thought on Kabbalah. He had at this point met Scholem twice in Jerusalem and, beyond recommending his book *Major Trends in Jewish Mysticism*, what is interesting is that he now began to speak of them as friends. After repeating to Sosnowski the list of books he had read about the Kabbalah, and again emphasizing Scholem's work, he added a note about their relationship. "I have read and reread the books of Gerhard Scholem, *Major Trends in Jewish Mysticism*.[56] I have spoken with him twice. I believe we are truly friends and those conversations in which I for my own benefit spoke little and listened and learned much, were two felicities for me."[57]

Similarly, he tells Alazraki, "I consider him a friend of mine and I believe he considers me a friend although in total we have seen each other eight hours in our entire life, but since I read him and reread him so much."[58] The feeling was evidently mutual. In 1969, after their first encounter, Scholem shared his experience of meeting Borges in an exchange he had with the poet John Hollander. Scholem wrote: "I was very much taken by Mr. Borges' visit in Jerusalem and the only thing I regretted was that I met him so late. I should have known him twenty years ago, and I'm sure both of us would have gained by it. I have not read much of his writings, but what I have read has attracted me very much by the sheer power of imagination."[59]

Beyond the amicable feelings they developed for each other, Borges also began to reflect on Scholem's work intellectually. This was cited above in Borges's 1970 lecture where he reports discussing his question about procedure and doctrine with Scholem, and it continues in his comments in both 1971 interviews. In comparing Bischoff and Scholem, he tells Alazraki, "different from Scholem, for example, [Bischoff] doesn't explain anything, he states how things are and no more."[60] In his interview with Sosnowski he explains further: "I believe Scholem is superior to other authors about the Kabbalah . . . the others expound the system, but one must accept what they say. . . . In contradistinction Scholem expounds the system and in a way he rationalizes it, he justifies it."[61] Again we see Borges's selective appropriation of Scholem, as he projects his own concerns with justifying or "vindicating" the Kabbalah onto Scholem's scholarship.

Another example of this comes in the interview with Alazraki, when he confronts Borges about the misattribution we have already noted in the poem "The Golem."

> J.A.: I recall that in the poem "The Golem" you wrote: "these truths are conveyed by Scholem . . ." Now, those who have done the work of reading *Major Trends in Jewish Mysticism* will note that that is not in the book.
> BORGES: No, no, no. It's not in Scholem, it's in Trachtenberg, but the rhyme, caramba . . . And I also believe Scholem is a more important author than Trachtenberg, no?[62]

Borges is confirming both the poetic utility of Scholem (as a rhyme) and the effect that mentioning Scholem's name (as an important author) would have on his readers and reception. These examples demonstrate that Borges cannot be seen as simply embracing Scholem's view of the Kabbalah. He remains focused on his own concerns with authorship and uses both the Kabbalah and Scholem to express those. As Borges continued to speak about the Kabbalah in coming years, he continued to mention Scholem while insisting on reading his own concerns into its doctrines and procedures.

The abovementioned lecture delivered in 1970 was revised and delivered again as part of a series of lectures that Borges gave over the summer of 1977, which were published as the collection *Siete Noches* (1980). In several of these lectures, Borges returns to the idea of Scripture as infinitely interpretable, both in order to discuss its implications and to distinguish it from Western concepts of "classical literature." In two of the lectures that mention this understanding of Scripture, Borges attributes the evolution of this idea to sources that again confound his knowledge of Scholem's work with his own interest in Kabbalah as a mode of authorship. Thus, in his lecture "The Divine Comedy" he states: "We should mention here Scotus Erigena, who said that Scripture is a text that encloses infinite meanings and that can be compared with the iridescent plumage of a peacock. The Hebrew Kabbalists maintained that Scripture has been written for each one of the faithful."[63] And again, in his lecture "Poetry" he adds: "The Irish pantheist Scotus Erigena said that the Sacred Scripture encloses an infinite number of meanings and compared it with the iridescent plumage of a peacock. Centuries later a Spanish Kabbalist said that God made the Scriptures for each one of the people of Israel and as a consequence there are as many Bibles as there are readers of the Bible."[64]

Borges's 1977 lectures also include the aforementioned (and cited) lecture titled "The Kabbalah," in which he revisits the theme of his 1932 essay. In this late lecture Borges is no longer concerned with the mechanisms and procedures of Kabbalistic interpretation. Kabbalistic now indicates a quality, expressed here as a doctrine, which is "alien to the Western mind." This is how Borges introduces his topic in 1977: "The diverse, and occasionally contradictory, teachings grouped under the name of the Kabbalah derive from a concept alien to the Western mind, that of the sacred book. We have an analogous concept of the classic book."[65]

The analogy is important, but so too is the difference, and Borges's intellectual-narrator-approximating-God should not be understood as the author of some "classical" literature. Such classical books are "seen as something changeable . . . studied in historical fashion . . . placed within a context. The concept of a sacred book is something entirely different."[66] Borges is circling the point that the Kabbalistic story he is after maintains a distance from history, from social context—not a chronological distance but an intellectual distance. "I am not dealing with a museum piece from the history of philosophy. I believe the system has an application: it can serve as a means of thinking, of trying to understand the universe."[67] Indeed, this system underlies the Kabbalists' attempt to understand the universe.

For Borges, however, this understanding is first and foremost an understanding of writing and authorship. The Kabbalists speculate on that which Borges wants to approximate, as something that can be approximated—the author. "By declaring that the universe is the work of a deficient Divinity, one whose fraction of Divinity approaches zero, of a god who is not *the* God. Of a god who is a distant descendant of God. I don't know if our minds can function with words as vast and as vague as God or Divinity. . . . But we can understand the idea of a deficient Divinity, one who must make this world out of shoddy materials."[68]

The materials of the world, the Kabbalists teach us, are words. A being whose divinity is reduced to zero, creating a world of shoddy materials, of words—which are, mystically, infinitely interpretable. This is very much what Borges wants to approximate as the intellectual narrator. The intention is the same: to create a narrative, a world, in which the fraction of divinity is reduced to zero, but which is nonetheless powerfully *meta*physical. This is poetically accomplished through the web of Kabbalistic allusions Borges so deeply embeds in his writing, and the way these are able to summon the latent Kabbalist within his readers. But this has not yet articulated the approximation he has in mind. Borges will go one step further in his 1977 lecture. "The idea is this: the Pentateuch, the Torah, is a sacred book. An infinite intelligence has condescended to the human task of producing a book. The Holy Spirit has condescended to literature, which is as incredible as imagining that God condescended to become a man. In that book, nothing can be accidental. (In human writing there is always something accidental.)"[69]

In setting up a parallel between these two images—on the one hand, divinity condescending to literature, conceding to descend, to lower itself into a book, and, on the other hand, divinity condescending into human form—Borges indicates the role of Scripture as a manifestation of divinity in the world. In terms of the intellectual author, this image completes the perspective shift Borges signaled in his 1932 vindication. From the Kabbalists' perspective, the doctrine may lead them to apply their cryptographic procedures to the text. But it is the successful application of such "alternatives to reading" that introduce the realm of irreality into the replete yet mundane world of the reader. For the Kabbalists, divinity precedes and encompasses the world. It needs to "condescend" into human forms of body and text in order to be encountered by the Kabbalists. For Borges it is narrative that precedes and encompasses the world. Through the activities of the intellectual author, the narrative is brought into worldly existence. Through the endless interpretive activities of the reader, narrative is manifest in the reality of the human world. Through these activities the intellectual author, like divinity, is vindicated in their narrative efforts.

After reading Borges mention Scholem in multiple interviews between 1969 and 1980, Edna Aizenberg took the question to Scholem himself. In June 1980, Aizenberg wrote Scholem directly to ask what he thought of Borges and the Kabbalah. Her letter reads:

> Earlier in the year I had the wonderful experience of speaking to Borges at length, and in the course of our conversation he mentioned that the "highlights" of his trips to Israel were his encounters with you.[70] On those occasions, he claimed, you spoke and he listened and learnt.
>
> I had, of course, known of your meetings from my research, but after hearing from Borges himself about them, my enthusiasm was fired.
>
> . . .
>
> I would be honored if you could comment on your encounters with Borges, on his Kabbalistic knowledge and his use of this knowledge, and on the affinities between the two of you. Do you think that each of you, one in the realm of historiography, the other in that of literature, are trying to answer the same impulses and achieve similar things?[71]

We will read Scholem's reply to Aizenberg in a moment. First, we must note the trend that this letter helps us identify. Alazraki in 1969, Sosnowski in 1971, and Aizenberg in 1980 all have an encounter with Borges, in which his mention of Scholem and their meetings encourages the development of their scholarship. Sosnowski published his book *Borges y la cábala: la busqueda del verbo* (1976) and Aizenberg published her book *The Aleph Weaver* (1984). Along with the aforementioned articles by Alazraki, these were the groundbreaking contributions to the study of Borges and the Kabbalah.[72] I bring these examples of Alazraki, Sosnowski, and Aizenberg not to critique the importance of their contributions—contributions that my own current project clearly builds on—but rather to highlight the way Borges was implicated in the development and promotion of the Kabbalistic line of inquiry into his own work, and to demonstrate the ways he accomplished this.

Interestingly, someone who rather insightfully perceived this relation that Borges develops to the Kabbalah was Scholem himself. Scholem replied to Aizenberg's letter immediately. But he refused to underwrite the perception these scholars had developed of an influence he may have had on Borges and his Kabbalism.[73] In June 1980 he replied:

> I cannot comment, as you wish, on my very pleasant encounters with Borges and on his Kabbalistic knowledge. I am not sure at what period or periods his Kabbalistic stories have been written and I cannot form a definite opinion whether he read my books before writing those stories or after it. What I can say is that they compare favorably with the mystical and partly Kabbalistical stories written in German by Gustav Meyrink. . . . As to your last question, I must say, that in the realm of historiography, I have not been trying to answer the same impulses as Borges and do not think that we have achieved similar things. Borges is a writer of considerable power of imagination and does not claim to represent a historical reality, but rather an insight into what the Cabbalists would have stood for in his own imagination.[74]

Scholem here opposes Borges's "power of imagination" to his own scholarly efforts "to represent a historical reality." As Scholem understands it, what the Kabbalists stood for in Borges's stories is not what he himself has shown them to stand for in his research. Scholem thus rejects the analogy between Borges's literary imagination and his own historiographical project, and perhaps also between literature and history more broadly. In fact, he seems to understand Aizenberg's question, in part, as a challenge to his own scholarly standards, as he continues: "What I did, was to try to describe the world of the Cabbalists by analyzing their own works and ideas without overstepping, essentially, these limits. It is only here and now, that, very rarely, I have made what I called 'a historical' assumptions about what the Cabbalists may have meant beyond a historical analysis."[75]

This reply is in line with Scholem's historiographic methodology and his definition of Kabbalah as a social-historical (rather than literary) text. His reply also demonstrates that Scholem himself does not understand Borges as trying to be a Kabbalist. Scholem would understand Borges as overstepping the limits of historical analysis and thus of Kabbalah. Of course, no one is holding

Borges to strict standards of historical analysis. Except, perhaps, for those readers who would apply Scholem's historiographic methods to an analysis of the influence of Scholem qua Kabbalah on Borges's writing. To repeat Sosnowski's invaluable point: "It is important to outline fields: Borges is not a philosopher, nor a theologian, nor a cabalist, nor an historian: He is a maker of fictions."[76] In these fictions, I would add, he conjures an imaginary reader-as-Kabbalist and then writes for them.

Kabbalah and Tradition

What we have skipped in our reading of Borges's discussions of Kabbalah, leaping from his stories in the 1940s to his interviews in the 1970s, is the intellectual development by which he comes to see the Kabbalists, like his own readers, as negotiating a complex relation with tradition. Here we encounter another aspect of Kabbalah that we have not dealt with in Borges's stories, nor seen expressed in "A Vindication if the Kabbalah"—its relation to a Jewish concept of tradition. Returning to Borges's comments in the early 1970s cited above, we find a clear expression of this connection. In his 1970 lecture "The Kabbalah" he commented: "Yet, once the doctrine was accepted, it either led to mystical experiences or, conversely, these mystical experiences led to the formulation of the doctrine. *The method was adopted so that the doctrine would remain within the confines of Jewish tradition.* Let us now examine the doctrine."[77]

The Kabbalists' reading practices are a result of the doctrine of a perfect text, but the doctrine of a perfect text is only an attempt to develop a language that would allow them to include their experiences within Jewish tradition. The challenge of the Kabbalists is here understood as the challenge of creating one's place in tradition, of belonging to a tradition that your experience is external to. The tension between interiority of tradition and exteriority of experience repeats in Borges's interview comments to Sosnowski: "I believe that the system, that the doctrine of the Kabbalah is independent of the procedures. . . . I believe that in the case of the Kabbalah, since [the Kabbalists] wanted in some way to connect to, or were within the Hebrew tradition, they invented this whole system of letters that seems arbitrary to me."[78]

In none of his earlier discussion on Kabbalah is there any mention of the Kabbalists as struggling to contain their experiences within their tradition. Where does this new observation come from? The trouble with tradition is a postwar problematic that emerges in Argentina, as elsewhere, in the context of postcolonial struggles with identifying, recuperating, and inventing local traditions. As we continue our reading into the 1950s, we will see Borges's concern with an Argentine literary tradition grow more prominent in his writing. In order to understand the significance of these comments about Kabbalah and tradition, we need to turn our attention to Borges's broader relation to the Judaic and contextualize his engagement with the question of tradition within it—an engagement that is notably a postwar intellectual effort on his part.

In his comments to Alazraki and Sosnowski, Borges is projecting backward from his 1970s moment a postwar concern with tradition onto the Kabbalists that were so valuable in shaping his perception of authorship before and during World War II. In these comments from the early 1970s, Borges is subsuming the Kabbalists into his engagement with the question of the Argentine literary tradition that came to the fore in the early 1950s, most notably in his 1951 lecture "The Argentine Writer and Tradition." In terms of Borges's allusions to the Judaic, this lecture will reveal both a continuation and a departure. It continues the significant yet idiosyncratic investment in the Judaic—both as a way of expressing himself intellectually and as a literary aesthetic in his stories—that we have seen Borges demonstrate thus far. At the same time, shifting his focus from Kabbalah to Jewish tradition highlights the extent of this investment and the fact that the Kabbalah is only one component of an evolving web of allusions to elements of a Judaic imaginary in Borges's writing.

This evolution is not motivated by historical developments in Jewish history or culture (as historically significant as such developments certainly were between 1932 and 1951), but by contextual developments in Borges's local intellectual environment. In that sense, what may seem like a departure in Borges's writing, most notable in the shift from a focus on mysticism in his 1949 "The God's Script" to a focus on tradition in his 1951 "The Argentine Writer and Tradition," is in fact further indication of the need to conceptualize a broader scholarly engagement with his thought about authorship, one that has its focus on the broad category of the Judaic in Borges's writing, rather than on discrete elements such as Kabbalah and tradition. I am arguing for a holistic approach to the Judaic in Borges, not because I ascribe a necessary intellectual coherence to the grouping of Kabbalah and tradition. As discussed previously, it is not my concern whether Borges understands Jews and Judaism correctly or incorrectly. I am here focused on a thick contextual understanding of those elements that have shaped what he thought about authorship and how he expressed those thoughts.

Leaping, then, from the late 1940s to the early 1970s: On his visit to Israel, Borges met with Scholem and discussed questions of authorship. On that same visit, he met with contemporary Israeli authors and discussed questions of literary tradition. It is in fact the juxtaposition of these two encounters that explains his projection of the question of tradition back onto the Kabbalists. Having identified the way the Kabbalah helped him articulate his notion of authorship in the context of World War II, and anticipating the way discussing Jewish tradition will help him articulate his notion of authorship in the context of the postcolonial question of literary tradition, it should not surprise us to see Borges seek (or imagine) a coherence to his thought on authorship, in part by conceiving a connection between Kabbalah and tradition. The next part in our discussion will lead us to this other central aspect of Borges's thought—the problem of literary tradition—and to a further exploration of the role of his Judaic imaginary in expressing his views on tradition and authorship.

Part 2

Tradition

The Trouble with Tradition

In 1951, Borges gave a lecture in the Colegio Libre de Estudios Superiores titled "El escritor Argentino y la tradición [The Argentine Writer and Tradition]."[1] This would become one of his best-known discussions of the question of Latin American literature and its place vis-à-vis what he perceived as European literary tradition.[2] As the epigraph above demonstrates, tradition was a question he continued to think about throughout his career. The 1951 lecture is also an important discussion of the social position and role of the intellectual author. A touchstone of Borges scholarship, scholars have looked to this lecture for an understanding of two major themes in Borges's writing. The first is his complex notion of literary tradition. In this lecture he frames his thoughts in opposition to what he calls "the Argentine cult of local color."[3] The second is his relation to the Judaic. Borges discusses this toward the end of the lecture by referring to the place of Jews and Irish in European intellectual history.[4] Borges suggests the possibility of Argentine writers mimicking this position in their own relation to European literature. Structurally, then, the lecture has been commonly read as moving from a rejection of "local color" to an embrace of "the Judaic" as models for Argentine, and even Latin American, letters.

Throughout the lecture, Borges maintains an ongoing reference to two texts that shape the lecture both structurally and intellectually. The first, already implied in the title of the lecture, is T. S. Eliot's essay "Tradition and the Individual Talent."[5] The second reference is to the sociologist Thorstein Veblen and his essay "The Intellectual Pre-Eminence of Jews in Modern Europe," which Borges names explicitly only toward the end of the lecture.[6] The former is invaluable in understanding Borges's thoughts about identifying or inventing an Argentine literary tradition and the place it would have in world literature. The latter is essential to understanding the way Borges's representation of the relation between Jewish intellectuals and their tradition informs his self-positioning as a writer and intellectual. The possibility of embracing the Judaic as a model for the Argentine writer's attitude toward Western literary tradition is the point of contact between the topics of literary tradition and the Judaic, and seems to serve as the conclusion to the lecture. That is, the nexus between Borges's notions of tradition and the Judaic is where his thought about authorship is most insightful in this lecture.

In order to fully appreciate the intertextuality that Borges's lecture maintains with Eliot and Veblen, it is essential first to identify the multiple contextual references that this essay develops. By 1951 Borges had been thinking and writing about literary tradition, and in particular Argentine literary tradition, for nearly three decades. It is important to locate this lecture along the development of Borges's thought on this question. Equally important is to locate this lecture along the development of Borges's conceptualization of the Judaic, which had been—at least since his 1932 essay "A Vindication of the Kabbalah" (if not earlier)—an important touchpoint for his thought on authorship and the role of the author. The postwar developments in Borges's thought about tradition and the Judaic will become apparent by tracking his engagement with Eliot and Veblen.

Borges's investment in questions of literary tradition and its problematic goes back to the 1920s, and the early role Eliot played in his thought is unmistakable. Noting Eliot's intertextual presence in "The Argentine Writer and Tradition" will highlight the differences between Borges's early engagement with these questions and the manner in which he resolves them in the 1950s.

Over the same three decades, Borges had assimilated the Judaic as a way to discuss the author and the author's position in society. While the Kabbalah was a central component of this early articulation, it was by no means coterminous with Borges's understanding of the Judaic, nor with his conceptualization of authorship. The 1951 intertextual reference to Veblen helps broaden our view of Borges's Judaic imaginary as well as nuance our understanding of his thoughts on authorship.

The immediate context in which "The Argentine Writer and Tradition" marks a development in Borges's thought and writing is the changing political landscape in postwar Argentina. This included the evolving debate between Borges's cosmopolitan circle and the local intellectuals he refers to in this lecture as "the nationalists," a debate that had already spanned nearly three decades as well.[7] One of the main targets of Borges's polemic on this front (though he is never named) is his contemporary Eduardo Mallea. In fact, "The Argentine Writer and Tradition" directly engages Mallea's lecture "The Writer and Our Times," published in his 1947 book *El sayal y la purpura*.[8] This is the third intertextual reference of Borges's lecture and will be essential to our understanding of his engagement with "the nationalists."

Before turning to a detailed discussion of these three interlocutors—Eliot, Veblen, and Mallea—and their relation to Borges's 1951 lecture, I will outline here the three corresponding intellectual contexts within which Borges's lecture must be read: literary tradition, Jewish tradition, and national tradition. In outlining these contexts, I offer a road map for the discussion ahead, as we expand on each of these frames for reading "The Argentine Writer and Tradition."

Literary Tradition

In the scholarly reception of Borges, "the edge" has played an important role in the discourse of locating Borges and his writing. In studies of Borges, we find that the edge denotes both a spatial relation—drawing on questions of center and periphery, the relations between a post-colony (Argentina) and the European center—and a temporal relation—where it draws on questions of postcolonial modernity and history. In both senses, Borges is seen as writing from "the edge," configured as a question of his relation to tradition, or a lack thereof. In fact, Borges himself identifies the question of his relation to tradition as a productive way of engaging his own spatial and temporal position.

In her book, *Jorge Luis Borges: A Writer on the Edge*, Beatriz Sarlo situates Borges as "a marginal [figure] making use of all cultures. . . . From the margin, Borges is able to place his literature in dialogue, as among equals, with Western literature. He made of the margin an aesthetic principle."[9] Sarlo does not pass inadvertently from "the edge" to "the margin." This transition encompasses her argument about Borges, namely that he encounters the edges of Buenos Aires as a demarcation between two sets of dichotomies. On the one hand, the limits of Buenos Aires mark the line between civilization and barbarism, cosmopolitans and gauchos, urban and rural epistemologies. On the other hand, this limit is also the demarcation between Argentina and Europe, between the post-colony and the traditions of the colonizer. What Borges does, states Sarlo, is to "inscribe a literature at the limit."[10] Through this inscription, Borges breaks apart the dual binary epistemologies of "the edge" and creates a space in-between the oppositions—a space Sarlo refers to as "the margin"— from which he will write an Argentine literature that is fully, paradoxically invested in both the particularity of Argentina and the universality of Europe.[11]

In this sense, Borges's self-made position is a defining trope for students of Latin American literature studying the relation between the perceived lack of distinctly Argentine literary traditions and the embeddedness of Argentine writing within the traditions of European literature. In his book *Cosmopolitan Desires*, Mariano Siskind frames his study with a reading of "The Argentine Writer and Tradition" that sees in it "a cosmopolitan attempt to undo the antagonistic structures of a world literary field organized around the notions of cultural difference that Latin American writers perceive to be the source of their marginality, in order to stake a claim on Literature with a capital L."[12] Similarly focused on the way Borges challenges antagonistic or dichotomous postcolonial structures, Sarlo argues that what takes place in the space of the Borgesian margin is not marginalization, not the devaluation of its occupants, but rather their constitution as alternatives. This is Borges's hallmark operation in Argentine culture and beyond, introducing alternatives—to the canon, to reading, and to tradition.

What the present study adds to this discussion is the observation that Borges's own articulation of this opening of the edge onto an in-between position, the conceptualization of a marginal space he can inhabit as a Latin American author, draws significant nuance from his investment in an analogy to the Judaic. When Borges depicts Jews as marginal in Europe, he does not mean it in the sense of unimportant, or excluded from the centers of cultural production. Quite the contrary. Figures such as Baruch Spinoza and Heinrich Heine— whom Borges identifies as quintessentially Judaic—are so, in his mind, precisely because of their importance as *European* figures.[13] What draws Borges to such figures is their existence as an alternative within the hegemonic culture. Marginality is thus a term for this position vis-à-vis Europe that has by now become commonplace in Borges research, designating what Borges perceives as the paradoxical relation between Argentina and Europe. This insight is a significant contribution of Sarlo's book, which has laid the intellectual framework for identifying the margin as a position quintessentially Borgesian.[14]

This leads to an important intervention of the present study. Subsequent scholarship in Latin American Jewish studies—in drawing attention to the role that Borges's understanding of Judaism played in the articulation of his position—has retrojected a notion of Jewish marginality that is uncritically analogized to Borges's own marginality, and which is then assumed as an equally quintessential Jewish position.[15] In her reading of "The Argentine Writer and Tradition," for example, Evelyn Fishburn states that "Borges puts forward the idea that Jews have played such an important role in their relationship to Western culture precisely because of their position of marginality."[16] This "position of marginality" is presented as a social historical fact and Borges's view of European Jews, rather than a projection of his insights about contemporary Argentine questions, is thus presented as offering a key to understanding the historical reality of Jewish marginality. Commenting on the same essay, and in similar terms, Erin Graff Zivin restates Borges's argument: "The Argentine, as a marginal citizen of the West, is actually more capable of innovation because of his simultaneous status as insider and outsider. In order to substantiate his argument further, Borges turns to the figure of the 'Jew' in Western culture."[17]

I would like to note my reservations about such statements. While Graff Zivin does put the "Jew" in quotation marks, I believe that further critical distance is required. It is neither the historical Jew, nor the figurative "Jew" that Borges refers to in his lecture. In our reading of Borges's interlocutors, our interpretation must pursue a fuller appreciation of the idiosyncratic nature of the Judaic in Borges. We must thus bracket any premature implication of a self-evident Jewish marginality. I want to keep this position, this opening of "the edge" onto an in-between location, in focus here as an aesthetically and discursively constructed space of, and relation to, tradition. In other words, when Borges speaks of Jews as marginal we should not assume this designation has a facile referent. Understanding the constitution of this "Jewish model" will require an understanding of the many interlocutors Borges engages, their intellectual context, and the way in which Borges reads and misreads their implications as he constructs his equally idiosyncratic notion of tradition.

Nor is it my intention to derive from Borges's engagement with the Judaic a definition of Jewish literature. While there may be compelling research that demonstrates Sarlo's understanding of the margin as an aesthetic principle for Borges, this does not simply translate into an aesthetic principle of Jewish letters.[18] As I proceed to use these words—in-between, margin, edge—my intention is not to offer them as an explanation (neither sociohistorical nor literary-poetic) but as a trigger for recurring and persistent questions about location, identification, and difference. I find Sarlo's argument about turning the edge into a margin a very productive lens through which to introduce these questions.

The second reservation I have regarding statements such as Fishburn's and Graff Zivin's relates to defining a role for "the Jews" in Borges's endeavor. I prefer to use Edna Aizenberg's term "the Judaic" ("lo judío") as referent to the object Borges constructs, imagines, and engages, as he reflects on its relation to the Argentine writer and his tradition. I do so in order to leave open the question of Borges's idiosyncratic identification, prioritization, and selection of themes related to the Jews in his conceptualization of the Judaic. This is to say that, as we did with knowledge of the Kabbalah, if we discover certain tensions between Borges's representation of Jewish marginality and our historical knowledge of the Jews, we will bracket them for now, as it is precisely the representation that I am interested in. I do not want to ask if Jews were marginal or not, at the edge or not, but rather, first, how Borges represents the position he ascribes to Jews, Irish, and Argentines and, second, what notion of tradition this implies. The answers to these questions will tell us very little about "the Jews," but hopefully a great deal about Borges.

Jewish Tradition

One of the earliest texts to address these issues is Borges's well-known 1934 polemical piece "Yo, Judío."[19] This short essay is recognized as one of his most explicit expressions of support for Judaism in the face of Argentine antisemitism in the 1930s. It is part of a brief but telling exchange between Borges, publishing in the journal *Megáfono* (Megaphone), and the editors of *Crisol* (Crucible), a right-wing paper of the time. In an editorial, *Crisol* had claimed Borges was concealing his Jewish roots: "As to Borges, we recognize his literary value, which no one can negate, his moral sordidness, also public and his Jewish descendance, maliciously occluded, but poorly dissimulated, since even his poems have that Psalmic accent characteristic of Hebrew poetry."[20]

The accusation here is double. First, Borges is guilty simply of being Jewish. Second, he is guilty of maliciously concealing this fact. "Yo, Judío" is Borges's response to these accusations, and in it he replies that he had been searching for such roots but has come to the conclusion that he has no such genealogical links. He was descended, he concludes, from "an ancestor, in short, irreparably Spanish."[21] However, debunking *Crisol*'s accusations in his typical tongue-in-cheek manner is not the main point of this text. Borges's broader point is to counter the negative valuation of Jews presupposed by the *Crisol* editors: "Who has not, at one time or another, played with thoughts of his ancestors, with the prehistory of his flesh and blood? I have done so many times, and many times it has not displeased me to think of myself as Jewish. . . . I am grateful for the stimulus provided by *Crisol*, but hope is dimming that I will ever be able to discover my link . . . to Heine, Gleizer, and the ten *Sefiroth*; to Ecclesiastes and Chaplin."[22]

Borges's reply is also double. To the first accusation he responds that the thought of his being Jewish is not an unpleasing thought. That is, Borges turns the accusation around, stating that it is not an accusation at all but rather a compliment. There is nothing surprising about this first accusation and reply—the ideological differences between Borges and *Crisol* are clear. Beyond this, Borges seems to reply by denying having any Jewish roots. This denial, however, still relates only to the first accusation, that of being Jewish. Borges says nothing to the second accusation, which is not that of having Jewish roots but of having concealed such roots. Of his Judaism "maliciously occluded" Borges replies only parenthetically—"(the participle and the adverb amaze and delight me)," he states.[23]

The *Crisol* editors pick up on this very point a month later, when they publish a subsequent editorial responding to Borges's reply. "[Borges] tells us he is descended from 'the Catalan Don Pedro de Acevedo' and thus has a grandfather 'irreparably Spanish.' He does not prove that [his grandfather] was not Jewish, and on our part we do not deny [Borges's ancestry] was Spanish and Catalonian. Being Spanish was not and is not an obstacle to being a Semite as well, just as Borges . . . being Argentine is not an obstacle for [his] being Jewish at the same time."[24]

How are we to understand this reply? Could the *Crisol* editors actually be preaching to Borges about the possibilities of Jewish integration into Argentine society? The magnanimity of allowing that one can be both Jewish and Argentine seems out of place for the editors of this openly antisemitic publication. What they are in fact implying is that only through becoming indistinguishable from their broader social setting—and thus accusable of hiding their Judaism— are Jews able to integrate into society. This integration, of course, is detrimental to society, according to the *Crisol* editors. The front page of the same edition that accused Borges of a Judaism maliciously concealed brandishes the title "The Jews bring corruption to the economic life of the towns," under which the feature article explains the corrupting effects of just such social integration.

Borges does not reply to this second *Crisol* editorial and, while certainly not opposed to such integration, we are left to wonder what he thought about the public invisibility that makes such accusations possible. Two decades later, in "The Argentine Writer and Tradition," Borges's reference to Veblen comes as a belated response to the questions this second accusation opens up. In the next chapter I will elaborate on the particular similarities Borges identifies between the Judaic and the Argentine situation. I will proceed to discuss his idea that these similarities imply a shared position and, therefore, the possibility that a certain way of acting within this position (which, he perceives, has proven propitious for modern Jewry) will serve Argentine writers as well. For now, however, one more point of context for the 1951 lecture is needed, in order to appreciate the full extent of the debates that Borges engages and summarizes in this lecture.

National Tradition

Borges was by no means the only Argentine intellectual concerned with the questions of tradition and the Judaic in those decades. He was merely the most notable of the cosmopolitan circle of intellectuals surrounding Victoria Ocampo and her publishing house Sur (South). Ocampo herself, as well as Borges's lifelong friend and collaborator Adolfo Bioy Casares, was part of a very active group of intellectuals, and the journal *Sur* was a major venue for their writing. Borges himself published many of his best-known stories in this journal, before collecting them into books (some of which were also published by *Sur*).

A notable counterpart to Borges on the question of Argentine literature was the literary critic and public intellectual Eduardo Mallea. Mallea was a persistent target of Borges's polemics going back to the early 1930s. Together with Borges, Mallea was one of the early contributors to *Sur* and the two maintained a long-standing intellectual rivalry. According to Judith Podlubne, who analyzes this rivalry, Mallea believed literature was an expression of the human spirit and "like Ocampo, Mallea appealed to spiritual values as a way of legitimizing the literary exercise because he believed these values would realize the authentic nature of humanity."[25] Borges saw literature as more formal and impersonal, and gained his prominent voice in *Sur* through his opposition to a kind of "moralizing humanism formulated by Mallea and vindicated by the other early members of Sur."[26]

Sur also published one of Mallea's most famous books, *Historia de una passión argentina* (1937).[27] The celebrated contribution of this book was Mallea's coinage of the nationalist essentialist term "argentinidad [Argentineity]." This, in the same years that Borges was cautioning against the dangers of essentialist notions of belonging, as he warned against the rise of Nazism almost daily in the pages of major (and minor) Argentine publications. Mallea in general, and this term in particular, came under persistent criticism by Borges in the years and decades that followed. Though he never mentions Mallea by name in his polemics, Borges directs much criticism at the nationalist essentialism promoted by "the nationalists." In "A Comment on August 23, 1944" we have already seen Borges mock "the infinite repetition of the interesting formula *I am Argentine*"—an interlinear allusion to Mellea's coinage.[28] Mallea's ideas about the human spirit would become ideas about the Argentine spirit and serve the nationalist ideology well in the decades to follow.

Turning to the genealogy of Borges's lecture, in 1935 Mallea gave a lecture titled "El escritor y nuestro tiempo [The Writer and Our Times]" to a group of university students. After World War II, he reprinted this lecture in his 1947 book *El sayal y la purpura*, where he also added a second chapter with the very same title: "El escritor y nuestro tiempo."[29] In these two chapters, Mallea warns of "the dis-harmony of a heterogeneous universe turning to anarchy and becoming unhinged."[30] Here he introduces the role of the author: "to intervene is the proper function of the writer in our times."[31] Later in the book he restates: "Hamlet said 'the time is out of joint,' our time is out of joint . . . for the extreme and profound [diversity] that we must now name and order."[32] To confront the threat of a heterogeneous universe, the Argentine author is tasked with reining in excessive diversity by focusing on his essential Argentineity. Mallea sees this as both a moral and a poetic mandate. Over the decade from the mid-1930s to the mid-1940s, the articulation of his position matured, as did his sense of urgency.

Mallea was not the only one dealing with the theme of the author's moral and poetic roles in the mid-1940s. In April 1946 the journal *Sur* had dedicated an issue to the same question, offering its readers the proceedings of a scholarly retreat hosting French writer Jean Guéhenno, which was held the previous year and titled "Free Literature and Committed Literature." The same issue also included a Spanish translation of Jean-Paul Sartre's "Portrait of an anti-Semite."[33] While in "The Writer and Our Times" Mallea is calling for authors to launch what he sees as a moral intervention into the dangerously heterogeneous reality of "our times," in the *Sur* conference, Guéhenno is discussing "how suspicious it becomes when one desires a committed literature: as if one wished to replace the aesthetic perspective with a moral one."[34] As this debate matured, it took the form of a more focused discussion on questions of literature, national tradition, and the role of the author. The maturation of this intellectual polemic in the postwar years is an important backdrop to our reading of "The Argentine Writer and Tradition."

These postwar debates are an important context for the moral and poetic corruption, of which Borges will accuse "the nationalists" in his own lecture a few years later. In fact, the Colegio lecture preceded a series of traveling lectures on the topic that Borges delivered over the subsequent two years, and which followed the same themes and arguments as the 1951 lecture. By the time this lecture was published in the journal of the Colegio in 1953 with the title "The Argentine Writer and Tradition," Borges had delivered at least four similar lectures traveling in Entre Rios. Interestingly, the title of the traveling lecture was "El escritor y nuestro tiempo," a far clearer reference to Mallea and his writing. These lectures formed a series of talks Borges gave between the winter of 1951 and the summer of 1952, all of which discuss the question of the relation between literature and national politics. Daniel Fitzgerald has reconstructed the traveling lecture and demonstrates that Borges's lecture "The Writer and Our Times" was a universalized discussion of the same questions that are discussed in particularly Argentine terms in "The Argentine Writer and Tradition."[35]

In the traveling lecture, Borges begins by dismissing certain modes of authorship as impossible. The first impossibility is detaching oneself from contemporary political reality. Referring to the metaphor of the ivory tower as signaling the total indifference of authors toward their contemporary moment, Borges states: "it is not possible to accept that literature does not reflect the clamor of anxiety [of our times]."[36] The second impossibility is writing what Borges calls "directed literature." Writing tributary literature in the service of the state is equally impossible, since literature "upon losing its independence also loses . . . beauty in order to serve a utilitarian end."[37] Third, Borges rejects "committed literature" as "always subordinated to other motivation," other than writing literature.[38] In this last reference to Sartre's recent articles on "committed literature," Borges signals his own lecture's engagement with the questions of his time and brings his audience and readers up to the early 1950s moment, in which he is discussing the relation between literature and national politics, in Argentina but also in a more global postwar moment. Borges's lecture should thus be read both in the context of the debate about the sociopolitical role of committed versus autonomous literature as well as in the context of postwar debates about antisemitism and nationalism. To complete the framing of this lecture, I turn now to discussing the context of Borges's ongoing engagement both with questions of literary tradition and with T. S. Eliot. "The Argentine Writer and Tradition" grows out of these two threads in Borges's thought.

Tradition in the Historical Sense

In his 1917 essay "Tradition and the Individual Talent," T. S. Eliot deals with what might appear as tension between a writer's talent and a writer's commitment to a literary tradition. Saying a writer is traditional, he explains, is seen as "some pleasing archaeological reconstruction, [a] comfortable reference to the reassuring science of archaeology."[39] Tradition, Eliot suggests, is perceived as disconnected from the writing of literature in the present and adherence to it implies a lack of originality, or what he is calling "talent." On the other hand, he continues, when "we praise a poet, upon those aspects of his work in which he least resembles anyone else . . . we pretend to find what is individual, what is the peculiar essence of the man."[40] Eliot does not so much contest this opposition between the imitation of archaic forms and the absolute individualism of literary innovation. Rather, he argues against the historical scheme such an opposition might suggest, namely, that tradition is a thing of the past, an archaeological artifact, while talent is a thing of the present, a total break from tradition.

Against such a scheme, Eliot proposes "the historical sense."[41] For the talented writer the past and the present are simultaneous.[42] "The whole of the literature of Europe from Homer and within it the whole of the literature of [one's] own country has a simultaneous existence and composes a simultaneous order."[43] Tradition is a cumulative thing of the present and talent consists in forming an innovative relationship to it, Eliot argues. Literary innovation is not a break with literary history and at the same time literary innovation is able to alter the historical sense of past texts. "What happens when a new work of art is created is something that happens simultaneously to all the works of art which preceded it. [We] will not find it preposterous that the past should be altered by the present as much as the present is directed by the past."[44]

Eliot very clearly shares the same concern Borges has for questions of literary tradition. Yet Eliot presumes a natural, uncritical link between literary tradition and the history from which the writer originates. His discussion does not address the case of a writer who does not have a clear sense of their history, or indeed "the literature of [their] own country," for whom the question of tradition remains undetermined.[45] In order to be part of a simultaneous order in the present, for such an order to allow the alteration of the past by means of the present, there must be a past, one's tradition must first be clearly identified. What of Latin American writers such as Borges, whose tradition has not been identified, or indeed may not be identifiable?

This lacuna in Eliot's essay concerned Borges for much of the first decade of his career. In fact, as Sarlo states, "the first thing Borges does is invent a cultural tradition for this ex-centric place that is his country. This aesthetic and ideological operation runs through his work in the twenties and the first half of the thirties, until *Historia Universal de la Infamia*."[46] From his very first publications, Borges not only set out to invent the missing tradition (as Sarlo points out) but also attempted a more theoretical reflection on the problem and imagined solutions to the lack of a properly Argentine tradition.[47] As early as his 1926 book *El tamaño de mi esperanza*, he states that, since Argentina does not have a tradition, his aim is to invent one.[48] "There are no legends in this land, and not a single ghost walks our streets. That is our dishonor . . . Buenos Aires is a country, and we must find for it the poetry, the music, the painting, the religion, and the metaphysics appropriate for its grandeur. This is the full extent of my hope (el tamaño de mi esperanza)."[49]

In the same essay, Borges then goes on to reject what at the time were considered properly Argentine cultural traditions. "I want neither progressivism nor *criollismo*. . . . The first means subjecting ourselves to being almost-North-Americans or almost-Europeans, a tenacious being almost-others. The second, once a word for action . . . is today a word for nostalgia (the slack appetite for the countryside). Not much fervor in either."[50] Borges does not want to imitate other literary traditions, nor does he want to encourage nostalgia for the rural culture of nineteenth-century Argentine ranchers (the gauchos). These are both options he will reject more comprehensively three decades later in "The Argentine Writer and Tradition." The former he will call "play at being European"[51] and the latter he will associate with "*gauchesco* poetry."[52] But in the mid-1920s he had not yet formulated the comprehensive argument of "The Argentine Writer and Tradition." And although he seeks to invent a "metaphysics" for Buenos Aires, it seems in 1926 there is no hint of perceiving the Judaic as a model for dealing with this question.

Borges's 1930 book *Evaristo Carriego* is seen as an example of his effort to find, or invent, the Argentine past.[53] In it, Borges directly engages the question of historical temporality.

> I maintain—and I wish neither coyly to evade nor boldly to parade paradox— that only new countries have a past; that is to say, an auto-biographical memory, a living history. If time is a succession of events, we must admit that where more things are happening more time is passing, and so it is on this inconsequential side of the world that time is most profuse. . . . Time—a European sentiment of people with a long past, and their very justification and glory—moves more boldly in the New World. . . . Over here we are contemporary with time, we are brothers of time.[54]

There are two points in which this passage is consistent with Eliot. First, in order to invent the content of an Argentine tradition, Borges must also affirm the existence of a past within which such an invention will be manifest. In these lines, Borges is conceptualizing a properly Argentine past, which maintains a tension with the kind of universal history he will later—as in "The Argentine Writer and Tradition"—identify as the locus (or lack) of Argentine tradition. Second, in this passage Borges maintains that such a properly Argentine past is essential for the existence of a properly Argentine tradition. It is an attempt to identify what Eliot describes as "the historical sense" of the literature of his own country, understood as the concomitant idiosyncrasy of a country's history with the idiosyncrasy of its literary tradition. His point of departure from Eliot's argument comes in a surprisingly competitive note added here to the discussion. Borges represents the past as a zero-sum game. Either it is the case that Europe has a past, full of nationally bound identifiable literary traditions, or it is that only the new countries of the Americas have a past at all. Borges clearly opts for the latter when he states, "over here we are contemporary with time."[55]

In the prologue to the 1955 edition of *Evaristo Carriego*, Borges reflects on the origin of this book and tries to phrase the question that the book was meant to answer, about his childhood neighborhood of Palermo and about Argentine history more broadly: "What was that [old] Palermo like or *what would it have been nice if it had been?* To these questions this book attempted to reply, less documentary than imaginative."[56] The subjunctive tense Borges uses in this question frames the past as a counterfactual moment. For Argentina there is no answer, outside of an imagined one, for the question of being rooted in a past. In the context of his 1950s concern with literary tradition, Borges understands his 1930 book as an effort to invent this past that is counterfactual. This effort is what Sarlo and others identify in his early literary works. For the present discussion, I am not concerned with these literary works as anything more than background.[57] My intention is to track a series of reflections on this question that leads Borges to his most emblematic—and, I will demonstrate, altered—articulation of literary tradition in "The Argentine Writer and Tradition."

Three years after his thoughts on the historical temporality of New World countries, in a 1933 essay titled "La eternidad y T. S. Eliot [Eternity and T. S. Eliot]," Borges quotes extensively from Eliot's essay, explaining the idea of "the historical sense" by identifying "the concepts [Eliot] attempts to consolidate or avoid."[58] These, Borges explains, are the ideas of progress and classicism. "One [concept Eliot wishes to avoid] is the idea of progress. . . . Indefinite progress makes of every book the draft of a successive book: a condition that, while it borders on the prophetic, is foolish and rudimentary as well. . . . The contrary hypothesis, that of the classics, is much more inept. . . . On the one hand it affirms that erudition and refined work are the conditions of art; on the other, that [the classics] have a secret and lasting significance."[59]

In this first direct engagement with Eliot's essay, Borges already signals the limitation of "the historical sense" in that, in its attempt to reconcile the motions of history, it is entirely predicated on a definition of that very term, to which the Latin American writer—individually talented as they may be—has no access. There is a tension between the idea that writers are constantly progressing, improving, innovating on their precursors, and the thought that the farther they get from their precursors the farther they get from the source of their own tradition. Borges's observation is that to be caught up within these tensions of historical tradition one must first be caught *within* a historical tradition.

It is also worth noting that this rejection of the classics as a paradigm for Latin American authorship comes just one year after we have seen Borges embrace the notion of a perfect text as just such a paradigm in "A Vindication of the Kabbalah." While we have only seen the explicit juxtaposition of these two concepts ("the sacred book" and "the classical book") occur in Borges's 1977 lecture "The Kabbalah," it is worth noting the extent to which the roots of this opposition are already present in Borges's writing in the early 1930s, during which time the stakes he saw for both authorship and literary tradition were being defined.[60]

After rejecting Eliot's attempted reconciliation of progress and classicism as inapplicable to his own circumstances, Borges goes on to identify the implications of Eliot's thesis for the possibility of a Latin American literary tradition. "I come to the thesis formulated by Eliot. . . . It does not propose to challenge the accumulated classical order, nor promise its clients a talisman that foretells glory. . . . The influence of the present upon the past—is of a literal veracity, though it may seem relativist mischief."[61] Juan de Castro demonstrates the manner in which Borges's selective and edited citations of Eliot's essay emphasize the idea of *the present changing the past* over other, more central arguments and proposals that Eliot makes in his essay. Borges's citation presents, "in a way more concise and vigorous than Eliot's original, the arguments that justify this notion."[62] This essay is also an early source for the thoughts Borges develops in "The Argentine Writer and Tradition," where "the idea that Borges encountered in 'Tradition and the Individual Talent,' of the influence of the present upon the past, had become a new proposal about literary history."[63]

It seems natural to insert "The Argentine Writer and Tradition" into the line of argument Borges was building in his writing in the 1920s and early 1930s. This would explain why, when the second edition of Borges's 1932 essay collection *Discusión* was published in 1957, it included the text of his 1951 lecture "The Argentine Writer and Tradition" alongside original first edition essays such as "A Vindication of the Kabbalah." As we have also seen in Borges's reflections in his 1955 prologue to the reprint of *Evaristo Carriego*, the 1950s were a moment when he reflected back on his activity in the 1920s and early 1930s and attempted to recast those older texts within the scope of his reinvigorated concerns with postcolonial literary tradition.

Nevertheless, there are important differences in this later articulation of the problem of Argentine tradition. Most obviously, the local social context had changed dramatically. As Annick Louis explains: "The decade of the 1920s was a golden age for cultural and literary journals. . . . The thirties, on the other hand, are marked by crisis, politicization and polarization of the media and the intellectuals while power was violently redistributed."[64] The 1920s saw the liberal governments of Hipólito Yrigoyen and Marcelo T. Alvear, but in September 1930 Yrigoyen was overthrown in a military coup by General José Uriburu, who effectively kicked off what has become known as "The Infamous Decade" in Argentine history. Moreover, by the early 1950s, when Borges delivered "The Argentine Writer and Tradition" as a lecture at the Colegio Libre de Estudios Superiores—an intellectual hub of anti-Peronist sentiment— World War II had left its mark on Argentina and the country was half a decade into the populist rule of General Juan Domingo Perón.[65]

Questions of national tradition received greater attention in the context of a conservative nationalist movement that had now gained substantial political power in the country. In this context, we should understand the 1951 lecture as an opportunity, in which Borges revisits his earlier thoughts on the question of Argentine tradition and attempts to rearticulate them as a commentary on the present national moment. His points of reference for what he previously rejected as progressivism and *criollismo* will become references to ideas he encountered in more contemporary intellectual circles. Thus, he will refer to the progressivism he rejected already in 1926 as "play at being European."[66] This is another reference to Eduardo Mallea's celebrated 1937 book *Historia de una pasión argentina*, in which Mallea rejects such "play" in favor of conformity to an essentialist Argentineity. Similarly, Borges's earlier rejection of *criollismo* will become a rejection of "the Argentine cult of local color," a reference to the

Peronist intellectuals of the time and to official state versions of Argentine tradition.[67] Clearly identifying this lecture as part of Borges's decades-long polemic against Mallea and "the nationalists" will help us make sense of the argument in "The Argentine Writer and Tradition." It will also further highlight the poetic significance of Veblen and the Judaic in this lecture.

The Postwar Question of Tradition

As Edna Aizenberg points out, World War II deeply affected Borges's thought about the Judaic and compelled him to rethink the (inevitable) Argentine relation to Europe as well.[68] His 1951 lecture is an example of the way in which these elements all come together. In this lecture, Borges moves away from the necessity of having a properly Argentine tradition. Unlike in *El tamaño de mi esperanza* and *Evaristo Carriego*, where his solution is to try to pull such a tradition out of imagination, from conjecture or from the past, in "The Argentine Writer and Tradition" he goes through the extant options for Argentine traditions and eventually questions the very necessity of having one's own tradition in the first place. Thus, from the very start of the lecture, Borges announces his skepticism about the existence of "the problem of the Argentine writer and tradition."[69] In the discussion that follows he breaks down this "appearance, a simulacrum," as he terms it, into the same two questions Eliot deals with.[70] What is literary tradition? What attitude should a writer have toward this tradition? But Borges rephrases the questions to apply specifically to the case of the Argentine writer. First, what is the Argentine writer's tradition? And, second, what should be the Argentine writer's proper attitude toward this tradition?

By calling the problem of tradition a "pseudo-problem," Borges attempts to adopt the easy tone with which Eliot answers the first question. Naturally, the Argentine writer's tradition is "the whole of the literature of Europe from Homer and within it the whole of the literature of [one's] own country."[71] The simulacrum of a problem arises for Borges not from the idea that there is in fact such a coherent whole, a body of tradition we might refer to as "the whole of the literature of Europe." This he seems to take for granted, as he did in "A Comment on August 23, 1944," where he stated that "for Europeans and Americans, one order and only one is possible; it used to be called Rome, and now it is called Western Culture."[72] The problem is that the second question—*what should be the Argentine writers' proper attitude toward their tradition?*—produces the entanglement of this coherent whole with the suggestion that there is a particularly Argentine literary tradition in the first place. That is, the particular Argentine tradition and the universal European tradition are coterminous and are thus indistinguishable from one another. Identifying the particular Argentine tradition is not possible because its very particularity is a simulacrum. "My skepticism is not related to the difficulty or impossibility of resolving the problem, but to its very existence," Borges explains.[73] Eliot does not consider any such problem of particularity. "The literature of [one's] own country," he states, is contained within "the whole of the literature of Europe."[74] This relationship of the part to the whole is something Eliot takes for granted.

The first part of Borges's lecture works through these two questions by reviewing the various contemporary suggestions as to what the Argentine tradition might be. In his attempt to separate the question whether Argentina has a literary tradition from the question of its relation to European tradition, Borges rejects as possible answers both the *gauchesco* genre of Argentina's nineteenth-century ranchers and the literary tradition of Spain, the founder of the Río de la Plata colonies. Nor can he accept the opinion that Argentina has no tradition, "that we Argentines are cut off from the past."[75] There is such a thing as an Argentine literary tradition, Borges asserts. One that is better perceived if we do not confuse its identification with its relation to European tradition. "What is Argentine tradition? I believe that this question poses no problem and can easily be answered. I believe that our tradition is the whole of Western culture," he states, repeating Eliot but with a difference.[76]

Borges adopts Eliot's idea of the simultaneity with which "the whole of the literature of Europe" presents itself to the writer. In this manner, Borges's answer avoids raising the question of a relation to the whole. The Argentine writer's tradition, he suggests, is the whole of European literature. The appearance of a pseudo-problem begins with the attempt to divide this whole into parts and continues with the attempt to locate the Argentine part within the whole—an attempt that results in the confusion of the very existence of such an Argentine part with its existence as a part of the whole.

After outlining "the historical sense," Eliot in his essay moves from tradition and talent to "the individual" and discusses the role of feelings and emotions in the work of art. He ends stating that "this essay proposes to halt at the frontier of metaphysics or mysticism."[77] Borges sees no reason to halt here. For him there is something inherently metaphysical about the idea that the past changes as a result of the present, and that the part and the whole are identical. He thus continues Eliot's discussion a bit further. "I believe that this problem of the Argentine and tradition is simply a contemporary and fleeting version of the eternal problem of determinism," he states.[78] This is a surprising connection to draw since the idea of determinism would seem to be the opposite of the idea that the present can change the past. Determinism holds that the past always leads, inevitably and irrevocably, to a single possible version of the present. Borges, tongue in cheek, explains as much.

> If I am going to touch this table with one of my hands, and I ask myself: "Will I touch it with the left hand or the right?" and I touch it with the right hand, the determinists will say that I could not have done otherwise and that the

whole prior history of the universe forced me to touch the table with my right hand, and that touching it with my left hand would have been a miracle. Yet if I had touched it with my left hand, they would have told me the same thing: that I was forced to touch it with that hand.[79]

In Borges's humorous portrayal, the determinists will always be right, since they are always only affirming the inevitability of the present ex post facto. They are unable to predict what will happen, but as soon as it happens, they state it could not have happened otherwise. This sort of logic would make the determinists an annoyingly-always-right bunch, if not for the added fact that (in Borges's depiction) they base their claim about the inevitability of the present on the past. This is the point at which Borges wants to appropriate the determinist logic for his argument. "The same occurs with literary subjects and techniques. Everything we Argentine writers do felicitously will belong to Argentine tradition."[80] If the present can alter the past, it is by retroactively making the past into that which predetermines the present.[81] This is what makes the Argentine tradition identifiable. The entire history of Europe has led inevitably to the present moment in Argentina. Everything Argentine writers do is ex post facto predetermined to form part of the simultaneous order that is Argentine tradition.

Thus far we have seen how, in dealing with his two questions, Borges successfully brackets the second (what should be the Argentine writer's proper attitude toward their tradition?) in order to answer the first: What is the Argentine writer's tradition? Borges suggests that Argentine writers have the whole of Western culture as their tradition and must operate therein. We come now to the second question: How ought they operate within this vast "simultaneous order"? In his answer to the second question, Borges recalls the essay "The Intellectual Pre-Eminence of Jews in Modern Europe" by the sociologist Thorstein Veblen.[82] This is where Borges will introduce his representation of the Judaic into the discussion of Argentine literary tradition. As Aizenberg notes, "Borges' application of a 'Jewish model' to the Latin American situation is his own, but the model he employs is borrowed from another thinker . . . the North American Thorstein Veblen."[83] We turn now to the question regarding the proper attitude toward tradition and discuss the intertextual relations that the Judaic maintains with Veblen, in "The Argentine Writer and Tradition" and beyond.

5

What Is Jewish Tradition?

Having discussed Borges's answer to the question "what is Argentine tradition?" in the previous chapter, we come now to the second question in "The Argentine Writer and Tradition," namely, what should be the Argentine writer's attitude toward their tradition? This question too is based on Borges's reading of T. S. Eliot, but the answer he offers is based on his reading of "The Intellectual Pre-Eminence of Jews in Modern Europe" by Thorstein Veblen.[1] In fact, the recollection of Veblen's article marks the moment that Borges's lecture transitions from the first to the second question. This happens toward the end of the lecture when Borges summarizes Veblen's article thus:

> Here I remember an essay by Thorstein Veblen, the North American sociologist, on the intellectual preeminence of Jews in Western culture . . . he says that Jews are prominent in Western culture because they act within that culture and at the same time do not feel bound to it by any special devotion. . . . We can say the same of the Irish in English culture . . . the fact of feeling themselves to be Irish, to be different, was enough to enable them to make innovations in English culture. I believe that Argentines, and South Americans in general, are in an analogous situation; we can take on all the European subjects, take them on without superstition and with an irreverence that can have, and already has had, fortunate consequences.[2]

Borges's answer to the second question is: irreverence. But in explaining and grounding this answer, he invokes the Jews and the Irish as examples to imitate, as differentiated cultural groups contained within Europe that operate within it very successfully. Within the broader culture of Europe, the mere "fact of feeling themselves . . . to be different, was enough to enable them to make innovations."[3] Having located the Argentine writer within the whole of Western culture, it is this feeling of difference that Borges wishes to promote among Argentines. Veblen's understanding of the preeminence of Jews in Europe offers Borges what he perceives as an attractive model of cultural difference, not because it dwells on the fact of cultural difference—Borges and Veblen take this difference for granted—but because it presents to him an account of the underlying social conditions of the feeling of difference that he wishes to inspire in his Argentine audience.

To understand the basis for the analogy Borges is drawing between Jews, Irish, and Argentines, we need to take a closer look at Veblen's argument and track the ways that his sociological observations inspire the analogy Borges is suggesting. In reviewing Veblen's article, we will also find that while explicit reference to Veblen comes only at the end of Borges's lecture, Veblen's article is pertinent to the structure of Borges's entire argument in "The Argentine Writer and Tradition" and, in fact, accompanies the argument of the lecture from its very beginning. Veblen's article reviews a series of possible explanations for Jewish preeminence, rejecting them one after the other, until it arrives at the explanation referenced by Borges. As we will see, Borges's lecture too proceeds along a similar structure, rejecting answers to his first question (what is Argentine literary tradition?) that are analogous to those rejected by Veblen. This structural similarity is an important backdrop for the final analogy Borges will suggest between Jews, Irish, and Argentines.

Though Borges does not mention it on the occasion of his lecture, the main concern of Veblen's essay is with the effects of Zionism on what he calls "Christendom." Beyond inspiring Borges's postwar articulation of the relation between the Judaic and questions of literary tradition, Veblen's understanding did also have an effect (unacknowledged in the present lecture) on Borges's own understanding of Zionism. This point will become clearer after comparing the structure of these two texts. For now, let us begin with the observation that, in order to elaborate his views on Zionism, Veblen attempts to outline "the conditioning circumstances . . . the nature and causes of Jewish achievement in Gentile Europe."[4] The overarching goal of his essay is to caution that the intellectual preeminence of Jews, as the title introduces it, is precisely what will be undone by the success of the Zionist project, which Veblen sees as "a project for withdrawal upon themselves, a scheme of national demarkation [sic] between Jew and gentile."[5]

In order to explain this predicted outcome of Zionism (the disappearance of Jewish preeminence), Veblen discusses the circumstances within which "the

Jewish people have contributed much more than an even share to the intellectual life of modern Europe."[6] This contribution is a basic assumption and point of departure. It is not detailed in any significant way, although we may recall Borges's list of notable Jewish figures in his essay "Yo, Judío" to realize that he already shared this assumption two decades before delivering "The Argentine Writer and Tradition." At the same time, the postwar context of this lecture is an important frame for understanding the way Borges implicates the Judaic in questions of tradition. While Borges is speaking in the aftermath of World War II, Veblen's article was clearly written in the aftermath of World War I. After clarifying the structural similarities between these texts and developing more nuance about the analogy Borges is suggesting, we will also have to review the points at which Borges's effort to construct an analogy between Veblen's prewar European Jewish condition and his own postwar Argentine moment is strained. This too will provide nuance to our understanding of Borges's attitude toward tradition and authorship, and the role of the Judaic in articulating this attitude.

First, however, we turn to a comparative reading of these texts. As mentioned, Veblen proposes a series of possible explanations for this preeminence and rejects them one by one. Having determined in advance that the grounds for these achievements lie in a certain mode of interaction—under the circumstances of Jewish existence within, and attitude toward, gentile Europe—the explanations Veblen raises and rejects are all possible answers to a question rather similar to Borges's second question: What is the relation to Western culture that has been so advantageous for the Jews and Irish? It is here that a comparison of Veblen's and Borges's rejected answers will illuminate just how much Borges's lecture was influenced by the line of argumentation through which Veblen explains his basic assumption about Jewish contributions to Europe.

First Rejection: The Essential

The first explanation for Jewish preeminence that Veblen rejects is a racial-essential answer. The idea that the Jewish gene itself conveys a special endowment. The question, as Veblen states it, is "whether the Jewish strain itself, racially speaking, can at all reasonably be held to account for . . . the pedigree of the Jewish nation as it stands."[7] Veblen rejects a racial explanation outright, arguing that, racially speaking, there is no such thing as the Jewish gene. "The Jewish people are a nation of hybrids . . . gentile blood of many kinds has been infused into the people in large proportions in the course of time. Indeed, none of the peoples of Christendom has been more unremittingly exposed to hybridization."[8] The hybridity of the Jewish population of Europe does not allow for any essentialist explanation for their preeminence.

Nor is hybridity itself a possible explanation for Jewish preeminence. Veblen rejects this proposition as well. There are other hybrid peoples in Europe who have not attained the same preeminence. So the fact of hybridity has "its bearing on the case of the Jews only in the same manner and degree as it is of consequence for any other hybrid people."[9] Veblen insists on rejecting any theory that would locate the explanation for preeminence within the community rather than in the mode of interaction between the community and its surrounding environment.

In his lecture, Borges follows Veblen in rejecting any answer that does not assume—for Argentines and Jews alike—that interaction with Europe is inevitable and, furthermore, that their success is predicated on the manner in which Argentines admit and embrace this interaction. The answer to the question regarding the Argentine writer's tradition cannot be that the Argentine writer is confined by what is essentially Argentine. Thus, the first answer Borges rejects in his own lecture is the *gauchesco* genre, which attempts to imitate the poetry of nineteenth-century Argentine ranchers (the gauchos).[10] In its particularistic imitation of such narrow subject matter, the *gauchesco* genre would only relapse Argentine literature into an obsession with essentialist notions of "local color." Such a circumscribed set of themes and references produces literature for which one "needs a glossary in order to reach even an approximate understanding."[11]

The debate about local color relates to the aforementioned intellectual confrontation between Borges, Eduardo Mallea, and their respective intellectual circles. Mallea's ideas were aligned with the Peronist intellectuals who espoused nationalist essentialist views of Argentine identity. Mallea's call for what Borges dubs "a committed literature" is what Borges mocks as an obsession with local color. In line with the terms of the debate, Borges's attack against "the cult of local color" is both moral and literary: "I do not know if it needs to be said that the idea that a literature must define itself by the differential traits of the country that produces it is a relatively new one, and the idea that writers must seek out subjects local to their countries is also new and arbitrary."[12] In using the terms "local color" and "differential traits" to describe the object of national essentialist thought, Borges is echoing the connection to Veblen's rejection of essential genetic traits.

Borges continues with a jab at the intellectual inconsistency of the nationalists' xenophobia, stating: "The Argentine cult of local color is a recent European cult that nationalists should reject as a foreign import."[13] Beyond the typical Borgesian metareflexive viewpoint, this critique also indicates the moral dimension of Borges's polemics. Borges's remark, that the thought one must espouse local color is an entirely nonlocal idea, is also a comment on the inevitable interaction between Argentina and Europe and its results. Argentine "local" ideas will never be detached from the influence "foreign" Europe exerts on them.[14]

Borges's lecture proceeds with his well-known confabulation about there being no camels in the Koran.[15] This is of course false, but the point about local color is well taken: When one is secure enough in their affiliation that they can take their belonging for granted, there is no need to emphasize this belonging. Only someone who is insecure about their belonging, Borges implies, would compensate by overrepresenting their local color. In terms of Veblen's importance to Borges's lecture, we can state that Borges is of course not denying that local Argentine dialects such as porteñol or lunfardo exist, or that they are characteristic of local porteños and Argentines. But he is resisting the appropriation of this local color by an inward-gazing celebration of the idiosyncratic elements of Argentine identity. What he is opposing is not that an Argentine write about the slums or the gauchos (as he himself did), but the claim that this is what defines an Argentine. "I believe that we Argentines [he concludes] can believe in the possibility of being Argentine without abounding in local color."[16] The fear of course is that one would lose their Argentine identity if it was not undergirded by a local, that is Argentine, poetics. This is where Veblen offers Borges a powerful analogy. The first explanation Veblen discards is that there is an essential, internal quality to the Jews that accounts for their preeminence. Along the same lines, the first idea Borges rejects is that what distinguishes the Argentine is essential or local to Argentina.

Second Rejection: The Original

The next answer Borges rejects is the proposition that a return to the historical origins of Argentina might produce the desired tradition. This second rejection is in line with the progression of Veblen's argument. As Veblen sees it, "the Zionists aspire to bring to full fruition all that massive endowment of spiritual and intellectual capacities of which their people have given evidence throughout their troubled history."[17] Yet this history has been one of growing distance between the Jews and their "home-bred Jewish scheme of things," and the intellectual capacities Veblen discusses arose precisely as a result of this distancing.[18] After all, "the days of Solomon and the caravan trade . . . are long past," he observes.[19] Jewish preeminence does not stem from a link to the "oriental twelfth century BC," which he believes the Zionists wish to revive.[20] That historical link is "of an archaic fashion . . . it all bears the date-mark, 'B.C.' . . . no longer of the substance of those things that are inquired into by men to whom the ever increasingly mechanistic orientation of the modern time becomes habitual."[21] The history of Jewish preeminence is a history of moving away from their ancient Near Eastern origins and its historical B.C. marker.

Therefore, Veblen reasons, any regression to a notion of origins will result in a move away from the preeminence that currently exists.

In step with Veblen's argument, the second answer Borges rejects is the idea that the Argentine writer's tradition ought to be the literary tradition of Spain. "Argentine history can unequivocally be defined as a desire to move away from Spain, as a willed distancing from Spain," he objects.[22] Borges thus concludes, "the fact that certain illustrious Argentine writers write like Spaniards is not so much a testimony to some inherited capacity as it is evidence of Argentine versatility."[23] Reading Veblen alongside Borges's lecture highlights the objection to such a return to the historical inheritance of Spanish tradition (or the days of King Solomon). First, it is still too narrow a proposition to be the source of Argentine tradition or future preeminence. Borges has already identified the Argentine's tradition as the whole of Western culture. Spanish tradition is subsumed by the broader category he has already proposed. Second, the return implied by selecting this particular historicity stands in contrast to the movement away from particularistic history. Searching for an Argentine application for the social structure underpinning Veblen's Jewish preeminence, Borges is objecting to the construction of a national–ideological narrative of "return to the source" that Veblen identifies with Zionism. As already stated, the place of Zionism as an opposite solution to the one Borges borrows from Veblen is not explicit in Borges's lecture.[24] Yet the structure of the lecture mimics the flow of Veblen's argument both rhetorically, in surveying and rejecting solutions, and in the content of the solutions surveyed.

Third Rejection: The Rupture

Veblen's article goes on to argue that Jewish preeminence is not due to inherent features but to a particular mode of interaction with European culture. This mode of interaction is what Borges will soon call for as Argentine irreverence. In Veblen's account, Jewish preeminence is achieved only by embracing the interaction with Europe, not by attempting to avoid or deny it. That is, the preeminence of Jews is only realized through immersion in the culture from which they are to be differentiated. "This intellectual pre-eminence of the Jews has come into bearing *within* the gentile community of peoples, not from the outside . . . the men who have been its bearers have been men immersed in this gentile culture," Veblen states.[25] Just as Veblen rejects what he sees as the isolationism of Zionism, so Borges will reject the notion that Argentina is, or should be, isolated from Europe. The third and final answer Borges rejects in his lecture is that there is no Argentine history or tradition, and that Argentina (and perhaps all New World countries) is involved in a project of radical innovation of history and tradition: "The opinion that we Argentines are cut off from the past; that there has been some sort of rupture between ourselves and Europe.

According to this singular point of view, we Argentines are as if in the first days of creation; our search for European subject matters and techniques is an illusion, an error; we must understand that we are essentially alone, and cannot play at being European."[26]

This imagined rupture between Argentina and Europe is both spatial and temporal. It sees both a radical distancing of Argentina from Europe and a radical break from European history. This is as close as Borges gets to echoing Veblen's rejection of Zionism. In describing Zionism's prospects, Veblen states: "There runs through it all a dominant bias of isolation and in-breeding, and a confident persuasion that this isolation and in-breeding will bring great and good results for all concerned."[27] While they have established that interaction with Europe is not only given but desirable, neither Borges nor Veblen will argue that this interaction cannot be broken. The argument is that such a disconnect is not desirable since the preeminence of Jews is predicated on the particular kind of cultural immersion Veblen will describe shortly. For Borges, the fortunate consequences he imagines for Argentine literature will come precisely from imitating that same cultural immersion.

To the suggestion that Argentina is a radical innovation Borges counters: "Everything that has happened in Europe, the dramatic events there in recent years, has resonated deeply here. This would not happen if we were detached from Europe."[28] Borges is referring to the divisive effects that World War II had in Argentina. Though the country remained neutral for most of the war, joining the Allies only months before it ended, the popular press was rife with debate over Argentina's "natural" affiliations.[29] This is not what radical distance looks like. It is what inextricable, unavoidable interaction looks like.

While Borges's objection is that such profound affects would not have been felt if Argentina was detached from Europe, it also references the difficulty Argentines have felt in being European. This existence within Europe, which at the same time is experienced as a difficulty, segues Borges's lecture into Veblen's account of European Jewry. Borges does not reject the difficulty that exists for Argentines when they "play at being European." What Borges rejects in this third answer is the idea that this feeling of difficulty implies Argentines are cut off from Europe and the past. On the contrary, he will affirm, as for the Jews and the Irish, the difficulty involved in this play stems from the very fact that it is inevitable, while at the same time always involves "feeling themselves . . . to be different."[30]

By comparing these rejected answers, we see how Borges's desire to mimic Veblen's ideas of Jewish difference in Argentine letters entails the rejection of other, perhaps equally feasible, models that Veblen also posited as alternative accounts for Jewish preeminence. Neither Veblen nor Borges say it is impossible to establish a Jewish nation in isolation or to found an Argentine literature on the *gauchesco* genre. They say only that such solutions would not be fortuitous for Jews or Argentines. Both Veblen's depiction of Zionism and Borges's rejected literary traditions were equally feasible, extant solutions, but they are understood as models of isolation rather than interaction. There is a particular social structure of inclusion and difference that Borges sees (through Veblen) in the Jews and Irish, and which he attempts to implement in the relationship between Argentina and Europe. But what is this social structure, within which Jews are immersed while feeling themselves to be different, and which Borges wants to model for the Argentine writer?

The Departure from Tradition

After rejecting inherent traits and historical origins as explanations of Jewish preeminence, and insisting self-isolation would undo this preeminence, Veblen proceeds to detail the mode of social existence that has, in his view, given rise to Jewish preeminence in modern Europe. He characterizes this existence in two ways. First, it is a social existence "within the gentile community of peoples, not from the outside. [They are] immersed in this gentile culture."[31] The basic condition of successful Jews in Europe is immersion in the surrounding non-Jewish culture. Second, though they exist within the culture of Europe, Jews feel no attachment to it. "In their character of a Chosen People, it is not for them to take thought of their unblest neighbors," Veblen explains.[32]

We should qualify that this is not the existence of all Jews in Europe. Borges takes Veblen's explanation of individual preeminence to stand for the broader Jewish community in Western culture. This, however, is not Veblen's argument. "The cultural heritage of the Jewish people is large and rich," Veblen admits, but it "is also reputed to have run into lucubrations that have no significance for contemporary science or scholarship at large."[33] The group of Jews immersed in European culture that Veblen refers to is somewhat narrower. It is only those Jews who have removed themselves from the confines of their own tradition and entered the gentile culture in the particular way Veblen has characterized it—as immersion—that attain preeminence. Veblen offers a sociological model for the preeminence of Jews in modern Europe that is nonetheless based on the individual Jew as its basic social unit. The application of this model to the general population of European Jewry is a significant departure that Borges makes from Veblen's argument.

What is the auspicious place of the Jew in modern Europe? "Losing his secure place in the scheme of conventions into which he has been born," will land the Jew within broader Western culture.[34] But intellectual preeminence comes "at the cost, also, of finding no similarly secure place in that scheme of gentile conventions into which he is thrown."[35] Immersion is a position that is at once inevitable and unattainable to the Jew who steps out of the bounds of tradition. "There is nowhere else to go on this quest," says Veblen.[36] Thus, the

Jew "becomes a disturber of the intellectual peace, but only at the cost of becoming an intellectual wayfaring man, a wanderer in the intellectual no-man's-land."[37] It is clear from Veblen's depiction of the departure from tradition that this is an individual process (and not, as Borges will have it, a collective one). What the individual Jew is able to achieve is a radical break from all convention and tradition. This endows individual Jews with those traits that will benefit themselves as well as modern Europe, and that are so central to modern inquiry, prime among them "a skeptical frame of mind."[38]

It is important to emphasize that the question here is not one of identifying Jewish traits, but of evaluating them. This is true for both Borges and Veblen. Veblen has argued that it is "by force of a divided allegiance to the people of his origin, that [the Jew] finds himself in the vanguard of modern inquiry."[39] He acknowledges that this divided allegiance is held also toward the culture into which these Jews have entered and within which they operate. Borges states as much too in paraphrasing Veblen: "They act within that culture and at the same time do not feel bound to it by any special devotion."[40]

Suggestions of a divided allegiance may smack of antisemitism and bring to mind accusations of the kind presented against Alfred Dreyfus two decades before Veblen's article was published. In her reading of Jewish influences on Borges, Edna Aizenberg clearly perceives this, explaining that "for Borges, as for the Nazis, *Intellektueller* meant *Jude*."[41] Indeed, Aizenberg demonstrates, Borges did not combat antisemitism by rejecting this Jewish stereotype, but by arguing for its positive valuation. Borges's polemic against Nazism in the 1930s and 1940s did not so much dispute the Nazi's identification of Jewish divided allegiance as argue that this Jewish trait was advantageous to Western culture. To exemplify this positive valuation, Borges often refers to notable Jews whom he regards as major figures in Western culture. Having detailed Veblen's influence on Borges's understanding of Western Jewry, we will not be surprised to find that the poetry of Heinrich Heine and the philosophy of Baruch Spinoza remain throughout Borges's life prime examples of Jewish writing, and the names of Spinoza and Heine—both prominent examples of Jews that exited the confines of Jewish tradition—are to Borges almost synonymous with "Jew."

For instance, when accused by the right-wing publication *Crisol* in 1934 of "Jewish ancestry, maliciously hidden,"[42] we have seen Borges respond: "I am grateful for the stimulus provided by *Crisol*, but hope is dimming that I will ever be able to discover my link . . . to Heine, Gleizer, and the ten *Sefiroth*; to Ecclesiastes and Chaplin."[43] That Charlie Chaplin's Judaism was a rumor matters little more than that Spinoza was excommunicated, or that Heine converted to Christianity. These facts only make them all the more exemplary of the social position Borges cites from Veblen. They are more Jewish than any, precisely for existing in the space between a departure from Jewish tradition and impossible inclusion within European culture.

If Veblen's argument sounds like a program for Jewish secularization or modernization, that is because it is. Veblen is explicitly suggesting that, in lieu of what he sees as the isolationist nation-state project of Zionism, the most propitious path for Jews is to leave their tradition behind and embrace inevitable yet unattainable integration into modern Europe. The path that runs along the space between a lost Jewish tradition and an inaccessible Western culture "can have, and already has had, fortunate consequences," as Borges puts it to his Argentine listeners.[44]

The inevitability of Jewish immersion into Western culture is the basic assumption of Veblen's program. He does not fear that the isolationism of Jews within the West will be damaging to modern Europe. He sees this isolation as impossible. Recall his observation about Jewish hybridization: "No unbiased ethnologist will question the fact that the Jewish people are a nation of hybrids; that gentile blood of many kinds has been infused into the people in large proportions in the course of time. Indeed, none of the peoples of Christendom has been more unremittingly exposed to hybridization."[45]

That is why Veblen perceives the Zionists as a threat to the progress of Europe. In stark contrast to the immersion and hybridization process that has been so beneficial to Europe, the Zionists believe they "are due to achieve much greater things and to reach an unexampled prosperity so soon as they shall have a chance to follow their own devices untroubled within the shelter of their own frontiers."[46] Their aim is thus double: To achieve much greater things than they have been able to in the Diaspora and to establish their own demarcation and frontiers. "It is not so much a question of what is aimed at, as of the chances of its working-out," Veblen explains, suggesting we might read this not only as "a question" but also as a warning.[47]

What is at stake is the "intellectual advance of Christendom," Veblen makes clear.[48] The threat is that "as the Jewish people in this way turn inward on themselves, their prospective contribution to the world's intellectual output should . . . fairly be expected to take on the complexion of Talmudic lore."[49] As his argument progresses, Veblen becomes less concerned with stating the advantage Jews will find in their continued Diaspora existence and focuses more on the benefits Christendom has found in it. "It is plain that the civilization of Christendom continues today to draw heavily on the Jews for men devoted to science and scholarly pursuits."[50] If the statist project of Zionism came to fruition, "there should be some loss to Christendom at large, and there might be some gain to the repatriated Children of Israel," Veblen finally admits.[51]

How does Veblen explain the impossibility of full Jewish immersion into European culture? It is a personal (perhaps a national) tragedy that fuels Europe's innovators. Christendom is rather a passive character in Veblen's narrative. Its desire for progress finds a promising partner in another's active search—for from the very first step, that of leaving their tradition behind, the

Jew has been the active partner—and enjoys the fruit of that other's struggles. What makes Veblen's account of this entanglement so tragic is that the reason it is impossible for Jews to become fully included in Western culture, to the point of losing all Jewish identification, lies in the Jews themselves. The possibility of gentile resistance to Jewish integration is only hinted at in an accidental double entendre, as he states: "The most amiable share in the gentile community's life that is likely to fall to [the Jew's] lot is that of being interned."[52]

Of course, there is an air of remorse to Veblen's entire locution. It was published two years after the Balfour Declaration of 1917 made public the support of the British Empire for the kind of Jewish repatriation project Veblen opposed. Though he focuses more on the effort than on its predetermined impossibility, a redrawing of the demarcation between Jew and non-Jew has already begun. In that sense, Veblen's article can be read as something of a retrospective as well, a retrospective on the great tragedy of the Jews that has fueled modern Europe's intellectual pursuits. The Zionist movement is for him a statement about the failure of the European project of integration. Veblen's article offers a dual articulation, of a program and a retrospective, of the future and the past of what he calls Jewish "immersion."

On an individual level, the tragedy is that of being stuck between a lost tradition and an unaccepting broader culture. The resolution of this Jewish tragedy, Veblen states, would surely be tragic for Europe. Neither full integration nor refusal to depart from tradition would turn Jews into those intellectual innovators he perceives them to be. The irresolvable nature of the individual Jew's predicament is what drives the individual's contribution to progress, precisely because "there is nowhere else to go."[53]

On the collective level, the tragedy is the failure of emancipation due to the reluctance of the Jews themselves to leave their tradition behind en masse. Thus, in Veblen's argument, Zionism is another moment of collective refusal to integrate. While success has been individual, failure has been collective. Veblen's explanation of Jewish preeminence only accounts for one individual at a time. It never occurs to him to ask about the possibility of group existence after such an exodus from tradition. He is writing about "the Jews," but would they remain the Jews after following through with his program?

A community, it seems, could not leave all its ties of tradition and custom behind and still maintain its group designation. "They are neither a complaisant nor a contented lot, these aliens of the uneasy feet; but that is, after all, not the point in question," states Veblen, somewhat skirting the question of what the large-scale success of his suggestion would mean (or would have meant) for Jews as a group.[54] In an effort to focus on what Borges draws from Veblen's programmatic (and problematic) historical account, we might nonetheless offer an answer. The effect of belonging to the Jewish group would become its cause. The preeminence attained as an outcome of their individual circumstances as

Jews would become the only marker of their group existence, the sole source of any separateness Jews would maintain from Europe.[55] Veblen ends his article without commenting on the slippage his argument makes between the individual and collective aspects, nor between the present and the past efforts, of immersion.

The challenge Borges takes on in "The Argentine Writer and Tradition" is to pick up where Veblen left off. Borges takes an ex post facto explanation for Jewish preeminence, which bases itself on their attitudes and conditions of interaction, and turns these attitudes and conditions into a programmatic Argentine approach toward Europe. Borges's lecture signals this attempt in two ways. First, he argues that the Argentine writer's condition of acting within Eliot's simultaneousness of Western tradition has the potential for stimulating the kind of divided allegiance that Veblen praises. Though Borges does not elaborate on where the Argentine author departed *from* in order to arrive at this inevitable yet unfulfillable immersion into European tradition, it is clear he thinks Argentines do occupy a similar social position. Second, this sense of difference from (and lack of devotion to) European tradition, which has given rise to Jewish and Irish skepticism, will, in Borges's program, become Argentine irreverence.

The Jewish marginal location, in between their own tradition and broader European culture, is what draws Borges to Veblen's program as a model for the Argentine writer. However, the unattended slippage from individual to collective in Veblen's narrative is unproblematically assumed in Borges's suggestion for Argentina as well. For Borges, certain Jews (Spinoza, Heine) may be exemplary of a location he has identified through Veblen, but Borges's ability to move from example to model revolves around the collective imitability of this location. Beyond imploring his audience to be irreverent toward European tradition, Borges never really explains how the individual Jew's position will be imitated by an Argentine collective. Nor does he explain how the Argentine author arrived at this in-between position. What tradition did the Argentine author have to leave behind in order to discover that they can neither go back nor ever become fully European? Like Veblen, Borges's argument slips between "we Argentines" and "the (individual) Argentine writer."

The tension between individual immersion and collective isolation continued to exist in Borges's variable attitudes toward both Jewish Diaspora existence and the State of Israel. This dichotomy is a paradigm that shapes many of Borges's writings on Jews and Israel.[56] We will engage this directly when we discuss Borges's encounter with Israeli literature. When considering the Jewish Diaspora in relation to the Argentine writer, we see Borges generalize the conditions Veblen lays out, under which individual Jews may become preeminent in Europe, applying them to the collective existence of the Jewish Diaspora. At the same time, expanding Veblen's argument from the individual to the group is key for its adaptation to the Argentine condition, even as this is done uncritically. After all, Borges is concerned with something of a national literature in Argentina, not merely with the success of this or that individual writer. However, "The Argentine Writer and Tradition" does not resolve the problem of maintaining a group identity following such (necessarily individual) immersion.

The concern for the possibility of Jewish group existence after a departure from the traditional structure of community is, for Borges, also the question of a possible Argentine tradition true both to unavoidable inclusion in Europe and the impossibility of ever fully accomplishing immersion into Western culture. The expansion of Veblen's argument signals Borges's maintained concern for the Judaic as an inseparable part of his investment in questions of literary tradition. After all, it is as a model of authorship that Borges references the Jews and the Irish in his lecture. Both groups, in his perception, have exhibited a great openness to literary and intellectual engagement with colors that were anything but local. And both groups still maintain their distinctiveness. That is the model of the Judaic Borges ultimately proposes. "They act within that culture and at the same time do not feel bound to it by any special devotion. . . . I believe that Argentines, and South Americans in general, are in an analogous situation; we can take on all the European subjects, take them on without superstition and with an irreverence that can have, and already has had, fortunate consequences."[57] This conclusion registers on the poetic level as a call for Argentine writers to engage literary traditions beyond the local. But it also registers on the moral level, opposing Mallea's fear of heterogeneity with a celebration of the same.

Returning to the structural parallels between Veblen and Borges, the fact that "The Argentine Writer and Tradition" ends without clarifying the question of individual and collective is in part a reflection of Borges's reliance on the structure of Veblen's paper for his own lecture. More importantly, however, it reflects a similarly unresolved tension in Borges's own argument. While the title of the lecture addresses a single ("the") Argentine writer, the collective language Borges uses ("we Argentines") presumes a group that can and should mimic Veblen's wayfaring Jew. Borges's lecture thus lays out an understanding of Argentine tradition and an attitude toward it that he himself intends to maintain. The question is, whom does he mean by "we"? To whom does this lecture offer a solution to the question of tradition? While there is a generalizing instinct to talk about "we Argentines," both context and content make clear that the addressees of this lecture are other writers and public intellectuals.

When Borges proposes the Judaic as a model to imitate, he is outlining the social position of the same intellectual author we have seen him deal with in "A Vindication of the Kabbalah." And yet, as we have seen with his attitude to the Kabbalah, this social position is not a static concept in his thought. Like his ongoing, evolving, at times incongruous references to Gershom Scholem and the Kabbalah, so too are Borges's references to Veblen's thought, in the context of articulating his understanding of Jewish tradition, a mirror in which to analyze and historicize his thought about the question of Argentine literary tradition and, within it, his own role as an author.

Veblen, an Imbalanced Analogy

While "The Argentine Writer and Tradition" offers Borges's best-known reference to Veblen, it was by no means an isolated thought. References to Veblen appear in Borges's lectures and interviews soon after World War II and continue for the rest of his life. Reviewing the many mentions of Veblen will help us contextualize the reference in "The Argentine Writer and Tradition" within Borges's broader engagement with the idea of Jewish preeminence. It will also allow us to develop further nuance in our understanding of the analogy Borges is suggesting between Argentines, Jews, and Irish.

Veblen's presence in Borges's thought, and especially the link it elicited between conditions of the Judaic and questions of Argentine tradition, actually found its earliest expression two years before Borges delivered "The Argentine Writer and Tradition." In a lecture about Max Nordau delivered in 1949, Borges already made the connection—and far more explicitly than in his 1951 lecture—between Veblen's depiction of the Jewish condition and that of the Argentine writer.[58] As we have seen, the influence of Veblen's article on Borges's 1951 lecture consists of similarities unnoticeable to those audience members unfamiliar with the article. It is only toward the end of the lecture that Borges mentions Veblen by name. Moreover, while concluding "I believe that Argentines, and South Americans in general, are in an analogous situation," Borges does not detail the full range and depth of the analogy he suggests between "we Argentines" and the "Jews in Western culture" or the "Irish in English culture."[59]

In his 1949 lecture Borges is much clearer, though equally selective in his presentation and interpretation of Veblen's argument. In the very first lines of the lecture, he recalls the topic of Veblen's article being "the intellectual preeminence of European *and American* Jews."[60] He then goes on to summarizes its main argument thus: "Veblen recognizes that preeminence, but denies it is the result of innate superiority, and prefers to attribute it to a conjunction of favorable circumstances. [In contradistinction to the Westerner, Veblen argues, the Jew] gazes objectively at Western cultures; that is why he is able to innovate within them."[61]

As we have seen, Veblen notes that the circumstances of Jewish preeminence are more favorable for "Christendom" than they are for the Jews. Furthermore, the Zionist movement, the explicit polemic focus of Veblen's argument, is admittedly a result of anything but the kind of objective gaze Borges imagines. We have seen Veblen state quite clearly that the Jewish desire for "withdrawal upon themselves" is the result of a troubled history in European lands. The analogy Borges suggests is, in important ways, a result of his own selective reading and representation of Veblen's argument.

This selective reading, or creative misreading, of Veblen's argument is important for understanding Borges's perception and construction of the Judaic as a point of reference for the articulation of his own Argentine concerns. It is possible to date his idiosyncratic reading of Veblen to the earliest postwar years, in which Borges directly invokes the Judaic in his discussion of Argentine literary tradition. Plotting the intellectual history of this Borgesian analogy does not shed light on Borges's understanding of the Jewish condition so much as—by providing an anatomy, as it were, of the ongoing construction of the Judaic in his imagination and writings—it sheds light on his understanding of the Argentine condition and related questions of tradition. After introducing Veblen's article, Borges's lecture on Nordau continues:

> I want to formulate an observation that occurs to me in this moment. For other reasons, we Argentines find ourselves in an analogous situation to that of the Jews. For our language, we pertain to Spanish culture; at the same time, instinctively, we all understand that Spanish culture does not suffice, and we search for other cultures. . . . We pertain, thus, to a tradition that we dispense with, in order to assume for ourselves other traditions, without prejudice, without preconceived superstitions. The Argentine, thus, is in some way voluntarily French, voluntarily English, voluntarily Italian.[62]

These earlier comments clarify an outstanding question about Borges's analogy in "The Argentine Writer and Tradition." It was not fully clear from his brief mention of Veblen what tradition it is that he thinks Argentines left behind in order to enter the in-between position, where they can never be fully integrated into Europe yet never return to their origins. In his comments on Nordau, we learn that it is the Spanish tradition Borges believes was rejected by Argentines, analogous to the way Jewish tradition was rejected by Jews in modern Europe. On the level of historical coincidence, this analogy seems well aligned. Argentine independence was won in the early nineteenth century by rejecting the Spanish crown, around the same years that Jews were encountering the spread of emancipationist ideologies in Europe, from Napoleonic France to tzarist Russia. The possibilities and challenges of Jewish emancipation are what drive the rise to preeminence of Veblen's wayfaring Jew around the same time that the political detachment from Spain presents the young Argentine nation with the possibilities and challenges of developing its own local culture.[63]

However, while the seeds of Latin America's postcolonial problematic may have been planted well before the postcolonial era, it is only in the context of the postwar cultural and political realities that Veblen makes his appearance in Borges's writing. It is perhaps a Veblenian irony by which, after the widespread and resounding failure of Jewish integrationist and European emancipationist projects, the analogy between the Argentine and the Jew "occurs to me in this moment," as Borges puts it.[64] That is, what occurs to him is an analogy to prewar figures such as Nordau, adding to the lineup in his 1934 essay "Yo, Judío," where his affinity is for Jewish wayfarers such as Heine and even Chaplin. These figures and his attitude toward them are certainly instrumental in formulating Borges's thoughts on the Argentine condition. However, the persistence of these ad hominem analogies, as revealed by the 1949 analogy to Nordau, suggests an important observation that is missing from readings of "The Argentine Writer and Tradition." Borges's analogy is not simply between Jews and Argentines—it is between the *prewar* Jewish condition and the *postwar* Argentine condition.

World War II and the Holocaust were watershed moments in Borges's literary career, and the changes these events elicited in his poetic style and subject matter have been documented by many scholars.[65] And yet the analogy between Argentines and a particular condition of prewar Jewish figures, whom Borges had admired and cited for decades, "occurs" to him only after the war. This observation provided by Borges's lecture on Nordau has important implications for our reading of "The Argentine Writer and Tradition," as well as for our understanding of Borges's engagement with what we might now perhaps more properly call Argentine postwar tradition.[66] This analogy should not be read as Borges's reflection on the Jewish condition in the late 1940s. The discrepancies and misalignments in such a reading would be notable. Borges was well appraised of the implications of World War II for the Jewish diasporic existence he admired. He had spent a considerable amount of energy during the war detailing the objectionable ideologies that he saw arriving from Europe, and the reasons Argentines ought to reject them.[67] The occurrence of this analogy between Borges's postwar Argentine writer and Veblen's prewar Jewish wayfarer—at a moment in which any purchase of Veblen's program would seem to have expired—should suggest to us that the significance of this analogy lies elsewhere.

It seems out of place for Borges to invoke an integrationist such as Veblen just a few years after the majority of European Jewry had been exterminated in the Holocaust. Indeed, in the context of his remarks on Nordau, there is no acknowledgment of what in his 1951 lecture Borges refers to as "everything that has happened in Europe, the dramatic events there in recent years, [which have] resonated deeply here."[68] Furthermore, having framed his remarks with reference to Veblen's article, Borges celebrates Nordau as someone who "disapproved of almost all Occidental superstitions [making him] an admirable example of that type of objective Jew . . . of whom Thorstein Veblen spoke."[69]

This framing is undermined in the final paragraph of this 1949 lecture, when Borges relates the episode of Nordau, living in London, reading about a pogrom against Jews in the Russian Pale of Settlement. "In that moment," Borges judges, "Nordau returned to being Jewish . . . and became one of the leaders of Zionism."[70] There is no acknowledgment of the irony in celebrating a Zionist leader as a paradigmatic Jew according to Veblen, whose express purpose in his 1919 article is to polemicize against Zionism and offer as an alternative that very paradigm Borges was so inspired by. Nor is there any indication that the possibility of a return to being Jewish, exemplified in Borges's account of Nordau, poses a problem for the analogy at hand. Borges does not mean to suggest that the possibility of a return to being Spanish is available to the Argentine writer. This he will make clear in "The Argentine Writer and Tradition." Nor does he appreciate the fact that for Veblen's wayfarer there is no such possibility of a return from the in-between position. Veblen's article is clear on this point. Once the Jew has exited their tradition, "there is nowhere else to go on this quest."[71]

Two observations will help us move past the oddities in Borges's analogy between Veblen's Jew and the Argentine writer. First, we should notice that the analogy Borges sets up is to the kind of prewar Jewish figures that Veblen looks to as well to explain Jewish preeminence. The fact that such figures may not be contemporary is not important since it is not the figures themselves Borges wants to model but the context in which they attained their preeminence, and the irreverent attitudes that allowed this. That is, the invocation of Veblen's Jew is not meant to highlight a personal model of psychological dispositions but a social model of intellectual relations between margin and center. Second, the analogy Borges constructs is itself particular to the postwar Argentine writer—indeed, both the third opinion that Borges rejects in "The Argentine Writer and Tradition," and in particular the rejection he offers, would have been unimaginable in the prewar years. Recall Borges states that "everything that has happened in Europe, the dramatic events there in recent years, [have] resonated deeply here."[72] The resonance of World War II in Argentina is taken as proof that Argentina is not detached from Europe. This logic would have been inapplicable in the prewar years. Framing the analogy in this way highlights its motivation to discuss the particular postwar social context of Borges's contemporary Argentina. Borges's invocation of the Judaic in this context should be seen primarily as a commentary on the changing landscape of Argentine letters, and as part of the newfound urgency with which authors such as Borges (and Mallea as well, as we have seen) responded to the social and political climate of the moment. This may not have been clear to Borges's audience in his 1949 lecture on Nordau, but it was made abundantly clear in his 1951 lecture. What went missing in this latter lecture by the rather terse gloss on Veblen is the particularly prewar context of this analogy.

Observing the off-balance elements of this analogy can help explain two further developments in Borges's writing. First, in the decades to come he continues to depart further and further from Veblen's actual argument, even as he returns time and again to the article and the analogy it inspired. This should not seem strange. The ambiguation of the actual prewar Jewish conditions serves only to deepen the point about Borges's contemporary irreverence toward world literature. Second, the postwar Jewish condition, quite different from Veblen's world, with the founding of the State of Israel, will emerge as a challenge to the social and historical soundness of this analogy. Borges will have to contend with an Israeli tradition different from the Jewish diasporic tradition he analogized. Once again, the way he does this will continue to reveal more about his views on Argentine literature than on contemporary Jewish conditions.

Veblen, an Evolving Analogy

Veblen's influence on Borges's construction of the Judaic remains evident throughout his career. Borges returns to this argument on several occasions, in comments about contemporary Latin American literature, prewar Jewish figures, and, more belatedly, his thoughts on the literary tradition of the State of Israel. Equally persistent are the equivocation, generalization, and misreading of Veblen's article, which we have already noted in his 1949 and 1951 lectures. In a 1960 essay commemorating Mexican writer and intellectual Alfonso Reyes, who had died just a few months previously, Borges recalls Veblen's article once more.

> In 1919 Thorstein Veblen asked himself why the Jews, in spite of the many and notorious obstacles they must overcome, stand out intellectually in Europe. If memory does not deceive, he ends up attributing this primacy to the paradoxical situation, in which the Jew, in Western countries, deals with a culture that is foreign to him and in which it is not difficult for him to innovate, with good skepticism and with no superstitious fear. It's possible my summary mutilates or simplifies his thesis; just as he puts it, it would apply particularly well to the Irish in the Saxon sphere or to us, Americans of the North or of the South. This last case is the one I'm concerned with; in it I find, or want to find, the key.
>
> . . .
>
> We are heirs to the entire past and not to the habits or passions of this or that lineage. Like the Jew of Veblen's thesis, we deal with European culture with no excess of reverence.[73]

While Borges's comments largely repeat his argument in "The Argentine Writer and Tradition," they also state more explicitly his expansion of Veblen's argument from individual circumstances to group identity. "Like the Jew of Veblen's thesis, we deal with European culture," Borges summarizes, abstracting "the Jew" sufficiently to stand for the "we" that is Argentina, and forgetting it is only modern Europe Veblen talks about.[74] In a much later interview from 1978 Borges will again recall Veblen, again omitting the fact that it is the Jews of Europe Veblen was talking about.

> DIAMANT: When you think of Israel today, do you consider it a natural extension of the Jewish People of the Bible?
>
> BORGES: I, truthfully, am not a Zionist, but I want to explain in what sense. Some time ago I read a very nice article by Veblen about the intellectual superiority of Jews. Note it's not about a racial superiority, but rather intellectual. And this is due—he explains—to the fact that every Jew has two cultures, two traditions: his tradition and the tradition of the place in which he was born. And that's what makes them much richer. I fear Israel today will be a country like all others. Obviously, that shouldn't matter too much, since it is a very small country, there will always be Jews in the world that will be more important than the Israelis.[75]

Borges answers the question quite directly. What is evident is that the programmatic aspect of Veblen's argument remained with him throughout his career, as does the association between Veblen's article and his understanding of Zionism. While Borges's answers still make no reference to the possibility of the group existence that Veblen's argument may or may not allow for Diaspora Jewry, Veblen's argument does remain central to Borges's attitude toward Judaism as well. Furthermore, Borges had previously rephrased Veblen's view of the Jews as being stuck between traditions, the Jewish tradition they depart from and the unwelcoming traditions of "the gentile community of peoples," as Veblen puts it.[76] In these latest comments about Zionism, Borges describes the Jews in terms of their ability to straddle two traditions—from being stuck in-between traditions, they have in Borges's depiction now become an exemplary bridge over this cultural gap.[77]

Borges's evolving depiction of Veblen's argument demonstrates his developing understanding of Judaism in the postwar reality. From an off-balance analogy in his 1949 and 1951 lectures, he comes to see a more direct confrontation between Diaspora Jewish existence and Zionism. His emergent understanding of Zionism as a break from Jewish tradition is also evident in the poems Borges composed to the State of Israel around the time of his first visit.[78] What bears highlighting here, as Humberto Núñez-Faraco observes, is that "the break with tradition [that is so evident] in the poems about Israel had not yet taken root in Borges's conceptualization of Zionism in the early 1940s, that is, before the creation of the State of Israel" and, I would add, does not take root until some time after he delivers "The Argentine Writer and Tradition."[79] That is, Borges's conceptualization of Jewish tradition develops apace with the increasing urgency he felt of contending with the postcolonial question of Latin American literary tradition.

What these interviews add to our reading of "The Argentine Writer and Tradition" is that they demonstrate the intellectual developments behind the equivocations Borges makes regarding Veblen's argument. Between 1949 and 1951, he conflates the individual and the collective, presenting Veblen's argument regarding preeminent individuals as relating to the Jewish Diaspora at large. By 1978, Borges seems to assume that the program Veblen was promoting has already happened. That is, the Jewish Diaspora in his 1978 account occupies the space in which Veblen only hoped they would end up in 1919. It is not surprising, then, to learn that Borges follows Veblen one step further, identifying the Jewish Diaspora as the antithesis to Zionism—and perhaps even identifying Zionism as a threat to the Jewish Diaspora. Borges is thus in accord with Veblen that Zionism undermines those traits he values in Jewish existence. But he differs from Veblen in that he seems to think integration has been successful for the Jews in the Diaspora, that as a group they have attained "intellectual superiority," as he puts it, by having two traditions, the Judaic and "the gentile."[80]

This conclusion brings to mind another statement Borges made the very same year he delivered "The Argentine Writer and Tradition," in a speech to the Sociedad Hebraica Argentina on the occasion of their twenty-five-year anniversary dinner in 1951: "Our [Western] fusion with the Hebrews . . . is irrefutable and final. . . . Every Western person is Greek and Jewish."[81] The departure from Veblen's depiction, which Borges made in the 1978 interview cited above—seeing the Jew as straddling two traditions rather than stuck in between the two—is already present in his thought in 1951, just not in "The Argentine Writer and Tradition." Studying Borges's drafts of "The Argentine Writer and Tradition," Daniel Balderston recovers a line explaining the relevance of Veblen and his argument about the Jews with more clarity. This line was cut from the final delivery. It reads: "it is significant that [the Jews] reject tradition."[82] That is, in "The Argentine Writer and Tradition" Borges chooses to emphasize their distance from any tradition, while in other contexts he emphasizes their attachment to two traditions—and indeed, ultimately extends that to all of Western tradition.

The tensions of individual and collective, inevitability and impossibility, introduced by Borges's reading of Veblen continued to challenge Borges's readers as well, as they made sense of his self-fashioned inheritance of the Judaic. Lisa Block de Behar explains these tensions as resulting from Borges's insistence on "the firmness of a Jewish net that assimilated cultural differences in a single identity, whose differentiating feature is precisely that they are not different."[83] This paradoxical formulation offers a resolution to the question of collective departure from tradition. To the extent that Block de Behar does not acknowledge the postwar bifurcation that Borges contends with between the Judaic and Zionism, her formulation may harmonize the problematic of individual and collective as it pertains to the postwar Jewish condition. However, it falls short of explaining the complexity of Borges's position toward questions of tradition as they pertain to his own Argentine context.

In the years following 1951, the challenges to reconciling Jewish tradition and Jewish nationalism within the Veblenian framework Borges lays out in "The Argentine Writer and Tradition" continued to mount, as Borges's contact with the State of Israel and its cultural agents increased. The ways in which Borges continues to try, and sometimes fails, to apply this framework to his encounters with Israeli literature are telling. These encounters will be our opportunity to read his 1951 lecture as a comment not only on literary tradition and Jewish tradition, but also on national tradition. The force of Borges's intervention into his contemporary debates about Argentine nationalism becomes clearer and more nuanced when we read its implications for his understanding of Israeli literature and the way he works through its constitutive tensions between Jewish tradition and national tradition.

Tradition and Local Color

In the decades that followed, Borges was continuously confronted by the challenges of maintaining a representation of the Judaic along the lines of his ongoing analogy to Thorstein Veblen, on the one hand, while on the other hand, reconciling with the reality he was encountering in the State of Israel. The year 1951 should mark a baseline in our discussion not only for delivering "The Argentine Writer and Tradition" but also for comments such as those at the twenty-five-year anniversary celebration of the Sociedad Hebraica Argentina, "every Western person is Greek and Jewish."[1] Both the universalization of Jewish tradition and the Veblenian distance between Jews and their tradition would come under pressure in the decades that followed, as Borges's contact with the developing literature and culture of the State of Israel only increased, culminating in his two visits to the country. How did his encounter with Israeli literature affect the analogy he proposed in 1951? Given that his analogy was between a prewar European Jewish diasporic condition and the postwar Argentine national condition, how does Borges reconcile his exposure to Israeli literature with the Veblenian framing of the Judaic that he persisted in referencing throughout his life?

These questions are not meant to shed light on Israeli literature, nor is our discussion in this chapter primarily meant to contribute to an understanding of Borges's attitude toward Israeli literature per se (though here and there along the way it may do that as well). Rather, Borges's engagement with Israeli literature will limn the tensions and limits of his analogy to Veblen and, in so doing, further clarify his understanding of literary tradition and the role it plays in his polemics against the nationalists. This functioning of Israeli literature as a litmus test is evident in a 1971 interview, given in anticipation of receiving the Jerusalem Prize later that year. Borges briefly reports a discussion he had with Israeli writers on his 1969 visit (the same visit during which he met Gershom Scholem for the first time).[2]

> INTERVIEWER: Are you familiar with the new Israeli literature?
> BORGES: I don't know Hebrew, but I have spoken to Israeli writers who amazed me. I had supposed the literary tendency would be, naturally, to approach the Psalms, the Song of Songs. . . . But no. They told me they did not want to copy King David. They wanted to be modern. I answered them that being modern did not seem obligatory to me. From the moment you are born you are modern, like it or not. Why impose upon yourself a contemporaneousness, which you already possess in any event?[3]

The writers Borges met seem to express a desire to depart from Jewish tradition in a way reminiscent of Borges's desire for Argentine authors. We may have expected Borges to approve of such efforts not to limit one's literary engagement to one's national or local tradition. After all, this was the basis of his analogy to Veblen's wayfaring Jews. At the same time, his reading of T. S. Eliot would suggest that the only way for Israeli authors to express their talent would be to engage the literary tradition of "their own country" in a way that alters what Eliot terms its "historical sense."[4]

Borges's 1971 interview encapsulates the tension that emerges between these two references (Veblen and Eliot) as a result of his encounter with Israeli literature. Eliot rejects the idea that talent is expressed in the form of a radical break from one's literary tradition. Veblen, on the other hand, sees the break from tradition as the key cause of Jewish preeminence. While Argentina struggles to find its place within Eliot's scheme of the historical sense, Borges encounters an Israel full of Jewish writers who are entirely in possession of a literary tradition and insist on breaking with it. The Israeli authors force Borges to confront this contradiction. The resolution he develops is to shift the focus from a tension between Eliot and Veblen to one between the Judaic and Israel. Borges will thus reject the analogy between the Israeli condition and the Argentine in favor of maintaining the analogy between the Jewish Diaspora and Argentina.[5]

An interesting if peculiar part of his reported exchange with the Israeli writers is that Borges implies that he has an idea of how one ought to write from within the historical sense of Jewish tradition. He is "amazed" to learn these authors are not trying to produce what he thinks modern Jewish literature should be. His expectations about postwar Jewish literature, only hinted at here, certainly had an effect on Borges's writing and seem to set up an opposition between the Judaic mode of writing Borges wants to approximate and the Israeli authors' mode of writing. That is, following his own ongoing engagement with the concept of tradition, we may see Borges emerge from his encounter with the Israeli writers as the "true" author of modern Jewish literature among them.

More than this would tell us about modern Jewish or Israeli literature, it reinforces our reading of Borges's literature. An important point about his repeated reference to Veblen is that, as Edna Aizenberg notes, "when [Borges] tells his interviewers that he regrets not being Jewish, and that his books are 'profoundly Judaic,' he is referring largely to the Jew and the Judaism of Veblen."[6] Thus, as Borges's depiction of Veblen's argument evolves, so too does the way he attempts to make his writing "profoundly Judaic." The refocusing of his writerly concerns from Kabbalah toward the question of Jewish tradition is a prime example of this evolution. His disappointment with the Israeli authors, then, is less a comment on modern Israeli literature as it is a comment on Borges's self-perceived success at upholding his side of the analogy to Veblen's wayfaring Jew.

At the same time, in Borges's assumption about Israeli authors wanting to copy King David, he ends up echoing the characterization of Jewish literature in the *Crisol* editors' accusation against Borges himself four decades earlier: "even his poems have that Psalmic accent characteristic of Hebrew poetry."[7] If in "The Argentine Writer and Tradition" Borges argued that the tradition of Argentine literature should be the whole of European literature, and that this is similar to the Jews of Veblen, why then does he seem to take such a restrictive view of the tradition and themes of modern Israeli literature? Surely the whole of European literature is greater than the psalmic accent of King David.[8] Would such imitation of the Psalms not reduce the Israeli writers to the kind of narrowly national expression Borges so opposed in his lecture? To make sense of this apparent shift and contradiction, we need to go back and read Borges's encounter with Israeli literature over the twenty years between delivering "The Argentine Writer and Tradition" and these interview comments. Understanding his shifting attitude toward Israeli literature will ultimately allow us to go back to his polemics with the nationalists and understand the moral and aesthetic debate Borges maintained with "the Argentine cult of local color" in greater nuance.

Between Jewish and Israeli Literature

Borges's proximity to Israeli literature goes back at least a decade before the encounter with Israeli authors on his trips to the State of Israel. Already in 1958, the literary journal *Sur* dedicated an issue, titled "Israel," to Israeli literature and culture. The issue included translations of works by many contemporary Israeli authors, including S. Y. Agnon.[9] It also included reviews and surveys of contemporary Hebrew literature, with titles such as "Forty Years of Israeli Literature" and "The New Hebrew Prose."[10] The effort to subsume prestate Hebrew literature written in the "forty years" since the First World War, mostly in British Mandate Palestine, under the category of "Israeli literature" is certainly the kind of nationalist effort to essentialize the connection between Hebrew language, Jewish nationalism, and the Land of Israel that Borges would be skeptical of in the Argentine context. In the *Sur* issue, the richness of Israeli culture, in literature, art, music, and the modernization of the Hebrew language, are all presented as parts of a comprehensive cultural and political renewal of the Jewish nation.

The opening text of this special issue of *Sur* is an essay by Borges himself, also titled "Israel." In this essay, Borges ignores the concrete nation-state, framing his relationship to Israel as a relationship to an abstract and atemporal Judaic. This is already clearly expressed is his opening line: "Beyond the adventures of blood, beyond the almost infinite and certainly incalculable chance of marriage beds, every occidental person is Greek and Jewish."[11] It is an out-of-place introduction to a journal issue dedicated to the many facets of contemporary and particularly Israeli culture. Borges frames his relationship toward Israel as toward a tradition that cannot be mistaken for a particularly national tradition.

Borges then goes on to speak of "the fusion of the two cultures,"[12] echoing his comments just a few years earlier at the twenty-five-year anniversary of the Sociedad Hebraica Argentina: "this, our fusion with the Hebrews, beyond the opinions we profess, is irrefutable and inevitable."[13] In the *Sur* issue of 1958, Borges offers several examples of thinkers throughout history whose thought he believes demonstrates such a fusion, including Nietzsche, Milton, Philo of Alexandria, and Maimonides, concluding finally: "Beyond aversions or preferences, [beyond] philosemitism or antisemitism, we are irreparably Jewish and Greek or, if you prefer, Hellenistic Jews."[14] These comments are entirely in line with Borges's desire to irreverently claim all of Western tradition, and within it all of Jewish tradition, as his own. In fact, arguing for the fusion of Judaic and occidental culture is a way of staking a claim to the Judaic that circumvents narrow notions of tradition, be they national or ethnic. This is consistent with the way Eliot urges the talented writer to look outside of tradition toward the historical sense and with the way Veblen imagines his wayfaring Jews exiting their homegrown tradition on the path to preeminence. These comments are not out of place within Borges's oeuvre. They are out of place in a journal issue introducing the Argentine reader to the national literature and culture of the State of Israel, that is, to Israeli national tradition.

If this were the end of the essay, it would appear to present an attitude toward the Judaic that we have already seen Borges develop over the previous decades. But there is one more paragraph to this text, and one that seems out of place even within this very essay. In the final lines, Borges's rhetoric takes a poetic turn inconsistent with the previous style of the essay, in which he concludes by offering an alternate view to his own previous comments: "Thus far I have thought, or have tried to think, historically. There is another way to consider this issue, more atemporal and more intimate. We could say that Israel is not only an intonation, an exile, a few facial features; an irony, a tired sweetness, a will, a fire and a song; it is also a humiliation and an exaltation, to have dialogued with God, to feel in a pathetic[15] way the earth, water, bread, time, loneliness, mysterious blame, . . . to be father or to be son."[16]

This is very poetic, but what does it mean? Framing this meditation as an alternative to "thinking historically" highlights the specifically poetic attraction Borges expresses toward the Judaic as intonation, irony, song, and dialogue, and goes as far as to frame that attraction as incommensurate with an attraction toward a historically delimited, nationally defined tradition. In my reading of the text, this final paragraph signals a complete unwillingness on the part of Borges to engage with the Judaic as a particularly national tradition. Keeping in mind that Borges and Eduardo Mallea were both on the editorial board of *Sur* in these years, and that the debate with the nationalists was far from over, I propose to understand this final paragraph as a poetical-polemical statement that expresses Borges's resistance to the underlying logic of this *Sur* issue—a logic that would counterpose to his 1951 analogy between irreverent Argentines, Irish, and Jews, an implied analogy between the local cultural traditions producing Israeliness and Argentineity, respectively.

Also noteworthy is that the final paragraph of this essay, published the same year as the poem "The Golem" (where we have seen Borges mention Scholem for the first time), offers no associative link between Israel and the Kabbalah. We may have expected to see Borges's chain of Judaic associations lead to the Tetragrammaton, the Aleph, or the ten *sefirot*, as it did, for example, in his 1934 text "Yo, Judío."[17] Interestingly, the essay includes two allusions to Martin Buber in the final line. The first is to Buber's notion of Jewish tradition as a dialogue with God. The second is to the idea that the Jews are "pathetic," an idea that Borges had attributed to Buber in his 1952 text "The Sect of the Phoenix."[18] Borges's recourse to Buber and his notion of tradition, rather than to the Kabbalah or Scholem, in his chain of Judaic associations is noteworthy in this context. This demonstrates the turn from Kabbalah to tradition, which we have been following in Borges's engagement with the Judaic, as our readings take us well into the postwar years. Borges's evolving intellectual concerns with questions of Argentine tradition on the one hand, and his contact with Israeli literature on the other precipitate this reorientation, both in his construction of the Judaic and his attitude toward the State of Israel.

In the decade that followed, Borges warmed to the idea of seeing Israel as a modern nation with a local literary tradition, while simultaneously increasingly distancing this local tradition from the Judaic as he had conceived of it. As his recognition of the tension between Jewish Diaspora and Jewish nationalism grows, so does his dichotomous attitude toward this tension. He increasingly aligns his analogy with Jewish diasporic existence in contradistinction to Zionism and the State of Israel, and expresses this in both interviews and stories. For instance, in the story "El Indigno [Unworthy]," first published in 1970, he tells of a Jewish shop owner named Santiago Fishbein who expresses criticism of the Zionist project.[19] "Firm and calm, he would condemn Zionism, which would make of the Jew a common man, attached, like all others, to a single tradition and a single country, without the complexities and discordances that now enrich him."[20] It is significant that these lines were written between his two visits to the State of Israel and around the same time that he shares his disappointment with Israeli authors in the interview cited above.

In the previous chapter, we saw the culmination of this conceptual separation expressed in the cited 1978 interview, where Borges is compelled to explain in what sense he is not a Zionist, stating: "I fear Israel today will be a country like all others. Obviously, that shouldn't matter too much, since it is a very small country, there will always be Jews in the world that will be more important than the Israelis."[21] I propose to read these comments not as a statement of his distance from the State of Israel—he would of course visit a second time and enthusiastically speak of these visits for the rest of his life—but as a statement of his unwavering intellectual commitment to a universalizing (rather than nationalizing) notion of literary tradition and a project of expanding Argentine engagement with the whole of Western tradition (and within it, all of Jewish tradition), as outlined in "The Argentine Writer and Tradition." Borges's consistent refusal to undermine the analogy between the Jew and the Argentine speaks to the centrality of the Judaic as a model for this commitment in his literary and intellectual world, even if it casts a shadow on the importance of Israel in his contemporary political and historical world.

The shift in tone between Borges's comments in the 1958 *Sur* issue and his comments surrounding his visits to the State of Israel is clear. There is still another significant moment in his acknowledgment of the literary tradition of the State of Israel, which we must attend to before we can fully appreciate the nuance of this shift, and of Borges's polemics against the nationalists in "The Argentine Writer and Tradition" and beyond. This moment comes when Borges engages the writing of S. Y. Agnon, Israel's Nobel Prize laureate in literature. The text of this engagement is produced between the 1958 *Sur* issue, which included the translation of a story by Agnon, and Borges's trips to the State of Israel, during which (perhaps tellingly) Borges asked to meet Scholem and not Agnon.

"The Memory of Israel is in Agnon"

In December 1966, the Instituto de Intercambio Cultural Argentino-Israelí [Institute for Argentine-Israeli Cultural Exchange] held an event to celebrate the recipients of the 1966 Nobel Prize in Literature, the German Swedish Nelly Sachs and the Israeli Shmuel Yosef Agnon. Among the speakers that day were included the Swedish ambassador to Argentina, the Israeli ambassador to Argentina, and Borges.[22] Borges was an obvious choice of speaker for this event. Not only was his literary stature in Argentina well established, but he himself was on the short list for the Nobel Prize in those same years.[23] Moreover, his long-standing involvement with institutions promoting Jewish–Argentine cultural exchange was well known, including the Sociedad Hebraica Argentina and the Instituto de Intercambio Cultural Argentino-Israelí. In fact, he gave two other lectures at this institute that same year, one on the biblical book of Job and one on Baruch Spinoza.[24] Thus, inviting Borges to speak alongside the Swedish and Israeli ambassadors marks the recognition of both his importance as the preeminent Argentine author of the time and his investment in the Judaic as a literary and intellectual touchpoint.

In his remarks, Borges will have to negotiate between two positions in his appreciation of Agnon, between recognizing him as a preeminent Israeli author (with all the national connotations of that title) and recognizing him as a Jewish author (with all the Veblenian connotations that would imply). The tension between these two possibilities is not essential to Agnon himself or to his writing.[25] It is a tension that is potentiated by Borges's own thought, which has not yet made (perhaps has even resisted making) conceptual space for the notion of a postwar Jewish attitude toward tradition. The fact that we will see this negotiation take place in his remarks about Agnon also demonstrates that, as opposed to Borges's out-of-place, even resistant, comments in the 1958 *Sur* issue on Israeli literature, a real intellectual engagement with the possibility and significance of Israeli writing does emerge here. As does a need to redefine some of the coordinates of the Judaic expressed in "The Argentine Writer and Tradition." Thus, Borges begins his remarks about Agnon with a question that already signals this preoccupation: "Let us begin with a question, apparently simple and essentially complex, as all questions are. What is a nation?"[26]

In what way is defining "what is a nation" the starting point for appreciating Agnon's literature? It is not. A far better question for appreciating Agnon would be "what is tradition" and, I propose, Borges knows this as well. But the nation is a necessary starting point for Borges in an effort that will take place between the lines of this essay about Agnon, and in which Borges will work through his thoughts on the Jewish writer and tradition. That is to say, answering this question will not help Borges define Agnon's place in world literature so much as it will help Borges reconcile Agnon's place in Israeli national literature with his argument in "The Argentine Writer and Tradition" that sees in the Judaic tradition a counterpoint to the nationalists.

Borges thus spends the beginning of the essay defining what is a nation in a way that will allow this reconciliation. "The first temptation . . . is to give an answer of the geographical order. Evidently, that would be insufficient."[27] Borges will not endorse any answer that privileges the local in defining the national. This is consistent with his position on Argentine literature, and in this regard the Jewish nation is a convenient example since the aspects of the Jewish Diaspora he is drawn to took place outside of a national-territorial existence. He proceeds to a more abstract and aterritorial definition. "We must then think of [the nation as] the sum of memories that nest in the bosom of the people."[28] While we may sense that in these lines Borges is already pointing to a notion of tradition that goes beyond the local, he does not yet state this directly.

After proposing that a nation is the collective memories of a people, Borges goes on to state, "I believe there is no clearer example of a 'nation' than Israel, whose origins are almost confused with those of the world."[29] If this is the definition of a nation, and Israel is the clearest example, "what, then, is this nation?" Borges repeats the question, and replies: "It is the memory of successive generations."[30] In his comments on Agnon—which, we should note, have not yet begun to discuss Agnon—Borges proposes the concept of a nation as the multigenerational accumulation of a people's collective memory. It is an awkward conceptualization. Not only does it deterritorialize "the nation" in the context of a nation-state that had, since its very inception, been deeply implicated in explicitly territorial struggles. Beyond this, Borges's conceptualization also depersonalizes the nation, replacing "the Jew" that was the basic unit in Veblen's argument with "the memory" as the basic building block of the nation. In this conceptualization, a nation is not about a place or a person. It is about something Borges might far more easily call a tradition, if not for the fact that he has already conceptualized Argentine tradition as universal and, in so doing, as a counterpoint to the local obsession of the nationalists.

This definition raises yet another problem in Borges's thought about literary and national tradition. The connection he makes between nation and history is in clear contrast to Borges's rejection of history as the justification for Latin American national existence in his 1930 book *Evaristo Carriego*.[31] Recall Borges's remarks, where he states that "only new countries have a past; that is to say, an auto-biographical memory, a living history. . . . Time—a European sentiment of people with a long past, and their very justification and glory—moves more boldly in the New World."[32] In his comments on Agnon thirty-six years later, he seems to admit that Israel is the quintessential nation precisely because of their long autobiographical collective memory. So, is it the new or the old nations that have a past? Is Israel analogous to the new countries of the New World in having "an auto-biographical, a living memory"? Or is its "memory of successive generations" more akin to "a European sentiment of people with a long past"?

Having noted his investment in the Argentine analogy to Jewish tradition, we can certainly expect that Borges would seek to circumvent any implication that there is a contradiction between Argentine and Jewish attitudes toward tradition. Rather than see this as a contradiction, and thus as a problem, a few years later he offers the reconciliation of this contradiction as a paradox. Recalling his 1969 visit to Israel he states, "I brought home with me the conviction of having been in the oldest and the youngest of nations."[33] And in his poem "Israel 1969" he would repeat the paradox that "the most ancient of nations is also the youngest."[34] These statements have been read by Edna Aizenberg and Ilan Stavans as demonstrating Borges's affinity for the State of Israel.[35] While they certainly show his emotional reaction to the encounter with the country, the paradoxical nature of this reconciliation reverberates with Borges's effort to define the distance between Israel and the Judaic. As we have seen, this distance is necessary for maintaining the analogy between the Judaic and Argentina.

At the same time, reconciling the Judaic and the nation will ultimately allow Borges to recognize a distinctive feature of Agnon. Agnon's writing exists within the long history of Jewish textual traditions, exhibiting a great deal of expressed attachment to these traditions. As Murray Baumgarten explains, Agnon's stories "grow organically out of classical Jewish tradition, echo in their syntax the dialectical sentences of the Mishnah and the Talmud, as well as some Yiddish rhythms."[36] Baumgarten compares Agnon and Borges on this very instructive point. "Unlike Borges, Agnon does not begin with 'the almost infinite world of literature,' though he certainly has a wide knowledge of it. Instead his starting point is the world of classical Jewish literature."[37] Agnon does not so much operate within European tradition as he operates irreverently within Jewish tradition. Agnon is both entirely irreverent toward and, at the same time, squarely and "organically" (as Baumgarten puts it) committed to Jewish tradition.

Agnon's preeminence cannot be explained in terms of Veblen's wayfaring Jew breaking from his own tradition. Agnon has not attained his preeminence by departing from his homegrown Jewish tradition but by acting within it in a way consistent with what Eliot would call "talent" and Borges would call "irreverence." This is evident, for example, in the way Agnon applies traditional narrative tropes and religious language to modern themes such as intimacy and eroticism.[38] And yet by not acting within the whole of Western culture, along the lines of Borges's analogy between Argentine, Irish, and Jew, Agnon is set apart from what Borges has conceived as the Judaic, and has depicted as quintessentially Jewish, via the figures of Spinoza and Heinrich Heine. Appreciating Agnon's place in world literature does not so much challenge Borges's notion of Jewish irreverence as it does his notion that an engagement with the whole of Western culture is the defining feature of the Judaic. This comparison and contrast are summed up in Baumgarten's analysis: "[Agnon and Borges] share a common effort to revitalize their respective languages by connecting them not merely to the argot of the street—a concern of many Argentine and Israeli writers of this century—but to a classical tradition available to Agnon in Jewish sources and to Borges in certain favorable writers whom he claims with good reason form a dominant tradition in western culture."[39]

The very fact that Baumgarten is comparing Borges and Agnon would suggest Borges's successful approximation of Jewish literature. At the same time, it also highlights the difference between them. Borges irreverently appropriates Jewish tradition as part of an effort to incorporate all Western culture as his tradition. Agnon, on the other hand, operates within that very same Jewish tradition but, in contradistinction to a view that would see it subsumed by the whole of Western culture, his engagement with Jewish tradition keeps it alive (to borrow Borges's word) as a distinct, national, and thereby local tradition. Returning to his 1966 lecture on Agnon, then, it is noteworthy to find Borges stating his appreciation for Agnon in the same language, while using the word tradition to refer to what in 1930 he resisted understanding in terms of historical temporality. "There is another [sense of] tradition . . . something more profound, that doesn't repeat, but rather blossoms in a living way and this is, precisely, what we encounter in the work of Agnon. . . . In the work of Agnon we can appreciate like a series of changing mirrors, this Hebraic tradition across the centuries."[40]

In concluding his remarks on Agnon, Borges returns to nation and memory in the closing lines: "The memory of Israel is in Agnon. It's not an erudite memory: It's a living memory . . . the living memory of this admirable people to which we all belong beyond the vicissitudes of blood. I have spoken of Israel. That's all."[41] Borges has redefined tradition for the Israeli literary context in a way that appreciates Agnon's innovative literary expression from within a newly conceived historical sense of Jewish tradition. He has attempted to do so without imposing on Agnon the expectation of a Veblenian departure from tradition and, at the same time, without foreclosing his own Argentine analogy to prewar Jewish departures from such tradition.

Returning now to the 1971 interview comments about his encounter with Israeli authors, it should be clearer why the lack of such a Judaic historical sense catches Borges by surprise when he meets with the Israeli authors in 1969—he expected them to write like Agnon. We can see how, having read Agnon and appreciated him in the terms that he does, Borges would be surprised to find that Agnon is in fact unique among Israeli authors. Most of them will not quote Talmudic verses, Yiddishisms, or Hasidic tales in their writing, nor stand in for the living historical memory of the people, but rather seek to break with the tradition that Borges now comes to recognize as living and blossoming in Israeli literature. A new dimension to his disappointment with the new Israeli literature that he encounters in the State of Israel is, in short, that they are not Agnon. Or, more precisely, having made conceptual space in his analogy for a Judaic historical sense, one that allows for Jewish irreverence toward a Jewish national tradition, it now seems like intellectual backtracking to reconcile with Israeli authors who express their desire for a Veblenian departure from tradition.

To remain focused on Borges, the question we must proceed with is not about the Israeli authors' attitude toward their tradition. Rather, we need to recognize that Borges is able to acknowledge Agnon's commitment to Jewish tradition without criticizing this commitment as narrowly nationalist the way he did with "the Argentine cult of local color." Indeed, Baumgarten has depicted Agnon in terms of a poetics that "grow organically out of classical Jewish tradition, echo in their syntax the dialectical sentences of the Mishnah and the Talmud, as well as some Yiddish rhythms."[42] Borges's assessment in "The Argentine Writer and Tradition" may well have analogized these elements to an Argentine overcommitment to Spanish literary tradition, or to an imitation of *gauchesco* poetry, both of which he has rejected in favor of a broader engagement with all of Western tradition. As a result of his encounter with Agnon, Borges no longer thinks of copying the Psalms as an obsession with local color but as a first step into the Judaic historical sense.

We have seen Borges link "the cult of local color" to the nationalists and oppose the nationally restrictive poetics of the latter to the Irish and Jewish irreverent engagement with a broadly conceived Western tradition. Following his remarks on Agnon, however, it seems there is more nuance to the distinction between local color and tradition than may be expressed in "The Argentine Writer and Tradition." What is it about Borges's understanding of tradition that allows him to make space for Agnon without triggering his resistance to local color? Having glimpsed the possibility of reconciling Agnon's attachment to Jewish tradition with Borges's view of the Judaic as a broad engagement with all of Western culture, we must now further clarify Borges's understanding of "local color."

Between Tradition and Local Color

We are now in a better position to reevaluate the common readings of "The Argentine Writer and Tradition." These have tended to understand Borges's conceptions of local color and the Judaic as opposing ideas, the former narrow and nationalistic, the latter universal and irreverent. With this understanding, the lecture has been read as proceeding from a rejection of local color to its replacement with the Judaic model, as an alternative for Argentine letters. This reading draws some validity from a consistent pattern of rejecting "differential traits" and "local color" in Borges's writing. His 1951 lecture was not the first time he had spoken against local themes, and not only in literature. For example, in a 1946 interview he states: "I believe that Argentine filmmaking should, as things stand at the moment, limit itself to those themes that offer less patriotic and sentimental temptations. It would do it well, I believe, to avoid the vernacular themes. . . . I don't know how the production of 'An Ideal Husband' by Oscar Wilde, and of 'Madam Bovary' by Flaubert would turn out; . . . *a priori*, however, these projects appeal to me."[43]

Thus, reading "The Argentine Writer and Tradition" as a continuation of Borges's rejection of local color is certainly consistent with comments he had made previously. In the 1951 lecture as well, Borges is certainly suggesting the rejection and replacement of the nationalists' ideology with a more cosmopolitan model and, in that sense, the rejection-replacement reading accurately captures the moral dimension of the argument. This either-or logic is not out of place with regards to the moral dimension of Borges's polemics. But it leaves unaccounted the poetic dimension of the argument, in which the relation between local color and tradition is not as straightforward.

On the poetic level of the argument, the dichotomous understanding suggested by such a rejection-replacement reading would lead to the same misleading or oversimplified questions as the ones about Agnon and Israeli literature, which we have worked to deconstruct in the pages above. Borges's reading of Agnon allows us to return to his 1951 lecture with this insight. In order to further engage the question of tradition and local color, it is necessary to distinguish between the moral and the poetic dimensions of the argument in "The Argentine Writer and Tradition." We have already seen both of these dimensions expressed by Mallea, Jean Guéhenno, and Borges in the debate about committed literature in the mid-1940s. That there exist these two dimensions to the question of literature is agreed by all discussants, including the editorial board of *Crisol*, whom we have seen point both to Borges's "literary value" and to his "moral sordidness."[44]

The idea that these two are intertwined is shared by Borges and Mallea as well. We have seen Mallea argue that the author's moral responsibility is to poetically commit to the representation of the essentially Argentine. Borges's 1951 lecture certainly stages a moral confrontation with the nationalist view of literature as a local endeavor that ought to express essential or differential traits while rejecting foreign ones. But it is equally a poetic intervention, expressed in Borges's call to "try out every subject" and to "take on all the European subjects, take them on without superstition and with an irreverence."[45] This would also echo Borges's a priori interest in Argentine film productions of Wilde and Flaubert cited above. At the same time, it is clear Borges is not calling on his fellow authors to simply copy other literary traditions, such as the Spanish tradition, which he rejected earlier in the lecture. The lesson Borges draws from Veblen is to engage tradition from a distance, a marginal mode of representation that he calls irreverence, but which does not receive explicit articulation in the lecture.

What I want to note at this point is that our reading of the Judaic model Borges has constructed, based on his reading of Veblen, has largely attended to the moral dimension of the discussion. It has demonstrated the persistence of identity in the face of heterogeneity, and thus served Borges in mounting his argument against national essentialism and xenophobia, and in favor of the Argentine cosmopolitanism he has become emblematic of.[46] In terms of literary attitudes, however, we only see Borges reject the poetic commitment to overrepresentation of local color. In presenting a sociological analogy between the Argentines, Jews, and Irish, the lecture stops short of articulating the poetics of the Judaic model. What does irreverence mean in literary terms?

Borges's remarks about Israeli literature suggest we have not yet fully understood "The Argentine Writer and Tradition" as a literary intervention. In fact, Borges's comments about the Israeli authors echo a line from this lecture. Regarding Argentine literature, Borges had stated: "We cannot confine ourselves to what is Argentine in order to be Argentine because either it is our inevitable destiny to be Argentine, in which case we will be Argentine whatever we do, or being Argentine is a mere affectation, a mask."[47] This does not apply to the Israeli writers. They tell Borges something along the lines of: We cannot confine ourselves to what is Jewish, "that all bears the date-mark B.C."[48] We want to be modern. In his response, Borges seems to repeat and invert the statement from his lecture. "I answered them that being modern did not seem obligatory to me. From the moment you are born you are modern, like it or not. Why impose upon yourself a contemporaneousness, which you already possess in any event?"[49] To his audience in 1951 Borges seems to say: you are inevitably Argentine, what you need to work at is your broader relationship to European traditions. To the Israeli authors Borges seems to reply: you are already modern, what you need to work at is your narrower relationship to Jewish tradition. This reply would follow neatly from his expressed appreciation of Agnon as well.

The confrontation Borges outlines between "the cult of local color" and the irreverent Argentine author expresses his particularly poetic engagement with the Judaic. While this confrontation may seem derivative of the moral confrontation between Borges and the nationalists, our reading of Borges's engagement with Kabbalah, and in particular "A Comment on August 23, 1944," has already demonstrated that we should not assume it is the political confrontation that gives rise to literary representation. My intervention here is to point out that, while in moral terms the opposition is between the nationalists and the Judaic model—or indeed between the nationalists and the Jews, as is evident in Borges's polemic against *Crisol*—in poetic terms there is no such opposition. Borges highlights the different possibilities for literary engagement demonstrated in the way Argentine writers approach local color and the way Jewish or Irish authors approach tradition. While the nationalists' approach is restricted to a narrowly local set of themes, Jewish and Irish writing is full of irreverence toward any tradition. The Judaic does not come to replace local color but to offer an alternate mode of literary representation, one that replaces an overcommitment to the local with an irreverence toward one's tradition—be that tradition broadly or narrowly conceived. It bears repeating that we have distinguished between two questions Borges takes from Eliot. The first is about identifying the writer's tradition (all of Western literature). The second is about the proper attitude toward the writer's tradition (irreverence).

This attitude is certainly evident in Borges's own stories. It would be a mistake to assume Borges is suggesting that an Argentine author should ignore local Argentine realities, expressions, and history in order to focus their literature exclusively on non-Argentine themes. Borges's stories are full of Argentine slang and Lunfardo, knife fighters and gauchos, the minutest details about Buenos Aires locales, and episodes of Argentine national history. What is lacking from his representation of these local themes is a reverence toward the essential Argentine identity that these underwrite. To be clear, neither Borges nor the nationalists use the term "reverence" to describe the nationalist attitude toward local color. Yet in the terms of the debate with the nationalists, we can take Mallea's attitude as an articulation of such a proposition. The moral responsibility to one's essential character and the poetic responsibility to representing local color are co-constitutive. Borges's irreverence is toward the sacrality of the local and the essential, as much as it is toward the idea that they constitute each other. Being Argentine does not obligate one to recreate local color any more than representing local color makes one Argentine.

Borges's writing undermines the sacrality of the local and the essential as part of its larger project of undermining the constitution of these elements of Argentine identity in each other. Thus an episode in national history turns out to be fake (or deliberately falsified) as in "The Theme of the Traitor and the Hero"; the local realism in mentioning a specific Buenos Aires street address becomes parodic when it turns out to be the precise street address of the mystical Aleph; and, perhaps most emblematic of this irreverence, the main character of many of Borges's fantastical stories is a character named "Borges," who is scrutinized by Borges himself in an auto-irreverent gesture in "Borges y yo [Borges and I]."[50] That is, skepticism about the local and the essential underwriting identity is pervasive in Borges's writing and directed even at Borges himself. These and other examples have received many excellent scholarly readings in line with what I am suggesting here.[51] My own focus is on Borges's reflections on the role of the author, so I would like to remain focused on Borges's articulation of irreverence.

Bring on the Camels

Let us return to the lecture at hand and revisit the transition Borges makes from the moral to the poetic in his discussion of local color. The debate with the nationalists is presented first as a social issue, the moral dimension of writing. Borges begins with a rejection of the social demarcations implied by the nationalists. Thus, in typical style, both jocular and paradoxical, Borges comments: "I do not know if it needs to be said that the idea that a literature must define itself by the differential traits of the country that produces it is a relatively new one, and the idea that writers must seek out subjects local to their countries is also new and arbitrary. . . . The Argentine cult of local color is a recent European cult that nationalists should reject as a foreign import."[52]

His first rejection is not of local color but of the nationalist ideology, which he mocks as a cult. He does not begin by taking aim at their poetic imagination but at their social and political imagination. Only then does he reject the overcommitment to local color in literature, following up his political observation about social differentiation with a poetic observation. It is the most explicit poetic comment Borges makes in the lecture and one of its best-known lines—his confabulation about there being no camels in the Koran. This is where Borges offers the only clear literary example of what he has in mind as a specifically poetic rejection of local color.

> A few days ago, I discovered a curious confirmation of the way in which what is truly native can and often does dispense with local color; I found this confirmation in Gibbon's *Decline and Fall of the Roman Empire*. Gibbon observes that in the Arab book *par excellence*, the Koran, there are no camels; . . . Mohammed, as an Arab, had no reason to know that camels were particularly Arab; they were, for him, a part of reality, and he had no reason to single them out, while the first thing a forger, a tourist, or an Arab nationalist would do is bring on the camels, whole caravans of camels on every page; but Mohammed, as an Arab, was unconcerned; he knew he could be Arab without camels. I believe that we Argentines can be like Mohammed; we can believe in the possibility of being Argentine without abounding in local color.[53]

There are many problems with this example, not least that it is plainly wrong. There certainly are camels in the Koran.[54] It also appears that, in the beginning of the example, Borges ascribes the lack of camels to a blindness toward local color—"Mohammed, as an Arab, had no reason to know that camels were particularly Arab"—while a few lines later the analogy implies an intentional, even ideological omission of camels—"he knew he could be Arab without camels [and] we can believe in the possibility of being Argentine without abounding in local color." Having read the lecture to the end, we may look back to this example and note the misalignment in the analogy, which, for Argentines to be like Mohammed, would mean that omitting the camels was an act of irreverence. As with the Judaic, it should not surprise us to find that Borges imagines or invents other idiosyncratic references, and the Koran without camels is certainly another such example. But it is not the example we are concerned with here.[55] For our purposes, we should note that this imaginary Koran is presented as an example of literature that does not express its author's differential traits. Borges will reimagine this example as literature that in fact rejects "the differential traits of the country that produces it."[56]

The ideological rejection of both political and literary efforts to overemphasize differential traits helps frame this 1951 lecture within Borges's broader polemics against alternatives to cosmopolitanism. This goes back to his anti-Nazi activity as well. Though we cannot date Borges's encounter with Veblen's article, discussion of the literary representation of differential traits does predate the mention of Veblen in Borges's writing. Tracking the evolution of Borges's attitude toward differential traits in the decade before the lecture will help us further clarify this aspect of the argument.

In 1941, Borges published his essay "Two Books" as part of his ongoing polemics against the Germanophiles. The occasion is a review of two books, H. G. Wells's *Guide to the New World* and Bertrand Russell's *Let the People Think*, both published that same year.[57] In this text, Borges discusses "the Jewish question" more explicitly than in the other polemical texts we have read and relates these polemics to literature more explicitly as well. In fact, it is an observation about literature that (perhaps by now predictably) leads him to his comments about the Judaic: "Since 1925, no writer has failed to claim that the inevitable and trivial fact of having been born in a certain country and of belonging to a certain race (or certain mixture of races) is a singular privilege and an effective talisman. Defenders of democracy, who believe themselves to be quite different from Goebbels, urge their readers, in the same language as the enemy, to listen to the beating of a heart that answers the call of the blood and the land . . . of the Race and of the People."[58]

This observation seems to anticipate Borges's rejection of the cult of local color in "The Argentine Writer and Tradition." It offers more context to what in 1951 he calls a European import by making a general observation about the prevalence of literary national essentialism. It also demonstrates a change in the intellectual and historical environment, as Borges's 1941 interlocutors are "defenders of democracy" who, Borges believes, should not be speaking in these terms. In contrast, in 1951 his interlocutors are the nationalists, supporters of a populist national essentialism whom Borges fully expects to be speaking in these terms. What in 1941 seems a more earnest argument that, to paraphrase Borges, "if you took your own ideological position more rigorously, you would not support literary nationalist essentialism" becomes in 1951 a jocular paradox about the ideological inconsistency of an imported idea about "the local."

Borges then moves from literature to the Jewish question in a way that similarly seems to anticipate his reference to Veblen in "The Argentine Writer and

Tradition." Here again this essay offers more context to what in 1951 Borges will refer to as "differential traits," as well as an illustration of the changed intellectual environment Borges will be working in ten years later.

> I also remember with some amazement a certain assembly that was convoked to condemn anti-Semitism. For various reasons, I am not an anti-Semite; the principal one is that I find the difference between Jews and non-Jews generally insignificant, and sometimes illusory or imperceptible. No one, that day, wanted to share my opinion; they all swore that a German Jew was vastly different from a German. In vain I reminded them that Adolf Hitler said the same thing; in vain I suggested that an assembly against racism should not tolerate the doctrine of a Chosen People; in vain I quoted the wise words of Mark Twain: "I have no race prejudices . . . All that I care to know is that a man is a human being—that is enough for me; he can't be any worse." (*The Man that Corrupted Hadleyburg*, 204).[59]

The concern with Jewish social difference is clear here, as is Borges's insistence that such difference is insignificant, or should be regarded as insignificant. However, in 1941 Borges seems concerned only with the moral dimension of such difference, whether it exists and whether it matters. He is not yet concerned with the literary representation of such difference. The closest he comes to a literary insight is his summary of Wells: "Wells exhorts us to remember our essential humanity and to suppress our miserable differential traits, no matter how poignant or picturesque."[60] However, these comments are troubled by Veblen's own views, referenced a decade later. As opposed to Borges in this 1941 conversation, Veblen does believe there is a difference between Jews and non-Jews, and the purpose of his article is to elaborate the underlying social conditions of this difference. What he shares with Borges is the desire not to essentialize such difference, hence his rejection of explanations that rely on innate racial qualities for what he terms "Jewish preeminence." It may be imperceptible, but it is not insignificant, according to Veblen.

Moreover, in Borges's rejection of "the doctrine of a Chosen People" as racist essentialism, he ignores the fact that this doctrine is shared by some of his contemporary Jews as well. This fact is very clear to Veblen and is in fact one of the challenges he sees in carrying out his program. "In their character of a Chosen People, it is not for them to take thought of their unblest neighbors," Veblen states, explaining the challenge he foresees with the integration of European Jews.[61] This further accentuates the blind spot in Borges's thought, when he suggests Israeli writers should approach the Psalms, a text that clearly demonstrates sentiments about the Chosen People in verses such as: "Happy is the nation whose God is the Lord, the people whom He has chosen for His own inheritance."[62]

On the moral register, then, it may seem that Borges's 1951 lecture moves him closer to the position of his 1941 interlocutors. However, there is a strong shift of focus away from the moral register and toward a poetic register that takes place between his jab at the cult of local color and his confabulation about camels in the Koran. This, I would argue, signals Borges's effort to go beyond mere adherence to social reality in his debate with the nationalists and to arrive at its underlying literary forces. Borges would of course not become Jewish as a result of engaging the Judaic (*Crisol* accusation notwithstanding), any more than he thinks the nationalists will become Argentine as a result of engaging local color. However ironic it may seem, it is his effort to engage what he understands to be quintessentially Judaic that ultimately will make him Argentine. This view is the source of subsequent paradoxes in Borges's thought. Mimicking Jewish distance from Argentine tradition, he embraces the very same tradition from which Veblen's wayfaring Jews, in turn, take their distance.[63]

To conclude the discussion, we might paraphrase our question thus: Are there no camels in Borges's Judaic imaginary? Of course there are. Whole caravans of camels. The way Borges expresses his attraction to the Judaic is through allusions to some of its most familiar themes. What is striking about the Judaic as a literary object is that highlighting the differential Jewish traits has been an express intention of Borges. The complex relation of the Jews vis-à-vis tradition is their differential trait, in his mind, and we have seen Borges emphasize this repeatedly. By incorporating the Kabbalah, the *sefirot*, the Tetragrammaton, the *Zohar*, Scholem, Buber, and more, Borges's Judaic is full of elements of that very tradition that Veblen's wayfaring Jew must leave behind in order to achieve preeminence. How is it, then, that Borges can adopt as Judaic those same elements of tradition that the Jew must leave behind in order to transcend their local culture toward a traditionless irreverence?

What I want to argue is that Borges's literary object of the Judaic is overrun with local color. Just not Argentine color. The poetic conclusion is that local color should be treated skeptically in one's own locale, but freely adapted from other locations. This is the irreverence Borges speaks of, which also leads to the moral conclusion. Irreverently adopting non-Argentine local colors would create in Argentine literature a poetic celebration of heterogeneity. This is entirely in line with what Borges proposes in his lecture as the model for Argentine letters and highlights the scope of his polemic with the nationalists.

This conclusion also helps further explain the seemingly paradoxical attitude Borges had toward Zionism. Borges himself expresses (almost verbatim) the same concern as Fishbein in the story "El Indigno" (1970) in an interview with Edna Aizenberg. He tells of his fear that "Israel might eradicate these almost archetypal Jewish characteristics and make the Jew a man like the others, nationalistic, mono-lingual, and hence intellectually impoverished."[64] In other words, Borges fears that Jewish nationalism will make the Jews similar to the nationalists he is polemicizing against at home, or any nationalists for that matter. Balderston emphasizes the same, taking note of the way the traveling version of this lecture emphasized the polemics against the nationalists even more than the printed version. "It is a provocation that [Borges] prepared meticulously . . . and perhaps with an intuition that his words would resonate not only in Argentina: that these would be words put forward by authors in many countries when they would want to silence their own nationalists in turn."[65]

While the application of this antinationalist logic to the Jews (and the Irish) has been somewhat preempted in Borges's argument about Agnon, nevertheless his comments to Aizenberg should make it clear that what he fears is the production of Jewish local color by Jewish nationalists.[66] For a Jewish nationalist to go on writing about Kabbalah, for example, would be to focus on those differential traits, or local color, that underwrite an essential Jewish-Israeli identity. To paraphrase Borges's comments about Mohammed, "the first thing a forger, a tourist, or [a Jewish] nationalist would do is bring on the [Kabbalah], whole caravans of [Kabbalah] on every page"[67]

I am of course using the Kabbalah and irreverence toward tradition as proxies for those differentiating traits that Borges identifies as Judaic. It is not important whether Jewish nationalist authors do in fact reference Kabbalah or reject tradition on every page. Borges did not know many such authors, and admits he is not familiar with Israeli literature in the aforementioned interview. What matters is that Borges has created allusions to Kabbalah and discussions of Jewish tradition as proxies in use of his own reflections on his role as an Argentine writer and, in so doing, he has imbued this conversation with his own pressing concerns about literature. This is the intellectual context in which I propose to make sense of Borges's desire to emphasize that he is not a Jewish nationalist: "I, truthfully, am not a Zionist, but I want to explain in what sense. Some time ago I read a very nice article by Veblen."[68] Borges cannot be a Jewish nationalist because he is an irreverent Argentine.

In this, Borges exhibits a certain naïveté about Jewish nationalism and its own relation to Jewish tradition, which ultimately relegates Zionism to a blind spot in his thought. Borges (through Veblen) sees the modern Jewish break with tradition as proof of the persistence of Jewish identity in the face of an abandonment of local color. In contrast, Scholem, for example, sees this same break as a dialectical swing away from tradition, which will enable the historical emergence of Jewish nationalism. This is not the place to work through this paradox. But I wanted to point to it as a question, which I believe my proposed reading of Borges can elucidate. It should not surprise us, then, to find that T. S. Eliot and the question of tradition converge around yet another aspect of Borges's engagement with the Judaic—his reading of Martin Buber and his understanding of Hasidism.

Part 3

Authorship

7

Authorship and Its Metaphors

I live . . . so that Borges can plot his literature, and that literature justifies me . . . but those pages cannot save me, perhaps because [they are] now no-one's . . . other than language, or tradition.

—"Borges y yo," Borges, *Obras completas, 1923–1972*, 808.

Borges's collection *Otras Inquisiciones* (1952) compiles over a decade of essayistic reflections on literature.[1] Beyond the trouble with tradition, Borges would explore the relation of his own texts to language and to tradition, as expressed in the epigraph. About half of the texts included in his 1952 collection were published in the major daily newspaper *La Nación* between 1941 and 1952. Perhaps the most famous essay of this collection is "Kafka and His Precursors."[2] This collection marks the accumulation of Borges's thought on literature and writing and, in many ways, is the literary theoretical counterpart to his two major collections of stories published in the same period, *Ficciones* (1944) and *El Aleph* (1949). Together with the publication of many of Borges's most notable essays on literature ("The Argentine Writer and Tradition" is a prime, though by no means unique, example) this period is also characterized by Borges's engagement with the writings of Martin Buber, marked by multiple references to Buber's writings and thought. Lisa Block de Behar states of this period: "Without leaving aside Borges' own claims, it is possible to say that Buber had an intense influence in that area of his thought that cannot be separated from his imagination and that became the Borgesian jurisdiction par excellence, one of the regions of literary extraterritoriality that, if not his discovery or his invention, still remains his conquest."[3]

Buber had a marked influence on Borges's thought about literature and authorship in the postwar period.[4] In the present chapter, we will retrace Borges's encounter with what Block de Behar calls "the regions of literary extraterritoriality," point to the specific influences of Buber's texts, and note the consequent evolution of Borges's metaphor for authorship in the postwar years. As opposed to Gershom Scholem, whom Borges only first encountered in the years following World War II, and whom we have worked to distance from arguments of influence over Borges's thought in the first chapters of this study, Borges had been familiar with Buber's writing since his World War I years in Geneva. The teenaged Borges had even translated a text by Buber as early as 1916.[5]

Borges's first published reference to Buber comes in his 1938 essay "A Disturbing Exposition," where he decried the ideological revisions to a recent edition of *Geschichte der deutschen Nationalliteratur* (The History of German National Literature) by A.F.C. Vilmar.[6] Borges notes the exclusion of a long list of prominent writers such as Heine, Kafka, and Buber. "There is not one that in all honesty should be excluded from a history of German literature. The (unreasonable) reasons for this manifold silence are evident: most of those eliminated are Jewish," Borges writes.[7] Buber and Kafka thus make a brief appearance in Borges's early anti-Nazi polemics. While his attention soon turned to the Germanophiles, the connection established in Geneva between Kafka, Buber, and the Judaic would reemerge in the years after World War II, when their role in the articulation of Borges's evolving conception of authorship is most pronounced. In fact, it is the World War I era association of Kafka and Buber with questions of tradition that reemerges in Borges's writing in the late 1940s and will provide the final dimension to our understanding of Borges's notion of tradition.

It is thus important for the literary-intellectual trajectory we have introduced in the first chapters of this study—tracking Borges's familiarity with the Kabbalah and, later, with Scholem—to note that Borges was introduced to Buber's writing during his youth in Geneva. In the course of just a few years he translated Buber, read Meyrink's novel *Der Golem* (1915) and Bischoff's *Die Elemente der Kabbalah* (1913), and was acquainted with Kafka's early work. We have already discussed Borges's early encounters with Kabbalah. What I want to highlight here is that Buber and Kafka are part of that same early context. As we will see presently, Buber in particular is an important and largely overlooked component of Borges's developing Judaic imagination, going back to the earliest moments of this aspect of his writing. As with his broader engagement with the Judaic, Borges's engagement with Buber is also centered on questions of writing and authorship and—refracted through Buber's own interests—takes the form of an interest in Jewish tradition and Hasidism. In fact, Buber is well-known for his explicit reconceptualization of Jewish tradition for an acculturated Jewish readership. It is quite likely that it was Buber who first drew Borges's attention to the centrality of the concept of tradition in the Judaic, setting the stage for Borges's intellectual efforts to recast or appropriate this focus for the Argentine context.[8]

When in postwar years Borges's thought about authorship turns from a focus on Kabbalah to a focus on tradition, this precipitates a decade of engagement with Buber in essays and stories. His reading of Buber also frames a more specific shift in the focus of Borges's representation of authorship. In the early 1950s, twenty years after "A Vindication of the Kabbalah," Borges moves from representing the author as an approximation of divinity to representing the author as an interlocutor of divinity, participating in an ongoing dialogue with an absent counterpart that nonetheless produces a tradition. It is in Buber's philosophical writings that Borges encounters this new notion of tradition and its production, and from which his postwar metaphor of authorship emerges.

Buber depicts Jewish tradition as a dialogue that began when Moses spoke to God on Mount Sinai, and which, as long as the Jew keeps speaking to God, will be maintained as a dialogue, constituting Jewish tradition.[9] If in the 1932 "A Vindication of the Kabbalah" Borges wants to approximate divinity and be the author of the Kabbalists, in the years following World War II this metaphor is recast through this notion of dialogue, the continuities and discontinuities of which Borges conceives as literary tradition, and comes to a head in his 1951 essay "Kafka and His Precursors." By the time Borges mentions Scholem in his 1958 poem "The Golem," his decade of engagement with Buber is coming to an end.[10] And yet, as we will see shortly, even this poem (which we have already discussed and distanced from any Scholem influence) should be read within the context of Buber's thought and its deep influence on Borges's articulation of authorship.

The decade following World War II saw a wave of publications by Buber, which Borges followed closely. In the same years, Borges began to express his appreciation for the multifaceted contribution of Buber's intellectual project to an understanding of his own concerns with literature and writing. In the late 1940s, Borges delivered a lecture about Buber at the Colegio Libre de Estudios Superiores, the same crowd and venue for "The Argentine Writer and Tradition" a few years later.[11] The multiplication of Borges's references to Buber in this period corresponds to the wave of Buber's own postwar publications, among which are some of his most notable works. In 1946 Borges read Buber's

Vom Geists des Judentums (1921) and it is his marginalia in this volume that first references Scholem.[12]

The following year, Borges cites Buber's collection *The Tales of the Hasidim* (1947) in his 1947 essay "On Chesterton," that is, in the very same year it appeared in English.[13] Already in that essay Borges weaves together Buber, Kafka, and the question of authorship in a way that will persist into the 1950s and find clear expression in his collection *Otras Inquisiciones* (1952). While there are other passing references to Buber in *Otras Inquisiciones* and more generally in Borges's writing of this period, we will focus here on three essays by Borges that best demonstrate the influence of Buber on his postwar thought. All three are included in *Otras Inquisiciones*: "On Chesterton" (1947) and "Kafka and his Precursors" (1951) were included in the 1952 edition and the essay "History of the Echoes of a Name," originally published in 1955, was added to the 1960 edition of *Otras Inquisiciones*.[14] Through these essays we will trace Borges's encounter with Buber's "regions of literary extraterritoriality," its influence on his postwar notion of tradition, and the development of a concomitant metaphor for authorship.[15]

Hasidism

At the end of "On Chesterton," Borges recaps Kafka's well-known parable "Before the Law."[16] The parable tells the story of a man who waits all his life before an open gate. He is told by the guard that there are stronger and more heavily guarded gates within, and so he waits his whole life by the gate, never entering and never discovering what is beyond the first gate. In a footnote, Borges makes the connection between the image of gates within gates in Kafka's parable and the same image in Buber's *Tales of the Hasidim* (1947), stating "the notion of doors behind doors interposed between the sinner and glory is found in the *Zohar*. See Glatzer, *In Time and Eternity*, 30; also Martin Buber, *Tales of the Hasidim*, 92."[17] In this footnote, Borges introduces an interpretation of the gates in Kafka's parable as separating man and God. This is certainly in line with Buber's thought, but its relevance to Kafka's parable is not explained. In fact, the Buber reference is to a Hasidic tale titled "The Fiftieth Gate" that narrates the opposite encounter, in which the gates have all successfully been accessed and the protagonist must make the choice to turn back.[18]

In "The Fiftieth Gate," a Hasidic disciple has made his way through the fifty gates of reason. He stands before the fiftieth and final gate, beyond which he will have perfect knowledge of God. The gate is open and he must decide whether to enter. His rabbi tells him that the proper thing for the faithful to do is not to enter. Faith means you do not know. Not entering demonstrates true faith.

> "You have passed through the fifty gates of reason. You begin with a question and think, and think up an answer—and the first gate opens, and to a new

question! And again you plumb it, find the solution, fling open the second gate—and look into a new question. On and on like this, deeper and deeper, until you have forced open the fiftieth gate. . . . But if you dare to probe still further, you plunge into the abyss."

"So I should go back all the way, to the very beginning?" cried the disciple.

"If you turn, you will not be going back," said [the] Rabbi. "You will be standing beyond the last gate: you will stand in faith."[19]

By juxtaposing these seemingly opposing parables about doors within doors, Borges is not offering an interpretation of the parables as much as identifying a Judaic literary theme that brings together Kafka, the *Zohar*, and Buber's account of Hasidism. This chain of associations sets up for us the coordinates of a Judaic metaphor that Borges will develop and elaborate in *Otras Inquisiciones* (1952) and beyond. While this is not yet made clear in "On Chesterton," this metaphor will come to replace the God of the Kabbalists with the absent interlocutor as Borges's primary postwar metaphor for authorship.

Borges read Buber's work on Hasidism in two books, *Tales of the Hasidim* (1947) and *Hasidism* (1948). Buber introduced his readers to the legends and stories of Hasidism in many volumes dating back to the first years of the twentieth century, but he offers his most comprehensive conceptual introduction to the theme in his 1948 book *Hasidism*. Already in the very first pages of this book, Buber explains that "legend is our main source for understanding [Hasidism], and its theoretical literature comes only after its legend. The theoretical literature is the gloss, the legend is the text."[20] This privileging of narrative as a source for understanding the social movement is instructive for our understanding of what Borges takes up in Buber's writings and, in some cases, directly translates for his own readership.

Another relevant aspect of Buber's thought is that he ascribes the Jews a unique in-between existence. This is a central motif in Buber's depiction of European Jews in general and the Hasidic movement in particular. Buber sees the Jews as *Mittlervolk*, an in-between people that mediate between Orient and Occident. In his own annotations to Buber's *Vom Geist des Judentums* (1921), which Borges read in 1946, he took note of precisely this argument. Borges highlights a line in Buber that may well have been Thorstein Veblen's line: "Europe needed a middle-folk."[21] Buber sees the Jews as essential to European culture in that they mediate between the spirit of the Orient and the spirit of the Occident. Buber and Veblen do not cross paths in Borges's writing and yet the resonances between their views of European Jewry are notable. As is the fact that Borges seems to embrace both the view that Jews are stuck between two traditions (as Veblen sees it) and that Jews are mediators between two traditions (as Buber sees it).

Furthermore, for Buber and Veblen, the in-between position of the Jews defines an epistemology—*Mittlervolk*, wayfaring—that Borges wants to adapt or recreate in his own margin. In Buber's writing, the Hasidic movement is the most recent and clear example of successfully navigating the tensions that this in-between position produces, between East and West, between tradition and modernity, between God and the world. These are the tensions of Jewish existence Buber presents in his 1948 book and Hasidism, he argues, attains a unique synthesis of these. "The separation of 'living in God' from 'living in the world' is overcome in the Hasidic message, and a true, concrete unity takes its place."[22] This unity is not without its internal tensions, and—importantly, both to Buber's project as well as to Borges's intellectual narrator—these are expressed in literary form, in Hasidism's legends and tales.

Thus perceived, Hasidism offered Buber a model for his own cultural renewal project. "Hasidism helped Buber to realize two objectives: to foster a model for the new or rather renewed Jewish consciousness envisioned by cultural Zionism . . . and, concomitantly, . . . the creation of a distinctive Jewish modernism,"[23] explains Martina Urban in *Aesthetics of Renewal: Martin Buber's Early Representation of Hasidism as Kulturkritik* (2008). There are two aspects that Urban focuses on in Buber's project. One aspect is that, from the very beginning, Buber's publications of Hasidic legends and tales "were considered contributions to these larger efforts to overcome assimilation in favor of acculturation."[24] Another aspect is that "Buber was part of a larger effort of restructuring Jewish memory and reconstructing Jewish identity through the creation of new forms of culture in the Diaspora."[25] Here again we find echoes of Borges's own cultural project as he attempts to invent an Argentine identity that resists assimilation into European tradition and yet recognizes its inevitable interaction with Europe. In "The Argentine Writer and Tradition," Borges argues this can be accomplished in the realm of literature.

Buber offers Borges the conceptualization of a tradition to be developed (or renewed) that can in fact only emerge out of such in-between space. Buber's audience, explains Urban, "no longer shared the same cultural and symbolic landscape inhabited by traditional Judaism."[26] At the same time, however, Buber did not arrive at a conclusion that would involve withdrawal from the cultures into which these modern Jews had been acculturated. This dynamic clearly echoes in Borges's concerns with the cultural relation between Argentina and Europe that we have seen him express in this same period. For the present, the point to emphasize is that Buber fills this in-between space with the rich cultural tradition of Hasidic narrative. In filling this space, Buber too must tackle the questions of authorship and tradition that Borges is most concerned with in his own reflections on literature at the time: "Through the aesthetic mode of representation Buber adopted, he sought to address the challenge faced by synchronic transmission. He well realized that the 'chain of tradition' or diachronic transmission had been broken. The modern acculturated Jew no longer shared the same cultural and symbolic landscape inhabited by traditional Judaism. To fill this vacuum and recreate a sense of Jewishness, Buber sought to reestablish a new mode of transmission."[27]

Urban's analysis helps us identify the point at which Borges takes up Buber's thought in his own reflections on writing and the Argentine intellectual. "By making retelling and not literal or faithful translation the mode of representation, Buber sanctions moderate decontextualization. . . . Hence, retelling is a form of synchronic transmission."[28] This is a practice Borges too had already adopted in his collection *Historia universal de la infamia* (1935) and expressed in various stories, such as "Pierre Menard, Author of the Quixote" and "The Gospel According to Mark."[29] It is here that we begin to see Buber's influence on Borges's intellectual narrator: Decontextualization as a form of appropriating literary traditions and recontextualization as the inscription of these traditions into the "margin" as Argentine literature. These are the points at which the space of social existence is mirrored by a question of literary tradition.

In Buber's *Tales of the Hasidim* (1947), Borges finds tales that relate such decontextualized spaces, whose connection to the broader context turns out to have been powerfully understated. Borges translated two such tales for his 1955 collection *Cuentos breves y extraordinarios*.[30] The tales are "A Transaction" and "Upsetting the Bowl."[31] He had already recounted the latter in full as part of his lecture on Buber in the late 1940s.[32] In both tales, an action by a Hasidic rabbi that seems at first disconnected from his social-political context turns out to have been affecting the very heart of decision-making in the emperor's court.

The story "A Transaction" opens with the emperor issuing "an edict which was bound to make thoroughly miserable the already oppressed Jews."[33] A disciple of the Hasidic rabbi Elimelekh is upset by this, approaches his master, and declares, "I have a suit against God."[34] The next day, Rabbi Elimelekh convenes a court of three rabbis to hear the suit. The plaintiff's argument is that, since God has commanded the Jews to follow His laws, therefore, "even though he has sent us to alien lands, still, wherever we are, he must leave us full freedom to serve him."[35] God cannot both command the Jews to follow His laws and place them in a situation that makes it impossible to follow those same laws. The audacity of this scene is typical of the Hasidic tale, as is its resolution. The court of three rabbis considers the plaintiff's claims as well as God's defense, which they find in scripture. "Then the three sat in judgment, silently and with closed eyes. After an hour, they called in [the plaintiff] and gave him the verdict: that he was in the right. In the same hour, the edict in Vienna was cancelled."[36]

The story "Upsetting the Bowl" has a similar conceit. In this story, Rabbi Elimelekh is the protagonist whose strange behavior turns out to have far-reaching effects. "Once Rabbi Elimelekh was eating the sabbath meal with his disciples. The servant set the soup bowl down before him. Rabbi Elimelekh raised it and upset it, so that the soup poured over the table."[37] One disciple is worried and confused, but the other disciples know better. As decontextualized as the rabbi's actions seem, they know that they have a purpose and an addressee. The story concludes: "Some time after this, it became known that on that day an edict directed against the Jews of the whole country had been presented to the emperor for his signature. Time after time he took up his pen, but something always happened to interrupt him. Finally he signed the paper. Then he reached for the sand-container but took the inkwell instead and upset it on the document. Hereupon he tore it up and forbade them to put the edict before him again."[38]

Whereas the English titles "A Transaction" and "Upsetting the Bowl" focus on the occurrence within the Hasidic court, Borges's translation of these titles (the only place he takes creative liberty in the translation of these tales) refocuses them on what Borges is interested in, namely the manner in which these supposedly decontextualized events extend from arbitrariness to fate. The first is thus retitled "The Accused," referring to God as the defendant before the tribunal of Hasidic rabbis. The second is retitled "The Distraction" or "The Neglect," for the consequence the rabbi's actions have in the emperor's court, causing a distraction that ultimately leads the emperor to neglect his edict against the Jews. The Hasidic rabbis in these tales act within an existentially isolated space where the only certainty is that actions will have consequences beyond the solipsistic existence of their protagonist. What characterizes Hasidism in these stories is the faith they depict in the broader effects of their protagonists' actions, even if they cannot comprehend these actions at the outset, beyond their seemingly decontextualized occurrences.

The Sphere of In-Between

In May 1948 Borges acquired Buber's book *Between Man and Man* (1947).[39] His marginalia show two ideas in the book that he was particularly drawn to, noting the same two passages multiple times and developing a web of associations and references around each. The first marginalia reference begins with Kafka and, by association, proceeds to Robert Browning, W. B. Yeats (via the work of literary scholar Richard Ellmann[40]), and then to a verse from the biblical book of Genesis.[41] This chain of associations is an important background for Borges's essay "Kafka and His Precursors" and we will discuss it shortly. I would like to focus first on the next idea Borges is drawn to in the book, as it gives an overview of Borges's encounter with Buber's thought in these years. The passage relates to Buber's conceptualization of the in-between space in which human interaction takes place. Borges's marginalia return three times to the discussion on page 203 of the book. The first line Borges notes is: "I call this sphere, which is established with the existence of man as man but which is conceptually still uncomprehended, *the sphere of 'between.'*"[42]

If in Borges's 1946 reading of Buber we found resonances with Veblen's view of the Jews as an in-between people (a "Mittlervolk," in Buber's words), here we find a universalization of the in-between space as a basic tenet of Buber's existentialist philosophy. In the next reference to page 203, Borges adds his own words: "The *between* is the essential, but it has not been perceived because it constantly varies."[43] Borges is paraphrasing the next passage on the page, where Buber further explains his concept of "between."

> The view which establishes the concept of "between" is to be acquired by no longer localizing the relation between human beings, as is customary, either within individual souls or in a general world which embraces and determines them, but in actual fact *between* them.
>
> "Between" is not an auxiliary construction, but the real place and bearer of what happens between men; it has received no specific attention because, in distinction from the individual soul and its context, it does not exhibit a smooth continuity, but is ever and again re-constituted in accordance with men's meetings with one another.[44]

Buber is conceptualizing the interpersonal space where dialogue takes place. Buber's notion of dialogue—famously encapsulated in his distinction between I–thou and I–it relationships—is where there is an encounter with some other, not as an object but as an interlocutor that is expected to meet you where you are, so to speak, between the individual, stable existences of both.[45] The third passage Borges references in his marginalia encapsulates this point: "In a real conversation . . . , a real lesson . . . , a real embrace and not one of mere habit, a real duel and not a mere game—in all these what is essential does not take place in each of the participants or in a neutral world which includes the two and all other things; but it takes place between them in the most precise sense."[46]

In Buber's book *Dialogisches Leben* (1947), he conceptualizes such an encounter as "dialogue." Buber understands dialogue as the act of entering into a relationship with another by stepping into the in-between space described above. The relationship between a self and an object (I–it) does not produce such a space. Only the encounter between a self and another self (I–thou) will open the in-between space where two subjectivities meet, that is, the in-between of dialogue is the product of an intersubjective encounter. As we have seen, Buber thinks of this as a real place, hard to pin down since it is always in flux, constituted and reconstituted with every interpersonal encounter.

Buber's concepts of "between" and "dialogue" are building blocks for his existentialist philosophy as well as for his theorization of Jewish tradition. The temporality of Jewish tradition is not chronological but dialogical, according to Buber. As long as Jews continue to address God as an interlocutor, they will perpetuate the tradition-as-dialogue that began when Moses first addressed God on Mount Sinai. When Borges summarizes Buber's philosophy to his friend Adolfo Bioy Casares in December 1954, he emphasized this point as well: "For Martin Buber the present is [made up of] the moments that are occurring or that have occurred, in which there is an encounter with someone, something: [that is the] dialogue I-thou; the past is [made up of] moments that are occurring or that have occurred, in which there is no encounter: I-it. The idea comes, according to Borges, from the desire to encounter a Jewish philosophy; to think about the encounter between Moses and God; from this, the importance of dialogue."[47]

Borges's attention to the temporal aspects of the argument set us up for appreciating the way this reading of Buber fits within his own thoughts about tradition, history, and the Judaic. This connection is expressed and elaborated within the frame of Borges's more immediate postwar concerns. In Borges's writing of the period, Buber's notion of dialogue is transformed into a metaphor for the intellectual author's position. This takes place most explicitly in two essays of the period, "Kafka and His Precursors" and "History of the Echoes of a Name."

Kafka and His Precursors

The essay "Kafka and His Precursors" is well-known for its rethinking and expansion of the notion of literary tradition. Like "The Argentine Writer and Tradition," this essay too can be read within the three contexts we have laid out previously: literary tradition, Jewish tradition, and national tradition. We have already seen the early connection between Kafka, Buber, and notions of tradition in Borges's thought going back to his youth in Geneva. So it is no surprise to see Kafka star in an essay that, between the lines, references T. S. Eliot's "Tradition and the Individual Talent," Buber's notion of Jewish tradition, and Eduardo Mallea's literary-nationalist views.

We have clarified the stakes of Borges's effort to reframe the notion of national tradition in opposition to the nationalists in the context of "The Argentine Writer and Tradition." But the relation between that effort and a reading of Kafka still needs some clarification. What is less obvious in this essay is its role within Borges's polemics against the nationalists. I want to first outline briefly what is at stake for Borges in pulling Kafka into his debate with the nationalists at this postwar moment and in these terms of literary tradition and its creation. After that, we will move on to the roles of Eliot and Buber in the essay.

The debate between Borges and Mallea goes back to the earliest years of the journal *Sur*, when they were both early members of the literary group that founded the publication and contributed regularly to its pages. Among its early members, Borges stood out for his "perception of the literary act and . . . conception of what a writer ought to be [that were] opposed to those expressed by the majority of its members."[48] Even among this majority group, Mallea stands out as a representative of the humanist view of literature and as an interlocutor against whom Borges would develop and define his more formalist view of literature. Judith Podlubne argues that "'against' this humanist ethics, 'against' the special recognition that Mallea achieved for being its most representative figure, Borges defined his controversial place in the journal," in the early years of his career.[49]

The debate between Borges and Mallea—which, as we have seen, was as much literary as it was moral—finds a focal point in the late 1930s in their respective engagement with Kafka, and their competitive pretentions to be the translator, editor, and general presenter of this author to the Argentine reading public. Podlubne details and analyzes several such literary confrontations that took place between Borges and Mallea.[50] What I want to highlight here is the way Mallea's attitude would lionize the person of Kafka through a humanistic reading of his work, while Borges's formalist attitude would attempt a deconstruction of that same person to the point that Kafka the author is no longer the precursor of Kafka the text. Mallea oversaw the first translations of Kafka to appear in Argentina, published in 1936 in *Sur*. In it, he presented Kafka to the Argentine readership of the time as "the most original writer of our times."[51]

The stakes of engaging Kafka, like the stakes of Argentineity, were not fully articulated in the 1930s. And perhaps they could not have been, since it is only after the war that Borges returns to many of these debates with renewed urgency and vigor. We have already seen Borges return to the debate about national literature and local color in "The Argentine Writer and Tradition." A few months before delivering the lecture, he had already published this essay on Kafka.[52] It is in the context of Borges's postwar rearticulation of his positions on authorship, refracted, as we have seen, through the questions of tradition, local color, and postcolonial writing, that both of these texts should be read.

When Borges proposes an amusingly heterogeneous list of Kafka's precursors, or states that "the first Kafka of *Betrachtung* is less a precursor of [Kafka] than is Browning," he is, through the same formalist attitude Mallea would reject, deconstructing Kafka's work to the point of resisting any humanistic reading of it.[53] Most importantly for his postwar debates with the nationalists, Borges's presumption to deconstruct Kafka is also his way of staking a claim to the writer. Kafka does not emerge from this essay as the precursor to the postwar nationalists, represented by Kafka's 1930s translator Mallea, whom Borges would argue against yet again a few months later in "The Argentine Writer and Tradition." Kafka emerges as a precursor to Borges.

Another point of convergence between "Kafka and His Precursors" and "The Argentine Writer and Tradition" is the role of Eliot's "Tradition and the Individual Talent." Both texts build on the idea that the present modifies the past. Unlike "The Argentine Writer and Tradition," where Eliot's influence is not explicitly acknowledged, in "Kafka and His Precursors" Borges cites this source more clearly. In a footnote to the line "his work modifies our conception of the past, as it will modify the future," Borges notes: "See T. S. Eliot, *Points of View* (1941), 25–26."[54] The reference directs to the precise pages in Eliot's "Tradition and the Individual Talent" where the argument about the historical sense is made.

Beyond citing his source, what is interesting in the essay by Borges is what it adds to his reading of Eliot. In this essay, Borges proposes a list of writers that are "precursors" of Kafka. They have little to do with each other but, after reading Kafka, it is clear they prefigure Kafka's work in some way. Kafka's work is what creates the connection between them as they form the group "Kafka's precursors." This is an example of Eliot's historical sense, where the new work of art modifies the significance of the works of art that preceded it. But Borges takes Eliot's argument one step further in this essay. "The fact is that each writer creates his precursors. His work modifies our conception of the past, *as it will modify the future*," Borges states.[55]

What Borges in this essay adds to Eliot's idea is the thought that a modification of the past can include the retroactive creation of a tradition, in which the author will operate going forward. And this tradition can be as idiosyncratic as the writer's individual talent. Thus, in Borges's account, Kafka has created an unlikely literary tradition of precursors spanning Zeno and Aristotle, Han Yu, Kierkegaard, Robert Browning, Leon Bloy, and Lord Dunsany. The randomness of these precursors serves both to create a comic effect in Borges's analysis of Kafka, and to suggest a much more far-reaching conclusion, namely, that by simply writing, an author from no identifiable tradition creates the tradition within which they operate, and will continue to operate, through constant and unknowable links that form their precursors.

One such precursor Borges suggests for Kafka is Robert Browning's poem "Fears and Scruples."[56] This poem, which Borges returns to twice over the course of his essay, is not only a precursor to Kafka, but also itself a discussion of what it means to create one's tradition. Borges summarizes the poem thus: "A man has, or thinks he has, a famous friend. He has never seen this friend, and the fact is that this friend has never been able to help him, but he knows that the friend has very noble qualities, and he shows others the letters his friend has written. Some have doubts about his nobility, and handwriting experts declare the letters to be fake. In the last line, the man asks: 'What if this friend happened to be—God?'"[57]

The epistolary relationship between the man and his friend exists, so it is suspected, entirely within the man's own library. The only certainty in the poem is that the man writes letters to his friend. Even the friend's replies, some suspect, may be fake. In the final line, the man wonders whether his elusive friend might be God. In this elusiveness Borges identifies Browning's poem as a precursor not only to Kafka but also to Buber. Here we come to the second passage Borges was drawn to in Buber's *Between Man and Man* (1947), what Buber calls the "strange room of the spirit." At first glance, Buber may seem entirely absent from this essay on Kafka. Yet in his thorough annotations to this volume by Buber, Borges indicates his own chain of associations, leading from Buber's text back to Browning's poem and forward again to Kafka. This association between Kafka and Browning is made in reference to Buber's lines: "Life is not lived by my playing the enigmatic game on a board by myself, but by my being placed in the presence of a being with whom I have agreed on no rules for the game and with whom no rules can be agreed on."[58]

Borges makes this connection explicit in his marginalia to Buber's book. In reference to the passage from Buber cited above, he writes: "166—life is not lived . . . Cf. Kafka, Browning."[59] Buber's suggestion that the other player—who we never meet and whose existence we only contrive from the fact that a game is in play—is God leads Borges to Browning's poem, in which the same is suggested by the protagonist after a lifetime of correspondence with an absent other. This room of the spirit, in which the game is played blindly, is also reminiscent of the room in which the idiosyncratic actions of the Hasidic rabbis proved part of an ongoing game that finally influences God to change the emperor's mind in the story Borges translates as "The Accused."

In the next line of his marginalia, Borges's concern with the activities of the intellectual narrator leads him from Browning's poem to a particular image in Buber, of the space from within which he might operate. This is the second passage Borges references in his marginalia:

> We enter a strange room of the spirit, but we feel as if the ground we tread is the board on which a game is being played whose rules we learn as we advance, deep rules which we ponder, and must ponder, but which arose and which persist only through a decision having once been reached to play this intellectual game, and to play it in this very way. And at the same time, it is true, we feel that this game is not arbitrarily chosen by the player, but he is under necessity, it is his fate.[60]

To this passage, Borges adds a reference to page 199 of Richard Ellmann's book *Yeats: The Man and the Masks* (1948). Borges is referring to an episode in Yeats's career, detailed by Ellmann, where Yeats comes to believe that the spirit of a deceased geographer named Johannes Leo Africanus is his otherworldly guide.[61] The relationship between them takes the form of Yeats writing letters to himself as Leo and then replying to Leo as Yeats. Between the episodes of writing to an absent friend, writing to God, and writing to a spirit that is oneself, Borges is characterizing the strange room of the spirit as the space from which to write. The room of the spirit is detached from the outside world and yet this decontextualized space nonetheless maintains unimaginable ties to other players. It is a small self-reflective step for Borges to identify this room of the spirit as the epistemic position of the intellectual author. As we will see, this image from Buber's *Between Man and Man* (1947) appears in several of Borges's texts from the postwar period.

What Borges adds to Buber's room of the spirit is the suggestion that the moves in the game that is taking place are made by writing. The dialogue between Browning and his elusive friend, between Yeats-as-Yeats and Yeats-as-Leo, between Kafka and his precursors, is a game of letters, in which the writer must never interrupt their side of the dialogue. The elusiveness of what is beyond the space we live in, along with the inevitability of our contact with it—Buber teaches that these are of the essence in understanding the dialogue that is Jewish tradition. This ongoing dialogue began between God and Moses in a moment of evasion, which Borges takes up in 1955, in his essay "History of the Echoes of a Name."

A New Metaphor for Authorship

"Isolated in time and in space, a God, a dream and a man who is mad, and who does not ignore it, repeat an obscure declaration; to relate and to weigh these words, and their two echoes, is the aim of this page."[62] In these opening lines of his 1955 essay "History of the Echoes of a Name," Borges is referring to the episode in the third chapter of the biblical book of Exodus where, as he concisely summarizes it, "Moses, author and protagonist of the book, asked God for His name, and He tells him: *I Am that I Am*."[63] This phrase has found many echoes in subsequent generations and translations, but only two interpretations, proposes Borges. His essay discusses these two interpretations.

The first interpretation understands God's reply, "I Am that I Am," as an "ontological affirmation," Borges explains. In its translation as "I Am that I Am," it affirms God as the essence of existence, the prime being. This is the interpretation that persists in the various translations, "multiplied by human languages—*Ich bin der ich bin, Ego sum qui sum, I am that I am*."[64] It is also true of everywhere this name echoes through its multiple intertextual references. One such echo Borges identifies is a line from Shakespeare's *All's Well that Ends Well*: "simply the thing I am shall make me live."[65] These are "words that reflect . . . those others that the divinity said on the mountain,"[66] Borges writes. He is conflating two central moments in Buber's thought. The first is God's reply "I Am that I Am" at the burning bush. The second is the encounter between Moses and God on the mountain, which Buber understands as the beginning of the dialogue of Jewish tradition.

This leads to the second interpretation of these words, which, as Borges presents it, belongs only to Buber. It sees God's response as an evasion. This phrase is not a name at all. It is God's attempt to avoid answering the question, to conceal His name: "Others have understood that the reply eludes the question. . . . Martin Buber indicates that *Ehyeh asher ehyeh* can also be translated as *I Am what I will be* or as *I shall be where I shall be*. Moses, following the Egyptian magicians, would have asked God for His name in order to have Him in his power; God would have answered, in fact: *Today I speak with you, but tomorrow I can re-dress myself in any form, even in forms of oppression, of injustice and of adversity*. This we read in *Gog und Magog*."[67] In these lines, Borges paraphrases an entire paragraph from Buber's 1928 lecture "The Faith of Judaism," without citing the source.[68]

> According to the usage common to primitive peoples, once they seized the secret of the name, they could conjure the god, and thus coerce him . . . but when Moses voices his scruple [God answers him] not "I am that I am" as alleged by the metaphysicians—God does not make theological statements— but the answer which his creatures need, and which benefits them: "I shall be there as I there shall be" (Ex. 3:14). That is: you need not conjure me, for I am here, I am with you; but you cannot conjure me, for I am with you time and again in the form in which I choose to be with you time and again; I myself do not anticipate any of my manifestations; you cannot learn to meet me; you meet me, when *you* meet me.[69]

Borges references Buber's novel *Gog und Magog* (1949), a historical fiction about the reaction of the Hasidic movement to the emergence of Napoleon and the internal rift this created in the movement.[70] Borges thus ties Buber's interpretation of "I Am that I Am" to his writings on Hasidism. At the same time, in his footnote to these lines from "History of the Echoes of a Name," Borges connects Buber's interpretation of God's reply back to the strange room of the spirit. His footnote reads: "Buber (*Was Ist der Mensch?* 1938) writes that to live is to enter a strange room of the spirit, whose floor is a board on which we play an inevitable and unfamiliar game against a changing and sometimes terrifying adversary."[71] Borges does not elaborate on the connection he is making between Hasidism and the strange room of the spirit.

These associations certainly suggest an interpretation of Buber's novel *Gog und Magog* that is in line with the understanding of Hasidism Borges finds in Buber more broadly. The Hasidic master, occupying this room of the spirit, is forced to contend with a terrifying adversary. The ambiguity that surrounds this adversary in the novel—taking the form of Napoleon but suggesting a divine agent, blurring the distinction between oppression and redemption—is the elusiveness Borges identifies in Buber's interpretation of "I Am that I Am." By circling back to *Between Man and Man* in his footnote, Borges closes the loop here between Buber, Browning, and Kafka. The elusiveness Buber attributes to God's reply is the elusiveness of Browning's famous friend, the elusive addressee of any author. Borges is crafting his metaphor of the author as the emblematic resident of Buber's strange room of the spirit.

This metaphor for authorship persists in Borges's texts beyond the period of his engagement with Buber. Having reviewed the genealogy of this metaphor, we can now demonstrate its presence in fuller form in later texts by Borges, where the protagonist is placed in the strange room of the spirit, on a board, playing a game. The first is the poem "Ajedrez" (Chess) published in 1960 in the collection *El Hacedor*.[72] It has two parts, and each takes the form of a sonnet. The poem repeats Buber's individual playing a game on a board by creating the image of a chess player who himself is a piece on a board, played by another player who (in Borgesian style) himself may be yet another piece on a larger board.

The first sonnet describes the game of chess in the first two stanzas and then offers its twist: "Once the players have gone, / Once time has consumed them, / Certainly the rite goes on."[73] The suggestion that the game is bigger than the players is emphasized in the closing line of the first sonnet: "Like that other, this game is infinite."[74] The first sonnet closes by making the move from the game of chess to the game of life. The instinctive reading would perhaps be to understand this closing line as a restatement of the idea that life is but a game. Having noted the way Borges has embraced Buber's room of the spirit as a metaphor for writing, we might also expect to find that the central analogy is not between the games of chess and life, but between the pawn and the person, both trapped on a board they cannot escape and forced to "play an inevitable and unfamiliar game against a changing and sometimes terrifying adversary."[75] When the human player looks up from the chess board (or in this case the sonnet about the chess board) to realize life is a game, it reinforces their own location in Buber's strange room of the spirit.

Following the chain of associations that brought Buber, Browning, and Kafka together, the second sonnet will pursue the metaphor further, introducing God as the absent interlocutor or opponent. The first two stanzas of the second sonnet continue the analogy between humans and chess pieces. Not only are they both pawns in a game that is infinite, but "They do not know that the signaled hand / Of the player governs their destiny."[76] In this line, Borges transforms the analogy into a regressive metaphor. The pawn is oblivious to the human player, just as the human is oblivious to the elusive player that controls their moves on the board. Who is the player that moves the human in the game of life? The third stanza does not offer the answer. It begins by offering what seems like a continuation of the analogy between the pawn and the human:

"The player too is a prisoner / . . . upon another board."[77] Yet the next link in this regressive chain has already been implied. Like the human that moves the pawn, the player who moves the human is also trapped. The final stanza offers this as the final twist to this metaphoric chain. "God moves the player, and they, the piece. / What God behind God begins the plot[78] / of dust and time and dream and death?"[79]

Jaime Alazraki has already connected this poem to Borges's interest in the figure of the Golem and associated the chess player with a "golem-maker [that] is a mere link in a long golem-making chain."[80] And indeed, it is useful now to return our attention to Borges's poem "The Golem," written in 1958.[81] We have already discussed this poem for its mention of Scholem. What has not yet been noted are its echoes of Browning's poem and of this metaphor for writing that Borges develops from reading Buber. In the final three stanzas of the poem, Borges introduces a twist similar to the ending of "Ajedrez."

> The Rabbi watched it with tenderness
> And with some horror. *How* (he said)
> *Could I have engendered this pitiful child*
> *And given up inaction, which made good sense?*
>
> *Why did I add to the infinite*
> *Series one symbol more? Why to the futile*
> *Skein that winds in eternity,*
> *Did I add more cause, effect and grief?*[82]

The first of these stanzas introduces the rabbi's gaze as it falls on the Golem. The poem then transitions to an internal monologue, set apart from the rest of the poem by the use of italics. It is an internal monologue of regret for creating the creature. When the internal monologue ends, the reader is no longer viewing the Golem through the rabbi's eyes. The gaze of the rabbi has been replaced with the gaze of God on the rabbi. This is not revealed to the reader until the last two lines of the stanza. The poem even prolongs the reader's ignorance of the shift by referring to the rabbi as "his Golem." The internal monologue divides between the rabbi's gaze in the previous stanza and God's gaze in the following. But it is the overlapping nature of this monologue, and its application to both sets of creator-Golem couples, that most closely anticipates the twist at the end of "Ajedrez."

> In the hour of anguish and dim light,
> Upon his Golem his eyes fell.
> Who will tell us the emotions felt
> By God, watching his rabbi in Prague?[83]

The closing lines of the poem juxtapose the relation between the rabbi and his Golem with the relation between God and the rabbi. The resonance of the rabbi's doubt and regret in God's gaze is the surprising twist that concludes the poem. Structurally, this chain is similar to the chain in the poem "Ajedrez," where the human moves the pawn, God moves the human, and the poem concludes by asking how far the chain extends. Is there a god behind the god that moves the player? This same chain may be familiar to readers from Borges's 1940 story "The Circular Ruins," where a similar conceit is developed between the magician who creates a dream child out of dirt, a Golem, and the divinity that has granted the magician such powers of creation. The story ends with the magician realizing he himself is a Golem of the god, a link in a chain of Golem-gods.

The introduction of the game element into this chain in "Ajedrez" is an echo of Buber's strange room of the spirit. The human player sees themselves reflected in the pawn trapped on the board upon which a game with unknown rules is being played. What I want to highlight is the similar conceit at the end of the poem "The Golem," which suggests that there is an echo of Buber in this poem as well. This poem has received attention for its Kabbalistic topic, its mention of Scholem, and the recurrent theme of the Golem in Borges's work. As we have discussed, Borges discovered the Golem and Buber around the same years in Geneva, and it is through Buber's writing that the Golem is integrated into a metaphor for writing. The image of the Golem as a metaphor for the written text, which has already been noted by Borges scholars, adds to the richness of the image of the author as emblematic resident of Buber's strange room of the spirit.[84]

Around the same time that Scholem's name first appears in Borges's writing, in the 1958 poem, references to Buber become less frequent in Borges's texts. We have already seen Borges mention reading Buber in his 1966 letter to David Ben Gurion and a few months later in his comments on Agnon.[85] Borges returns to the image of "A man . . . who spoke with God on a mountaintop" in his 1967 poem "Israel."[86] And again to the evasive answer "I Am that I Am" in his 1977 poem "The Thing I Am," where he recalls Buber's interpretation in a note.[87] Although such continuities persist, they do not represent a shift in Borges's understanding of Buber nor in this metaphor for authorship. The major engagement with Buber took place over about a decade, between 1946 and 1955. These were the years that Borges was most concerned with the question of literary tradition and was reorienting his thought, apace with developments in the postwar attitudes of Argentine nationalists and the broader postcolonial moment. The engagement with Buber has a central role, beyond rethinking the role of the author, in reconceiving the metaphor for authorship. From the god of the Kabbalists challenging the banal narratives of the Germanophiles, the author has become the isolated player writing a tradition from within the strange room of the spirit.

I wanted to end the final chapter of this book by returning to the Golem, to close the literary circle, as it were, from Kabbalah, through tradition, to authorship. And thus to highlight that articulating a conception of authorship—socially, poetically, metaphorically—was a constant and evolving effort in Borges's thought and writing. This effort frames our reading of Borges's engagement with Kabbalah, Jewish tradition, and Buber, producing an idiosyncratic notion of the Judaic. The developments in this engagement, constantly constructing and deconstructing this very same Judaic, lead us finally to a conclusion that goes beyond the vicissitudes of blood, as Borges would put it. "The Judaic" is imagined in order to answer a question about writing, which is also a question about Borges—God of the Kabbalists, conspiracy theorist, emblematic resident of the strange room of the spirit, player of this intellectual game, partner to a one-sided dialogue—that is, about authorship.

Conclusion

Borges and His
Kafkaesque Precursors

"Perhaps universal history is the history of the diverse intonation of a few metaphors," Borges suggests in the final line of his 1951 essay "Pascal's Sphere."[1] Reading Borges's Judaic imaginaries has been a project in tracking the diverse intonation of a few metaphors for authorship. One central insight the current project strives to offer the field of Borges studies is that this diversity is instructive and the methodological engagement it elicits is productive in reading Borges's texts. Scholarship sometimes takes "Borges" (a proxy for his oeuvre) as a fixed set of coherent, recurring, or recursive metaphors, studying with an Aleph-like gaze the way labyrinths, mirrors, circular time, Kabbalah, and the Judaic proliferate in his writing. While this attitude has been very productive in scholarship, I have shown that Borges himself was implicated in suggesting and promoting this interpretive practice. To the extent that Borges has succeeded in eliciting the Kabbalist or conspiracy theorist within us, he has succeeded at his effort to approximate the god of the Kabbalists.

Nonetheless, the bold observation with which Borges concludes his essay about Kafka—"The first Kafka . . . is less a precursor of the [later Kafka] than is Browning"[2]—should suggest to us a question about our reading of Borges's

"

own authorial activity. The god of the Kabbalists may have delivered Scripture all at once in a single event, but Borges the human approximating divinity did not. There is a dimension to Borges's writerly project that is fleeting, contextual, historicized, and which can be read with equal discernment as a progression of shifting positions. Drawing out this dimension has been the project of the current book.

This does not diminish the persistence with which Borges was concerned with questions about authorship and literature. Nor does it obfuscate our view of his writing as an ongoing effort to answer these questions. It only makes clearer and more nuanced our understanding of his writing as an effort to think and rethink his view of the intellectual author, to intone and re-intone its metaphors. One such example we have followed throughout this book is that of divinity as an author, whom Borges wishes to approximate. This metaphor remains constant throughout his writing, even as the intonations of divinity change from the god of the Kabbalists in "A Vindication of the Kabbalah," to the deficient and conspiratorial divinity of his anti-Nazi polemics, to the delinquent pen pal that is the god of Browning, and to Buber's god beyond the game that plays with humans as chess pieces.

Writing as a game is another example of such metaphorical variations. The ambiguity of the interlocutor, addressee, referent—this is the condition of writing that Buber conceptualizes for Borges, basing himself on interpretations of the Hasidic movement and the dialogical nature of Jewish tradition. Borges takes this a step further in his quest for a productive position to occupy in his own search for a tradition. Writing is a game that produces tradition, a web of allusions, an ex post facto inheritance. The act of writing already generates innumerable, unlikely, and inexhaustible references to unknown precursors who deterministically emerge as such in the moment of writing. Writing from within Buber's "strange room of the spirit," not knowing the rules of this game, which oblige one to make reference to something outside this space without understanding the effects of such allusion—at one moment creating a precursor, at another causing the emperor to cancel his edict—this is how one begins to write a tradition.[3] But more fundamental still, this is the position of the intellectual author. The game of chess, the game of the intellectual author, the game of inheritance, these are all intonations of Borges's metaphor for the authorial creation of literary tradition.

In "Kafka and His Precursors," Borges describes the idiosyncratic group of precursors that emerge as Kafka's ex post facto tradition. In so doing, he is also certainly casting Kafka as his own precursor. After all, what do Browning, Kafka, Veblen, Scholem, Eliot, Buber, Mallea, and Agnon have in common? To paraphrase Borges: "If I am not mistaken, the heterogenous pieces I have listed resemble [Borges]; if I am not mistaken, not all of them resemble each other. This last fact is what is most significant."[4] They are Borges's Kafkaesque precursors.

A Sidenote on Another Precursor

There is another precursor that has gone unmentioned in this study. One that stands at the beginning of Buber's own thought, informing his appreciation of the Hasidic movement and inspiring his efforts toward a Jewish cultural renaissance. It is Nachman of Braslav, the early-nineteenth-century writer and Hasidic leader, whom Buber engaged as early as his 1906 *Die Geschichten des Rabbi Nachman*.[5] In this book, Buber describes Nachman as a figure who "stands at the end of an unbroken tradition."[6] The paradoxical nature of this location—unbroken, at the end—serves Buber to articulate the distance between himself and his contemporaries, on one side of a break from tradition and, on the other side, the traditions of Hasidism and the tales of Nachman. For Buber, it is a break that he seeks to overcome in his own moment through his own conceptualization of tradition.

Reading Borges (in Eliot's historical sense) retroactively alters the significance of his own precursors. Borges helps us recognize that tradition itself is neither stable nor invented. It materializes ex post facto, deterministically altering the historical significance of its past moments. Buber citing Nachman and Borges citing Buber are links in a chain of one-sided dialogue. I return to this chain at the end of my own study full of Borges citations in order to highlight another tradition—the tradition of seeing the Judaic as essentially a literary category. In the same years when Jean-Paul Sartre argued that antisemitism produces "the Jew," we have seen Borges propose an alternate view—literature produces "the Judaic."[7]

Relying on Buber for his path toward this literary argument, Borges highlights the proximity of Buber and Nachman, even while Buber himself saw his own location as radically disconnected from Nachman. I have explored this relation in my book *A Permanent Beginning: R. Nachman of Braslav and Jewish Literary Modernity*.[8] I raise the issue here again as an opportunity to close the loop on an argument that began in my 2016 dissertation about Borges and Nachman.[9] While this argument has now been published in separate books, I want to acknowledge (or create) its relation to these precursors. My analysis of Nachman's writing is the precursor to this book on Borges and the Judaic. Nachman inspires our reading of Borges by raising a question about tradition and its discontinuities, as much as Borges suggests a reading of Jewish literature as the ex post facto creation of tradition.

This concept of tradition has motivated my reading of Borges and the Judaic. To the extent that our reading has been able to shift focus from the Jew to the Judaic, it offers a way to broaden the nexus between literary studies and Jewish studies. Recognizing the literary production of Jewish tradition should force us to rethink the category of Jewish literature. In a very real historical sense, ex post facto, Borges is writing Jewish literature.

Jewish Literature after Borges

In this book I have held the line firmly separating the Jew of historical studies from the Judaic of Borges's imaginary. I have insisted on shifting focus away from questions of accuracy toward questions of aesthetics. What then might this study contribute to the field of Jewish studies? After all, Borges's reading of Veblen has little to do with those debates about Jewish emancipation and nationalism that Veblen was engaged with, for example. Nor has Borges's understanding of Zionism and Jewish tradition become a touchpoint for Jewish social history. What implications might this study purport to have for those debates? The questions we encounter, if we step beyond the line that separates the Jew from the Judaic, are literary by nature.

The first question would be about Borges's attitude toward Jewish Argentine letters, and Jewish Latin American letters more broadly. For instance, when Borges extols his friend the prominent Jewish Argentine author Alberto Gerchunoff (1883–1950) as a Jewish writer, he forgives a great deal of local color in Gerchunoff's work.[10] Gerchunoff's famous book *Los gauchos judíos* (The Jewish Gauchos) is full of local color—both Jewish and Argentine—of the kind Borges argued against in his 1951 lecture.[11] In Borges's eulogy for Gerchunoff, published the same year as "The Argentine Writer and Tradition," he ignores the famous Jewish gauchos. Instead, Borges focuses on Gerchunoff's interest in Cervantes and even compares Gerchunoff to Cervantes.[12] His reading of Gerchunoff helps frame the question: When a Jewish Latin American author utilizes Latin American local color, does that align the author with the nationalists or is it another example of irreverent engagement with non-Jewish cultures—of the kind Veblen celebrates and Borges wants to counterpose to the Argentine cult of local color?

"Jewish gauchos never existed," says Santiago Fischbein in Borges's story "El indigno," soon after renouncing Zionism.[13] Borges's attitude toward both Israeli literature and Jewish Latin American letters is not fully articulated. This makes such questions a productive place to identify the limits of Borges's conceptualization of tradition. More generally, it allows us to go back to the off-balance analogy we have seen Borges structure and formulate a broader question about diaspora and nationalism as perhaps diverse intonations of a similar metaphor for Jewish literature.

Beyond Latin America, if this study of Borges's Judaic imaginary is useful to Jewish studies more broadly, it is in another way. Studies of Jewish literature after Borges sometimes take his idiosyncratic Judaic as a model for understanding Jewish literature, and literature more broadly. He is juxtaposed with Kafka, Nachman of Braslav, Agnon, and others, and embraced by "Hebraist" literary critics like Harold Bloom, Geoffrey Hartman, and George Steiner. Although I have argued that his reasons for doing so were local and contextual, Borges consciously interpolates himself into Jewish literature. Provoked by Borges's own mentions of his dubious Jewishness, of Scholem and Kabbalah, his readers delight in being the Kabbalists to his approximation of divinity. These readerly practices interpretatively produce in Borges's writing a legibility as Jewish literature. In so doing, they not only challenge the boundaries of Argentine literature, but also push the delimitation of Jewish writing toward the horizon of world literature. Borges's reception by scholars of Jewish letters has made him a precursor of Jewish literary modernity. That past has already been altered.

Notes

Introduction

1   Jorge Luis Borges, *Selected Non-fictions*, trans. Eliot Weinberger (New York: Viking, 1999), 110.
2   Quoted in Ronald Christ, "Jorge Luis Borges, The Art of Fiction No. 39," *The Paris Review* 40 (1967), 162. All translations are my own unless otherwise noted.
3   Lisa Block de Behar, "Antecedents of an Unexpected Poetic Affinity: Jorge Luis Borges as Reader of Martin Buber," in *Thinking with Borges*, ed. William Egginton and David E. Johnson (Aurora, CO: The Davies Group, 2009), 185.
4   See Ricardo Piglia, "Ideología y ficción en Borges," *Punto de Vista* 2, no. 5 (1979).
5   Jorge Luis Borges, *Obras completas, 1923–1972* (Buenos Aires: Emecé, 1976), 86.
6   For a comprehensive history of Borges's British family, see Martín Hadis, *Literatos y excéntricos: los ancestros ingleses de Jorge Luis Borges* (Buenos Aires, Argentina: Editorial Sudamericana, 2006).
7   Jorge Luis Borges, *The Aleph and Other Stories 1933–1969*, ed. and trans. Norman Thomas Di Giovanni (New York: Bantam, 1971), 203–260.
8   Piglia, "Ideología y ficción en Borges," 3.
9   Beatriz Sarlo, *Jorge Luis Borges: A Writer on the Edge* (London: Verso, 1993), 47.
10 Dalia Wassner, "The Salience and Pervasiveness of the Literary Figure of the Jew in Latin America: From Sor Juana Inés de la Cruz to Jorge Luis Borges," *Latin American Research Review* 54, no. 2 (2019): 398.
11 Erin Graff Zivin, *The Wandering Signifier: Rhetoric of Jewishness in the Latin American Imaginary* (Durham, NC: Duke University Press, 2008).
12 Mariano Siskind, *Cosmopolitan Desires: Global Modernity and World Literature in Latin America* (Evanston, IL: Northwestern University Press, 2014), 8.
13 Jorge Luis Borges, *El tamaño de mi esperanza* (Buenos Aires, Argentina: Editorial Proa, 1926).
14 Borges, *Selected Non-fictions*, 17. Borges is referring to Erich Bischoff, *Die Elemente der Kabbalah* (Berlin: H. Barsdorf, 1913); and John Peter Stehelin, *The Traditions of the Jews; With the Expositions and Doctrines of the Rabbins, Contained in the Talmud and other Rabbinical Writings. Translated from the Hight Dutch* (London, 1732).

15 Johann Andreas Eisenmenger, *Endecktes Judenthum, oder: Grundlicher und wahrhaffter Bericht [. . .]*, 2 vols. (Frankfurt am Main, Germany: J. P. Andreae, 1700).

16 Stehelin, *The Traditions of the Jews*, a1–a2.

17 Jaime Alazraki, "Conversación con Borges sobre la Cábala: Entrevista inédita de 1971," *Variaciones Borges* 3 (1997): 167.

18 Examples are previous generations of Kabbalah scholars, whom Scholem clearly desired to break with, such as Bischoff (mentioned above), as well as contemporary scholars such as Joshua Trachtenberg (whom Borges also mentions, in Christ, "Jorge Luis Borges, The Art of Fiction No. 39"). See Joshua Trachtenberg, *Jewish Magic and Superstition: A Study in Folk Religion* (New York: Behrman's Jewish Book House, 1939). For a survey of the sources Borges mentions, see Saul Sosnowski, *Borges y la cábala: la búsqueda del verbo* (Buenos Aires, Argentina: Ed. Hispamérica, 1976), 13–15. For more on the differences between Scholem and previous generations of Kabbalah scholars, see Scholem's own reflections in Gershom Scholem, "The Science of Judaism—Then and Now," in *The Messianic Idea in Judaism* (New York: Schocken Books, 1995); and a discussion of this essay in David Biale, *Gershom Scholem: Kabbalah and Counter-History* (Cambridge, MA: Harvard University Press, 1979).

19 See Edna Aizenberg, "A 21st Century Note on Borges's Kabbalism," *Variaciones Borges* 39 (2015): 55–56. Aizenberg refers to Borges's essay "Partial Magic in the Quixote"; see Jorge Luis Borges, *Labyrinths: Selected Stories and Other Writings*, ed. James East Irby, André Maurois, and Donald Yates (New York: New Directions, 1964), 185–187.

20 For an example of the debate between Scholem and Buber, see Gershom Scholem, "Martin Buber's Hasidism," *Commentary Magazine*, 1961. For a study of this debate, see Claire E. Sufrin, "On Myth, History, and the Study of Hasidism: Martin Buber and Gershom Scholem," in *Encountering the Medieval in Modern Jewish Thought*, ed. James A. Diamond and Aaron W. Hughes (Leiden, the Netherlands: Brill, 2012).

21 Aizenberg, "A 21st Century Note on Borges's Kabbalism," 53.

22 For more on the Christian Hebraist strategy, in the context of the Reformation, of basing the authority of their contemporary social and political claims on the authenticity of the Hebrew sources they drew upon, see Eric Nelson, *The Hebrew Republic: Jewish Sources and the Tranformation of European Political Thought* (Cambridge, MA: Harvard University Press, 2011). For the sociocultural negotiations, enabled by claims to the authenticity of Hebrew texts, in the context of the Counter-Reformation, see Amnon Raz-Krakotzkin, *The Censor, the Editor, and the Text: The Catholic Church and the Shaping of the Jewish Canon in the Sixteenth Century, Jewish Culture and Contexts* (Philadelphia: University of Pennsylvania Press, 2007).

23 Jorge Luis Borges, *A Personal Anthology*, ed. Anthony Kerrigan (New York: Grove Press, 1967), ix–x.

24 I am referring to the well-known essay Roland Barthes, "The Death of the Author," trans. Stephen Heath, in *Image, Music, Text* (New York: Hill & Wang, 1978).

25 See the influential article William K. Wimsatt and M. C. Beardsley, "The Intentional Fallacy," *The Sewanee Review* 54, no. 3 (1946). Conversely, Borges exhibits this practice in his own engagement with the texts he reads. Emir Rodríguez Monegal advances the idea that Borges pretends to read even as he in fact writes ("Borges and Derrida: Apothecaries," in *Borges and His Successors: The*

Borgesian Impact on Literature and the Arts, ed. Edna Aizenberg [Columbia: University of Missouri Press, 1990]). For a broader account of Borges's reading practices, see Emir Rodríguez Monegal, *Jorge Luis Borges: A Literary Biography* (New York: Dutton, 1978).

26 Barthes, "The Death of the Author," 147.

27 In the present discussion of the Judaic in Borges, I will leave Scripture to the side for reasons outlined here briefly. Of all the Jewish texts Borges read, this was the least mediated. It was available to him in translation—many translations, in fact, as he collected Bibles and particularly enjoyed the comparative study of the various translations. There is thus less confusion as to what it was that made Scripture so Jewish in Borges's eyes. There was also plenty that made it Christian in his eyes, not least the many Christian translations he read, and the fact that "the Bible" refers, for him, to both the Hebrew Bible and the New Testament. This is also evident in the choice of themes Borges revisits as biblical—Cain and Abel, Adam and Jesus, Job, Judas—which exhibit the Christian elements he takes up.

　　As far as biblical interpretation, or the tradition of taking up biblical themes in literature, Borges's main referents were writers such as Dante and Milton, not Rashi or Abarbanel. The reader interested in the influence of Scripture on Borges's thought and writing may consult Aizenberg's work: Edna Aizenberg, *Borges, el tejedor del Aleph y otros ensayos: del hebraísmo al poscolonialismo* (Frankfurt am Maim, Germany: Vervuert, Iberoamericana, 1997); as well as the discussion of biblical themes in Borges's writing in Gonzalo Salvador, *Borges y la Biblia* (Madrid, Spain: Iberoamericana and Vervuert, 2011). For a discussion of the role of Scripture in twentieth-century Argentine literature more broadly, see Lucas Martín Adur Nobile, "Borges y el Cristianismo: Posiciones, Diálogos y Polémicas" (PhD dissertation, UBA, 2013); and Lucas Martín Adur Nobile, "Las biblias de Borges," *Variaciones Borges* 41 (2016).

28 Edna Aizenberg, "Borges, Postcolonial Precursor," *World Literature Today* 66, no. 1 (1992).

29 For a recent publication of Borges's drafts, see Daniel Balderston, *How Borges Wrote* (Charlottesville: University of Virginia Press, 2018). For a recent publication of his marginalia, see Laura Rosato and Germán Álvarez, eds., *Borges, libros y lecturas: catálogo de la colección Jorge Luis Borges en la Biblioteca Nacional* (Buenos Aires, Argentina: Ediciones Biblioteca Nacional, 2010). Borges's published lectures include Jorge Luis Borges, *This Craft of Verse*, The Charles Eliot Norton lectures, ed. Calin-Andrei Mihailescu (Cambridge, MA: Harvard University Press, 2000).

30 See Sosnowski, *Borges y la cábala*; Jaime Alazraki, "Kabbalistic Traits in Borges' Narration," *Studies in Short Fiction* 8, no. 1 (1971); Daniel Nahson, *La crítica del mito: Borges y la literatura como sueño de vida* (Madrid, Spain: Iberoamericana, Vervuert, 2009); as well as Shlomy Mualem, *Poets of the Ein-Sof: Borges and the Literature of Kabbalah* (Tel Aviv, Israel: Idra, 2019).

31 Jorge Luis Borges, "The God's Script," trans. L. A. Murillo, *Chicago Review* 17, no. 1 (1964): 7. Emphasis in the original.

Chapter 1　Kabbalistic Stories

1 I have discussed my intentional use of the term "allusion" in the introduction. As will become clear in the coming chapters, when we read Borges's poetic uses of the

Kabbalah, of Scholem, and of what in the next part will be termed "the Judaic,"
I use this word to describe a way of incorporating these elements into Borges's
writing that is primarily poetically motivated. It is therefore simplistic to call the
appearance of the Kabbalah or Scholem in Borges's stories a "reference," and it is
misleading to attribute to these appearances a bibliographic value. My hesitancy
regarding overdetermined Kabbalistic readings of literature has already been
expressed in my previous work, where I caution against the allegorical reading
of Kabbalistic content in literature and demonstrate the ways such a reading
obfuscates the poetic decisions made by the author. See Yitzhak Lewis,
A Permanent Beginning: R. Nachman of Braslav and Jewish Literary Modernity
(Albany: State University of New York Press, 2020), ch. 6.

2   Borges scholarship more readily deploys other adjectives, such as "irreal" and
"marginal." See Ana María Barrenechea, *La expresión de la irrealidad en la obra de
Jorge Luis Borges y otros ensayos* (Buenos Aires, Argentina: Ediciones del Cifrado,
1957); and Beatriz Sarlo, *Borges, un escritor en las orillas* (Buenos Aires, Argentina:
Ariel, 1995). "Kabbalistic" is a fruitful, if less utilized—and less questioned—
adjective, through which to examine Borges's writing.

3   Borges was not the only author who received this mystical valuation from critics at
the time. Nor is he the only author whose Kabbalism remains ill-defined. Another
writer who might come to mind in the context of Kabbalistic stories is Franz
Kafka, whose relation to the Kabbalah is raised in Gershom Scholem, *Zehn
unhistorische Sätze über Kabbala* (Zurich, Switzerland: Rhein-Verlag, 1958), Satz 10.
Commentators, however, have been doubtful as to its significance. David Biale
remarks that "Scholem's relationship to Franz Kafka as an unwitting product of a
'heretical Kabbalah' deserves an essay in its own right for *what it tells us about
Scholem himself*" ("Gershom Scholem's Ten Unhistorical Aphorisms on Kabbalah:
Text and Commentary," *Modern Judaism* 5, no. 1 [1985]. Emphasis added).

Moshe Idel, in a later article, spells out "what it tells us about Scholem himself,"
stating: "I would say that a vision of Kafka as representative of a secularized
Kabbalah is based upon a comparison of things that are incomparable. . . . Not too
much of Kabbalah is found in Kafka. . . . Much more of Kafka is found, however,
in Scholem's own understanding of Kabbalah" ("Hieroglyphs, Keys, Enigmas:
On G.G. Scholem's Vision of Kabbalah: Between Franz Molitor and Franz
Kafka," in *Arche Noah: die Idee der "Kultur" im deutsch-jüdischen Diskurs*, ed.
Bernhard Greiner and Christoph Schmidt [Freiburg, Germany: Rombach Verlag,
2002], 242). Biale, in the cited article, also implies a broader application of Idel's
insight, asking whether we might think of the modern philosophical categories
Scholem mentions in these aphorisms as models, through which he understood
the Kabbalists he studied. "Scholem boldly suggests parallels between modern
schools of thought and the Kabbalah: dialectical materialism and the Lurianic
Kabbalah, phenomenology and Moses Cordovero, Franz Kafka and the eighteenth
century Frankist, Jonas Wehle" (Biale, "Gershom Scholem's Ten Unhistorical
Aphorisms on Kabbalah," 67–68). For another interpretation of Scholem's "Ten
Unhistorical Aphorisms," see Joseph Dan, "Beyond the Kabbalistic Symbol,"
Jerusalem Studies in Jewish Thought 5 (1986).

Discussions of Borges's Kabbalistic stories lack the kind of ad hominem
dimension cited above. Much of the writing on Kafka and the Kabbalah takes
Scholem's observations on the matter as their starting point. See, for example,
Karl-Erich Grözinger, *Kafka and Kabbalah*, trans. Susan Hecker Ray (New York:

Continuum, 1994), 1–2. Or they offer an understanding of the Kabbalah that is already deeply indebted to an understanding of Kafka that is itself found, as Idel puts it, "in Scholem's own understanding of the Kabbalah." See, for example, the definition of Kabbalah offered by Walter Strauss. "The historical Kabbalah was intended to be a secret key to a revelation whose power . . . had already begun to weaken," he asserts in Walter A. Strauss, *On the Threshold of a New Kabbalah: Kafka's Later Tales* (New York: Peter Lang, 1988), 3. Idel, in the article referenced above, offers a critique of the metaphor of the Kabbalah as a "key," in Scholem's understanding of Kabbalah ("Hieroglyphs, Keys, Enigmas," 234–241).

Of course, the majority of scholarship on Kafka does not deal with the Kabbalistic question, even within the field of Jewish literature. See, for example, Dan Miron, *From Continuity to Contiguity: Toward a New Jewish Literary Thinking* (Stanford, CA: Stanford University Press, 2010), ch. 10–11; and Dan Miron, *The Animal in the Synagogue: Franz Kafka's Jewishness*, trans. Yitzhak Lewis, (Lanham, MD: Lexington Books, 2019). At any rate, the entanglement of Scholem and Kafka in these discussions raises methodological questions that are, as will become clear, not the ones I am dealing with here.

4 Jaime Alazraki, "Borges and the Kabbalah," *TriQuarterly* 25 (1972): 241.

5 Alazraki, "Borges and the Kabbalah," 241.

6 Alazraki, "Kabbalistic Traits in Borges' Narration," 78.

7 Saul Sosnowski, "El verbo cabalístico en la obra de Borges," *Hispamérica* 3, no. 9 (1975): 37.

8 Sosnowski, "El verbo cabalístico en la obra de Borges," 37.

9 This is evident in the references provided and the assumptions made about the textuality and canonicity of the Kabbalah, as well as a heavy reliance on Scholem in citations offered by Alazraki, Sosnowski, and others. The impact of Scholem on the study of Borges and the Kabbalah will be a recurring subject of this part.

10 Borges, "The God's Script."

11 See Saul Sosnowski, "'The God's Script'–A Kabbalistic Quest," *Modern Fiction Studies* 19, no. 3 (1973).

12 For a study of Borges that focuses on his allusive practices, see Ronald J. Christ, *The Narrow Act: Borges' Art of Allusion* (New York: New York University Press, 1969). And see also Evelyn Fishburn, "Hidden Pleasures in Borges's Allusions," in *Borges and Europe Revisited*, ed. Evelyn Fishburn (London: Institute of Latin American Studies, University of London, 1998).

13 Didier T. Jaén, *Borges' Esoteric Library: Metaphysics to Metafiction* (Lanham, MD: University Press of America, 1992), xvii.

14 Aizenberg, *Borges, el tejedor del Aleph y otros ensayos*, 65, ff.1.

15 Alazraki, "Borges and the Kabbalah," 242.

16 Borges, *Labyrinths: Selected Stories and & Other Writings*, 85–94.

17 Gershom Scholem, *Major Trends in Jewish Mysticism* (New York: Schocken Books, 1995), 3.

18 It is hard to find a single citation of a Kabbalistic text in any of the existing work on Borges and Kabbalah that is not cited as "Quoted by Scholem in . . ." Consider, for instance, that references to Scholem take up twenty-nine out of sixty-five footnotes in Alazraki's article "Borges and the Kabbalah," one of the groundbreaking works on the topic. Similarly, the two writers most widely referred to by Sosnowski are Borges and Scholem, each receiving an equal number of eleven bibliographic entries in his book: Sosnowski, *Borges y la cábala*.

19 Sosnowski, *Borges y la cábala*, 13.

20 Jaime Alazraki, *Borges and the Kabbalah: And Other Essays on his Fiction and Poetry* (New York: Cambridge University Press, 1988), 11.

21 See, for example, Sosnowski's detailed analysis of Borges's story "The God's Script" in Sosnowski, *Borges y la cábala*, 62–72.

22 Saul Sosnowski has made a similar observation with regard to the way Borges incorporates historical events and dates, thereby rendering the vocabulary of "certainty" and "veracity" as ways of aesthetically shaping his literary tropes. See Saul Sosnowski, "'Tlon, Uqbar, Orbis Tertius': Historia y desplazamientos," in *The Contemporary Latin American Short Story*, ed. Rose S. Minc (New York: Senda Nueva, 1979).

23 These are the parameters Scholem lays out already in the opening chapter of *Major Trends in Jewish Mysticism*, and which have been discussed and analyzed by David Biale, Joseph Dan, and others. See, for example, Biale, *Gershom Scholem*; Joseph Dan, *Al Gershom Shalom: Teresar Ma'amarim* (Jerusalem, Israel: Merkaz Zalman Shazar le-Toldot Yisrael, 2010); Paul Mendes-Flohr, *Gershom Scholem: The Man and his Work* (Albany, NY: SUNY Press and The Israel Academy of Sciences and Humanities, 1994).

24 Virginia Gutierrez Berner, "Mystical Laws: Borges and Kabbalah," *CR: The New Centennial Review* 9, no. 3 (2010): 137–138.

25 Gutierrez Berner, "Mystical Laws," 139.

26 Alazraki, "Kabbalistic Traits in Borges' Narration," 78.

27 The reader to whom this may seem an overgeneralization is invited to search any of the bibliographic references cited here for an example to the contrary. Though citations include numerous references to the works of major researchers in the field, as well as to several younger scholars, the reader will find this generalization is something of an "industry standard." Sosnowski is unique in quoting more extensively from traditional Jewish texts (especially the Talmud), but the structure of presenting stories by Borges alongside doctrinal texts of Kabbalah, cited as they appear in Scholem, still holds.

28 Gutierrez Berner, "Mystical Laws," 138. Borges encountered the figures of Abulafia and Cordovero in the fourth chapter and in the fifth and sixth chapters, respectively, of Scholem, *Major Trends in Jewish Mysticism*. Scholem's seems to be the first book Borges mentions reading on the Kabbalah that mentions these figures in any detail.

29 Scholem, *Major Trends in Jewish Mysticism*, 20.

30 Borges, *Selected Non-fictions*, 210–211.

31 Sosnowski, "El verbo cabalístico en la obra de Borges," 36.

32 Borges's reception in France and his influence on many of the major postwar French intellectuals is a fascinating topic but well beyond the present scope. For the early article on Borges and the Kabbalah, see Rabi, "Fascination de la Kabbale," *L'Herne* (1964). This article appeared in a special edition of *L'Herne* that compiled translations of Borges's texts and interviews alongside critical evaluations of his work. There is also a chapter titled "Borges y la Cábala, o el escritor frente a la palabra" in José Isaacson, *El poeta en la sociedad de masas; elementos para una antropología literaria*, Nueva biblioteca de cultura social (Buenos Aires, Argentina: Editorial Américalee, 1969). This chapter offers a Kabbalistic reading of Borges's writing rather than an analysis of the theme of Kabbalah in his work.

In that sense it is outside of the present considerations. However, the proximity of this publication to Borges's visit to the State of Israel still supports the argument that it was the encounter with Scholem that generated an interest in Borges and the Kabbalah in the first place.

33 Evelyn Fishburn, "Borges, Cabbala and 'Creative Misreading,'" *Ibero-Amerikanisches Archiv* 14, no. 4 (1988): 407.

34 Borges's own marginalia has been published in Rosato and Álvarez, *Borges, libros y lecturas: catálogo de la colección Jorge Luis Borges en la Biblioteca Nacional*. Some of his drafts and notes have been published in Balderston, *How Borges Wrote*.

35 An example of the former can be seen in the articles by Alazraki quoted throughout this chapter. An example of the latter can be found in Mualem, *Poets of the Ein-Sof: Borges and the Literature of Kabbalah*.

36 The juxtaposition of Borges's and Scholem's writings is a productive one in scholarship on literature, mysticism, and philosophy. In particular, this juxtaposition has helped raise important questions about the intellectual and literary limits of these genres. However, the success of this comparison in raising such questions is often extended into an argument about intellectual-historical causality, an influence that is simply unsupported by intellectual-historical record.

37 See Jorge Luis Borges, *Discusión* (Buenos Aires, Argentina: M. Gleizer, 1932); Jorge Luis Borges, *Ficciones, 1935–1944* (Buenos Aires, Argentina: Sur, 1944); Jorge Luis Borges, *El Aleph* (Buenos Aires, Argentina: Editorial Losada, 1949); Jorge Luis Borges, *Otras Inquisiciones* (Buenos Aires, Argentina: Sur, 1952).

38 Bischoff, *Die Elemente der Kabbalah*.

39 Both would also grow disillusioned with Buber later in their careers. The impact of Buber on Borges's thought and writing is the topic of the final chapter in this study.

40 See Scholem's account of this context and his commentary on it in his 1959 essay: Gershom Scholem, "The Science of Judaism—Then and Now," in *The Messianic Idea in Judaism* (New York: Schocken Books, 1995).

41 Originally published as "Una Vindicación de la Cábala." Translated as "A Defense of the Kabbalah" in Borges, *Selected Non-fictions*, 83–86.

42 See Christian D. Ginsburg, *The Kabbalah: Its Doctrines, Development, and Literature* (London: G. Routledge & Sons, 1920); Trachtenberg, *Jewish Magic and Superstition*; Gershom Scholem, *Major Trends in Jewish Mysticism: Based on the Hilda Strook Lectures Delivered at the Jewish Institute of Religion, New York* (New York: Schocken, 1941); S. L. MacGregor Mathers, *The Kabbalah Unveiled* (London: Routledge & Kegan Paul, 1957).

43 See Gershom Scholem, "Das Buch Bahir ein Schriftdenkmal aus der Frühzeit der Kabbala" (Aurinia, 1922); Gershom Scholem, "Rememption Through Sin," in *Messianic Idea in Judaism and Other Essays on Jewish Spirituality* (New York: Schocken Books, 1971).

44 Borges's 1941 story collection *The Garden of Forking Paths* was reprinted in its entirety as *Ficciones* in 1944, with the addition of other texts published in the interim. See Gershom Scholem, *Major Trends in Jewish Mysticism*; and Jorge Luis Borges, *El jardín de senderos que se bifurcan* (Buenos Aires, Argentina: Sur, 1941).

45 Published as "Historia de los ángeles" in Borges, *El tamaño de mi esperanza*. In this essay, Borges mentions John Peter Stehelin. The book he refers to is Stehelin,

The Traditions of the Jews. The origin and interest in this book was already discussed in the introduction.

46 Jorge Luis Borges, "Yo, Judío," *Megáfono*, no. 12 (April 1934).

47 Borges's copy was Martin Buber, *Vom Geist des Judentums* (Munich, Germany: Kurt Wolff Verlag, 1921). These notes appear in Rosato and Álvarez, *Borges, libros y lecturas.*

48 This volume is held in the "Fundacion Internacional Jorges Luis Borges," and I have a scan of the relevant pages.

49 Nahum N. Glatzer, *In Time and Eternity: A Jewish Reader* (New York: Schocken Books, 1946). The essay "On Chesterton" was originally published as Jorge Luis Borges, "Nota sobre Chesterton," *Los anales de Buenos Aires* 20–22 (1947).

50 The Sociedad Hebraica Argentina was formed in 1926, around the same years Borges returned to Argentina. For more on his activities in the 1920s, see Sarlo, *Jorge Luis Borges*; Graciela Montaldo, "Borges: una vanguardia criolla," in *Yrigoyen entre Borges y Arlt: 1916–1930*, ed. Graciela Montaldo (Buenos Aires, Argentina: Contrapunto, 1989).

51 An account of the twenty-fifth anniversary celebration, including Borges's remarks, appeared in the June 1951 bulletin of the Sociedad Hebraica Argentina. See *Boletin S.H.A.* 20, no. 338 (1951).

52 Glatzer's book was referenced in the essay "On Chesterton" (1947) as Borges's source on the *Zohar* and, in the same year, the *Zohar* was also mentioned in Borges's story "The Theologians" (1947).

53 See Jorge Luis Borges and Adolfo Bioy Casares, *Cuentos breves y extraordinarios (antologia)* (Buenos Aires, Argentina: Editorial Raigal, 1955); and Jorge Luis Borges and Margarita Guerrero, *Manual de zoología fantástica* (Mexico: Fondo de Cultura Económica, 1957).

54 I thank Professor Moshe Idel for drawing my attention to this early text by Scholem about the Golem. See Gershom Scholem, "Die Vorstellung des Golem in ihren tellurischen und magischen Beziehungen," *Eranos–Jahrbuch* 22 (1954). This early article would become the chapter "The Idea of the Golem" in Gershom Scholem, *On the Kabbalah and Its Symbolism* (New York: Schocken Books, 1965).

55 Maurice H. Harris, *Hebraic Literature: Translations from the Talmud, Midrashim and Kabbala* (New York: Tudor Publishing, 1944). For details of Borges's note, see Rosato and Álvarez, *Borges, libros y lecturas*, 182.

56 This poem is the only time Scholem is mentioned in any poem, story, or essay by Borges. As we will see, Borges mentions Scholem in lectures and interviews, many of which were collected and printed as well.

57 See Borges, *Obras completas, 1923–1972*, 886.

58 Alazraki, "Borges and the Kabbalah," 247–248.

59 Alazraki, "Borges and the Kabbalah," 248.

60 Scholem, *Major Trends in Jewish Mysticism*, 99.

61 Borges, *The Aleph and Other Stories 1933–1969*, 147.

62 See Scholem, "Die Vorstellung des Golem in ihren tellurischen und magischen Beziehungen."

63 Scholem reports this in a 1969 letter to John Hollander. See Gershom Scholem and John Hollander, Series 1: Correspondance: Hollander, John, 1969, ARC.4*

1599 01 1180, Gershom Gerhard Scholem Archive, The National Library of Israel, Jerusalem.

64 This volume is held at the Fundación Internacional Jorge Luis Borges, in Buenos Aires, Argentina.

Chapter 2   The Ideal Author

1 Block de Behar references recollections of Borges's lectures, where "people did not go to a lecture: they went to mass." See Block de Behar, "Antecedents of an Unexpected Poetic Affinity," 192.

2 See George Steiner, *After Babel: Aspects of Language and Translation* (London: Oxford University Press, 1975); Harold Bloom, *Kabbalah and Criticism* (New York: Seabury, 1975). Harold Bloom is an important figure to mention in the context of a relation between the 1970s identification of Borges's Kabbalistic stories and the broader understanding of Kabbalah as a mode of reading. See also Bloom's later notes on Borges in *Jorge Luis Borges* (New York: Chelsea House Publishers, 1986).

3 Alazraki, *Borges and the Kabbalah*, 9.

4 In the introduction to his book *Midrash and Literature*, Hartman grants Borges the rabbinic honorific "Reb Borges." See Geoffrey Hartman and Sanford Budick, eds., *Midrash and Literature* (New Haven, CT: Yale University Press, 1986), xi. In the same volume, the article by Myrna Solotorevsky demonstrates how a literary theorization of *Midrash* offers an interpretive lens for reading Borges. See Myrna Solotorevsky, "The Model of Midrash and Borges' Interpretative Tales and Essays," in *Midrash and Literature*, ed. Geoffrey Hartman and Sanford Budick (New Haven CT: Yale University Press, 1986). Aizenberg would push back, pointing out that Borges "anticipated and inspired" this theorization in the first place. See Aizenberg, *Borges, el tejedor del Aleph y otros ensayos*, 140.

5 Aizenberg, *Borges, el tejedor del Aleph y otros ensayos*, 140. Aizenberg is referring to Bloom's work cited above as well as the appearance of Borges in the introduction to Hartman and Budick, *Midrash and Literature*, and more generally to Borges's influence on the American school of Deconstruction and what she sees as its "Hebraic" influences.

6 See Borges, *Discusión*. This early collection was edited and published in a second edition in 1957, a few years after the publication of Borges's second essay collection. See Borges, *Otras Inquisiciones*.

7 Originally published in Borges, *Discusión*. See Borges, *Obras completas, 1923–1972*, 209–212. Translated as "A Defense of the Kabbalah" in Borges, *Selected Non-fictions*, 83–86. The Argentine context of Borges's thought is also evident in those years, as the editorial advertisement of the book promises in the same series forthcoming books by Eduardo Mallea, with whom Borges maintained an ongoing debate into the 1950s. More explicit references to Mallea will be given in subsequent chapters.

8 Originally published as Jorge Luis Borges, "La Cábala," *La Opinión*, 1977, and collected in Jorge Luis Borges, *Siete noches* (Mexico D.F.: Fondo de Cultura Economica, 1980). See Jorge Luis Borges, *Obras completas, 1975–1985* (Buenos Aires, Argentina: Emecé, 1989), 267–275. Translated as "The Kabbalah" in Jorge Luis Borges, *Seven Nights*, trans. Eliot Weinberger (New York: New Directions, 1984), 76–84.

9 Alazraki, "Kabbalistic Traits in Borges' Narration," 78–79.

10 Alazraki, "Kabbalistic Traits in Borges' Narration," 78.

11 Borges, *Selected Non-fictions*, 83. Emphasis added.

12 Borges, *Selected Non-fictions*, 83.

13 Cited in Alazraki, "Kabbalistic Traits in Borges' Narration," 78, ff.2. as "Gershom Scholem, *Major Trends, loc. cit.*"

14 The essay originally appeared in Borges, *Discusión*. It was revised for the second edition of this collection. See Jorge Luis Borges, *Discusión* (Buenos Aires, Argentina: Emecé Editores, 1957). This edition is also the first volume of Borges to include "The Argentine Writer and Tradition" (the central text we will discuss in the next part).

15 Borges, *Discusión*, 71–72. Emphasis added.

16 Borges, *Discusión*, 72.

17 Scholem, *Major Trends in Jewish Mysticism*, 100.

18 Borges, *Selected Non-fictions*, 83. Emphasis added.

19 Borges, *Selected Non-fictions*, 86.

20 Borges, *Discusión*, 71.

21 Borges, *Selected Non-fictions*, 84.

22 Borges, *Selected Non-fictions*, 85.

23 Borges, *Selected Non-fictions*, 85. Emphasis added.

24 Borges, *Selected Non-fictions*, 85.

25 Borges, *Selected Non-fictions*, 85.

26 Borges, *Selected Non-fictions*, 85.

27 I return here to the brief comment I made in the introduction regarding the death of the author. What Borges is appreciating and aspiring toward in this essay is to write a text that is infinitely interpretable, the interpretation of which will be entirely in the hands of each individual reader. This is how he understands the Kabbalists' attitude toward Scripture and their hermeneutical procedures. Writing in the 1930s, we might understand Borges as anticipating the argument in Roland Barthes's essay "The Death of the Author," depicting the readerly practice as generating the text's meaning, and the author's activity as what Barthes will call "the scriptor." At the same time, Borges ascribes this infinite interpretability of Scripture to the infinite intelligence of divinity. And he develops an image of the intellectual author as one aspiring to such intelligence. In this, he does not accord with Barthes's efforts to reduce the centrality of authorial intention within the act of reading. In that sense, Borges's position here may be better understood through its resonance in Edward W. Said's treatment of authorial intention in *Beginnings: Intention and Method* (New York: Basic Books, 1975). Said tries to walk the nuanced line between the inaccessibility of the author's intention and the fact that any work of literature is nonetheless a product of authorial intention. For Borges, authorial intention is completely accessible to the reader, because divinity-as-author has already intended every interpretation the reader may produce. We will see this come up in the representation of divinity as an author in "The God's Script" in chapter 3.

28 Borges, *Selected Non-fictions*, 85.

29 Alazraki, "Kabbalistic Traits in Borges' Narration," 92.

30 Edna Aizenberg, "'I, a Jew': Borges, Nazism and the Shoah," *Jewish Quarterly Review* 104, no. 3 (2014): 350.

31 For readings of the story in the context of Borges's polemics with Nazism, see Sosnowski, "'Tlon, Uqbar, Orbis Tertius': Historia y desplazamientos"; María

Díaz Pozueta, "From Philosophical Idealism to Political Ideology in 'Tlön, Uqbar, Orbis Tertius' and 'Deutsches Requiem'," *The New Centennial Review* 9, no. 2 (2009). And in the context of Argentine fascism, Annick Louis, *Borges ante el fascismo* (Bern, Switzerland: Peter Lang, 2007).

There are many other readings of this story. Examples include the following: In relation to mysticism, Jaén, *Borges' Esoteric Library*, ch. 9; in the context of debates about literary realism, Silvia Dapía, "'This Is Not a Universe': An Approach to Borges's 'Tlön, Uqbar, Orbis Tertius'," *Chasqui: revista de literatura latinoamericana* 26, no. 2 (1997); in the context of regionalist novels of the time, Roberto Gonzalez Echeverria, *Myth and Archive: A Theory of Latin American Narrative* (New York: Cambridge University Press, 1990), ch. 4. See also Iván Almeida and Cristina Parodi, eds., *El fragmento infinito: estudios sobre "Tlön, Uqbar, Orbis Tertius" de J. L. Borges*, 1st ed. (Zaragoza, Spain: Prensas Universitarias de Zaragoza, 2006).

32 Jorge Luis Borges, *Collected Fictions*, trans. Andrew Hurley (New York: Penguin Books, 1998), 72.

33 Borges, *Collected Fictions*, 69.

34 Borges, *Collected Fictions*, 74. Hurley translates "literatura fantástica" as "literature of fantasy."

35 Borges, *Collected Fictions*, 78.

36 Borges, *Collected Fictions*, 79. I depart slightly from Hurley's translation to maintain the original mood and emphasis on the creative activity of world-making.

37 Borges, *Selected Non-fictions*, 85.

38 Borges, *Selected Non-fictions*, 85.

39 Borges, *Collected Fictions*, 81.

40 Hurley has translated the word "idealistas" as "idealistic," but I keep the meaning closer to the Spanish intention of naming a philosophical school by translating it as "idealist."

41 Borges, *Collected Fictions*, 72. For discussions of this story in the context of philosophical idealism, see Pozueta, "From Philosophical Idealism to Political Ideology in 'Tlön, Uqbar, Orbis Tertius' and 'Deutsches Requiem'"; and Kleber Roberto Pirota, "This is the Universe: David Bohm, Borges and the Wholeness of the World in 'Tlon, Uqbar, Orbis Tertius'," *Variaciones Borges* 53 (2022).

42 Borges, *Collected Fictions*, 81. I translate the word "ceder" as "to cede," in keeping with the original sense.

43 Evelyn Fishburn, "Digging for Hrönir: A Second Reading of 'Tlön, Uqbar, Orbis Tertius'," *Variaciones Borges* 25 (2008): 54.

44 The story that creates its reality is an interpretive trope in Borges scholarship beyond his interest in Kabbalah. Jacques Rancière, for example, expresses this view as well, stating that: "Borges must bring off a special twist: the very working of fiction must produce the 'reality' it comes from, the circuit of experience by which the content of the story reveals itself to be anterior to the voice that narrates it." However, this trope has largely served to depoliticize Borges's stories. Rancière sees this "twist" as necessary, not for the grounding of fiction as anterior to politics, but precisely to free experience from its adherence to such "reality." Thus, the twist is necessary, in Rancière's argument, in order "to save both the power of invention peculiar to art and the impersonality that is its paradoxical complement." See Jacques Rancière, "Borges and French Disease," trans. Julie Rose, in *The Politics*

of Literature (Malden, MA: Polity Press, 2011), 142. For an early and influential decontextualizing reading of Borges, see Paul de Man, "A Modern Master," *The New York Review of Books* (November 19, 1964).

45 Borges, *Collected Fictions*, 80.

46 Ricardo Piglia, "Teoría del complot," *Ramona: revista de artes visuales* 23 (2002).

47 Jorge Luis Borges, "Anotación al 23 de Agosto de 1944," *Sur* No. 120 (1944). See Borges, *Selected Non-fictions*, 210–211.

48 For an insightful discussion of conspiracy in "Emma Zunz," see Josefina Ludmer, *The Corpus Delicti: A Manual of Argentine Fictions*, trans. Glen S. Close (Pittsburgh, PA: University of Pittsburgh Press, 2004), ch. 6. For a discussion of conspiracy in "The Man on the Threshold," see Daniel Balderston, *Out of Context: Historical Reference and the Representation of Reality in Borges* (Durham, NC: Duke University Press, 1993), ch. 7.

49 Piglia, "Teoría del complot," 4.

50 Alberto Moreiras, "The Villain at the Center: Infrapolitical Borges," in *Comparative Cultural Studies and Latin America*, ed. Sophia A. McClennen and Earl E. Fitz (West Lafayette, IN: Purdue University Press, 2002), 143.

51 Moreiras, "The Villain at the Center," 143.

52 Borges, "Anotación al 23 de Agosto de 1944." See Borges, *Selected Non-fictions*, 210–211.

53 *La Nación* (Buenos Aires, Argentina), "Los aliados desembarcan en Arcachon y han avanzado al sudeste de París y en Provenza," August 23, 1944.

54 *La Nación* (Buenos Aires, Argentina), "Paris fue liberado por las tropas francesas del interior y el alzamiento de su población. Luego entró una división," August 24, 1944.

55 *La Nación* (Buenos Aires, Argentina), "Buenos Aires celebró con júbilo la recuperación de la capital francesa," August 24, 1944.

56 *La Nación* (Buenos Aires, Argentina), "Muchas manifestaciones se improvisaron en la ciudad," August 24, 1944.

57 *La Nación* (Buenos Aires, Argentina), "Una multitud imponente y ferverosa rindió altísimo homenaje a Francia," August 25, 1944.

58 Borges, "Anotación al 23 de Agosto de 1944." See Borges, *Selected Non-fictions*, 210–211.

59 Jorge Luis Borges, "Ensayo de imparcialidad," *Sur* No. 61 (1939). See Borges, *Selected Non-fictions*, 202–203.

60 Borges, *Selected Non-fictions*, 202–203.

61 Jorge Luis Borges, "Definición del Germanófilo," *El Hogar*, December 13, 1940. See Borges, *Selected Non-fictions*, 203–205.

62 Borges, *Selected Non-fictions*, 204–205.

63 Jorge Luis Borges, "1941," *Sur* No. 87 (1941). See Borges, *Selected Non-fictions*, 206.

64 Maurice Leblanc (1896–1941) was the French novelist and creator of detective Arsène Lupin.

65 Borges, *Selected Non-fictions*, 206. The original Spanish version uses the word "complot" on the first line and has it in italics. The English version cited above translated the word as "conspiracy" and removed the italics.

66 Borges, *Selected Non-fictions*, 210.

67 Borges, *Selected Non-fictions*, 210. Emphasis in the original.

68 Mallea coined this term in 1937. See Eduardo Mallea, *Historia de una pasión Argentina* (Buenos Aires, Argentina: Sur, 1937). The polemics between Borges and

Mallea were ongoing and will be discussed in more detail in the next part of the book.

69 Borges, *Selected Non-fictions*, 210.

70 Borges, *Selected Non-fictions*, 210–211.

71 Borges, *Selected Non-fictions*, 211.

72 Borges, *Selected Non-fictions*, 211.

73 Annick Louis, "La adhesión a la realidad: las ficciones de Borges durante la Segunda Guerra Mundial," in *El enigma de lo real: las fronteras del realismo en la narrativa del siglo XX*, ed. Geneviève Fabry and Claudio Canaparo (Oxford, UK: Peter Lang, 2007), 124.

74 Borges, *Selected Non-fictions*, 211.

75 Borges, *Selected Non-fictions*, 211. Suzanne Jill Levine has translated "irrealidad" as "unreality." I have chosen to stay closer to the Spanish word by translating it as "irreality." As I will discuss shortly, this term does not denote opposition to, or negation of, reality. Borges is constructing a conceptual space that is beyond the initial dichotomy of reality and fantasy.

76 Borges, *Collected Fictions*, 70. Here too I translate "irrealidad" as "irreality."

77 Balderston, *Out of Context*, 1.

78 Balderston, *Out of Context*, 2.

79 Balderston, *Out of Context*, 10–11.

80 Borges, *Selected Non-fictions*, 206.

81 Borges, *Selected Non-fictions*, 211.

82 Balderston, *Out of Context*, 10–11. I am replacing the word "plot" with "complot." See my discussion above.

83 Borges, *Selected Non-fictions*, 211.

84 Lest the reader believe that Borges was irreverent toward the real historical atrocities perpetrated by the Nazis, I would refer the reader to the following accounts of Borges's attitude towards Nazism by Edna Aizenberg: Edna Aizenberg, *On the Edge of the Holocaust: The Shoah in Latin American Literature and Culture* (Waltham, MA: Brandeis University Press, 2016); Edna Aizenberg, "Postmodern or Post-Auschwitz, Borges and the Limits of Representation," *Variaciones Borges* 3 (1997); as well as Antonio Gómez López-Quiñones, *Borges y el nazismo: Sur (1937–1946)* (Granada, Spain: Universidad de Granada, 2004); Leonardo Senkman, "Borges y el mal del nazismo," in *Borges en Jerusalén*, ed. Myrna Solotorevsky and Ruth Fine (Madrid, Spain: Iberoamericana, 2003); Annick Louis, "Borges y el nazismo," *Variaciones Borges* 4 (1997).

85 Borges, *Selected Non-fictions*, 211. Emphasis in the original.

86 Sosnowski, "'The God's Script'–A Kabbalistic Quest."

87 See, for example, Boaz Huss, "The Mystification of the Kabbalah and the Myth of Jewish Mysticism," *Pe'amim*, no. 110 (2007); and Moran Gam-Hakohen, *Kabbalah Research in Israel: Historiography, Ideology and the Struggle for Cultural Capital* [in Hebrew] (Tel Aviv, Israel: Resling, 2016). While Balderston's study does not deal with Borges and the Kabbalah, I have followed his insight about the need for contextual readings of Borges.

Chapter 3   The Ideal Reader

1 Theodor W. Adorno, *Prisms*, trans. Samuel Weber and Sherry Weber (Cambridge, MA: MIT Press, 1981), 34.

2 Borges certainly continued to discuss Kabbalah in essays and, most prominently, in interviews throughout his life. But the days of his Kabbalistic stories, that is, narrative fictions that allude to Kabbalah, seem to have ended with the publication of *El Aleph* (1949).

3 There are certainly other stories with similar elements, such as the vision of the *ein sof* in "The Aleph," but the combination of a mystic as protagonist, who seeks a connection with divinity, and through that quest experiences *unio mystica* is the most comprehensive and "normative" representation of mysticism in Borges's writing.

4 Borges, "The God's Script," 8.

5 Scholem, *Major Trends in Jewish Mysticism*, 5. Mystical union is not absent from Kabbalah. It was a central component of the Kabbalah developed by Abraham Abulafia. Scholem mentions this as well and his students have pursued this further. See Moshe Idel, *The Mystical Experience in Abraham Abulafia* (Albany, NY: SUNY Press, 1988). However, some scholars (including Scholem) believe that Abulafia was an outlier in this regard in the field of Kabbalah. Boaz Huss has argued that an overemphasis on Abulafia's school in the study of Kabbalah has created the erroneous impression that mystical union is a common concern for Kabbalists. This, Huss argues, is part of a reorientation of Kabbalah studies toward categories of "mysticism" prevalent in the general study of religion. See Huss, "The Mystification of the Kabbalah and the Myth of Jewish Mysticism."

6 Scholem argues that the Hebrew term *Devekuth*, understood as a union between the believer and God, is not equivalent to the experience of *unio mystica* since it describes attainment of a perpetual state rather than a passing rapture or momentary union. "The Hebrew term which in our literature is generally used for what is otherwise called *unio mystica* [is] the word *devekuth*, which signifies 'adhesion,' or 'being joined,' viz., to God. This is regarded as the ultimate goal of religious perfection. *Devekuth* can be ecstasy, but its meaning is far more comprehensive. It is a perpetual being-with-God, an intimate union and conformity of the human and the divine will" (Scholem, *Major Trends in Jewish Mysticism*, 123). Sosnowski ignores these comments by Scholem in his own reading of "The God's Script" and presents it as a shared factor between Tzinacán and the Kabbalists, stating: "the search for God's script demands passing through the various stages that lead to *devekuth*" (Sosnowski, "'The God's Script'–A Kabbalistic Quest," 392).

7 Bischoff describes the unions of various *sefirot* with each other through prayer, the union of God and the world, and the union of the soul with its wellspring. See Bischoff, *Die Elemente der Kabbalah*. For further discussion about the place of mystical union in Kabbalah and its study, see Huss, "The Mystification of the Kabbalah and the Myth of Jewish Mysticism." Meyrink depicts the cration of the Golem as a magical act framed by its socio-politcal context, not as an ecstatic moment. See Meyrink, *Der Golem*.

8 Edna Aizenberg has argued that much of Borges's knowledge of mysticism comes from Christian and Christian Hebraist sources, a fact that has gone unacknowledged in the study of Borges and the Kabbalah. See Aizenberg, "A 21st Century Note on Borges's Kabbalism."

9 See Alazraki, "Kabbalistic Traits in Borges' Narration," 87, ff. 22. Borges's encounter with this book was discussed in the previous chapters.

10 Alazraki, "Kabbalistic Traits in Borges' Narration," 87.

11 A counterexample to this would be the appearance of the Tetragrammaton in "Death and the Compass," which is accompanied by many details and is clearly taken from Kabbalistic sources.

12 In the discussion and citations that follow, the reader will encounter references to both jaguar and tiger. Borges is inconsistent in this story, referring to both interchangeably. In both cases, the reference is to the big cat that shares the cell with Tzinacán, or to the species of that same big cat.

13 For more on the historical figures of Pedro de Alvaro and Tzinacán, as well as some Mesoamerican sources Borges alludes to in this story, see Nicolás Emilio Alvarez, "Borges y Tzinacán," *Revista Iberoamericana* 50, no. 127 (1984); and Balderston, *Out of Context*, ch. 5.

14 Borges, "The God's Script," 7.

15 Sosnowski, "'The God's Script'–A Kabbalistic Quest," 383. Emphasis added.

16 Alazraki, "Borges and the Kabbalah," 241.

17 Alazraki, "Kabbalistic Traits in Borges' Narration," 78.

18 Borges, *Obras completas, 1923–1972*, 629.

19 Sosnowski, "'The God's Script'–A Kabbalistic Quest."

20 Plato, *Republic, Volume II: Books 6-10*, ed. and trans. Christopher Emlyn-Jones and William Preddy (Cambridge, MA: Harvard University Press, 2013), 107–203. This analogy was previously proposed in Jaime Giordano, "Forma y sentido de 'La escritura del Dios' de Jorge Luis Borges," *Revista Iberoamericana* 38, no. 78 (1972).

21 Borges, "The God's Script," 5.

22 Alvarez, "Borges y Tzinacán," 464.

23 Borges, "The God's Script," 6. Emphasis added.

24 Borges, *Selected Non-fictions*, 86.

25 Sosnowski, "'The God's Script'–A Kabbalistic Quest," 383.

26 Borges, "The God's Script," 7.

27 Borges, *Selected Non-fictions*, 86.

28 Borges, "The God's Script," 7.

29 Sosnowski, "'The God's Script'–A Kabbalistic Quest," 387.

30 Borges, "The God's Script," 7.

31 Borges, "The God's Script," 7.

32 This educational philosophy was developed by Joseph Jacotot (1770–1840). See Jacques Rancière, *The Ignorant Schoolmaster: Five Lessons in Intellectual Emancipation* (Stanford, CA: Stanford University Press, 1991).

33 Sosnowski, "'The God's Script'–A Kabbalistic Quest," 388.

34 Borges, "The God's Script," 8.

35 Borges, "The God's Script," 8.

36 Borges, "The God's Script," 6. Emphasis added.

37 Borges, "The God's Script," 9.

38 Borges, "The God's Script," 9.

39 Sosnowski, "'The God's Script'–A Kabbalistic Quest," 384.

40 Sosnowski, "'The God's Script'–A Kabbalistic Quest," 390.

41 Sosnowski, "'The God's Script'–A Kabbalistic Quest," 390.

42 Sosnowski, "'The God's Script'–A Kabbalistic Quest," 388.

43 Christ, "Jorge Luis Borges, The Art of Fiction No. 39," 161–162.

44 Jorge Luis Borges, *El informe de Brodie* (Buenos Aires, Argentina: Emecé Editores, 1970).

45 Mario Eduardo Cohen, ed., *Borges, el judaísmo e Israel*, 2nd ed., Sefaradica (Buenos Aires, Argentina: Centro de Investigación y Difusión de la Cultura Sefardí, 1999), 42.

46 It is unclear where in Scholem's writing Borges read this. In *Major Trends in Jewish Mysticism* Scholem discusses Abulafia's prophetic Kabbalah and cites a tradition, according to which the prophet sees himself: "Know that the complete secret of prophecy consists for the prophet in that he suddenly sees the shape of his self standing before him" (Scholem, *Major Trends in Jewish Mysticism*, 142). In chapter 5 of *On the Kabbalah and Its Symbolism*, Scholem discusses the view that the Golem is the double of the rabbi that created it. By 1967 Borges was familiar with the former. In our discussion of his 1958 poem "The Golem" in chapter 1, we discussed the possibility that he may have been familiar with the latter as well.

47 Jorge Luis Borges, *The Book of Imaginary Beings*, trans. Andrew Hurley (New York: Penguin Books, 2005), 62.

48 Quoted in Alazraki, "Kabbalistic Traits in Borges' Narration," 79. And again in Alazraki, "Borges and the Kabbalah," 241.

49 Alazraki, *Borges and the Kabbalah*, 3.

50 Alazraki, *Borges and the Kabbalah*, 54–61.

51 Alazraki, *Borges and the Kabbalah*, 55–56.

52 Alazraki, *Borges and the Kabbalah*, 58.

53 Alazraki, *Borges and the Kabbalah*, 58.

54 Alazraki, *Borges and the Kabbalah*, 55.

55 Alazraki, *Borges and the Kabbalah*, 61.

56 As in his remarks at the twenty-five-year anniversary of the Sociedad Hebraica Argentina, Borges again says "books" in the plural but only mentions one book by Scholem.

57 Saul Sosnowski, *Borges, la letra y la Cábala* (Madrid, Spain: delCentro Editores, 2016), 268.

58 Alazraki, "Conversación con Borges sobre la Cábala: Entrevista inédita de 1971," 169.

59 Scholem and Hollander, Series 1: Correspondance: Hollander, John.

60 Alazraki, "Conversación con Borges sobre la Cábala: Entrevista inédita de 1971," 169.

61 Sosnowski, *Borges, la letra y la Cábala*, 269.

62 Alazraki, "Conversación con Borges sobre la Cábala: Entrevista inédita de 1971," 169. In his 1972 article, Alazraki proposed that Borges had found the information about the Golem in Meyrink's novel rather than Scholem's book. Here Borges admits having taken it from Trachtenberg. Although this interview was conducted in 1971, the article had already been submitted and Alazraki did not have the chance to correct this error. See Alazraki, "Borges and the Kabbalah," 247.

63 Borges, *Obras completas, 1975–1985*, 208.

64 Borges, *Obras completas, 1975–1985*, 254.

65 Borges, *Seven Nights*, 76.

66 Borges, *Seven Nights*, 76.

67 Borges, *Seven Nights*, 80.

68 Borges, *Seven Nights*, 82.

69 Borges, *Seven Nights*, 78.

70 To my knowledge, this interview was never transcribed and the recording of the conversation, which Edna mentioned to me on several occasions, has been lost.

71 Gershom Scholem and Edna Aizenberg, Series 1: Correspondance: Aizenberg, Edna, 1980, ARC.4* 1599 01 0026, Gershom Gerhard Scholem Archive, The National Library of Israel, Jerusalem.

72 Sosnowski, *Borges y la cábala*; Edna Aizenberg, *The Aleph Weaver: Biblical, Kabbalistic and Judaic Elements in Borges* (Potomac, MD: Scripta Humanistica, 1984).

73 Aizenberg does not quote her own letter, and only cites an excerpt of Scholem's reply in her book. See Aizenberg, *Borges, el tejedor del Aleph y otros ensayos*, 81, ff.2. The full correspondence is available in the Scholem Archive in the National Library of Israel.

74 Scholem and Aizenberg, Series 1: Correspondance: Aizenberg, Edna. Scholem here implies having read Borges's stories and, by comparing them to Meyrink, indicates he is familiar with Borges's literary treatment of the Golem character. This was also indicated by his choice to give Borges a copy of *On the Kabbalah and its Symbolism* (1965) during their 1969 meeting. Unfortunately, outside of this comment to Aizenberg, the Scholem archive has preserved no trace of what he thought about Borges's stories.

75 Scholem and Aizenberg, Series 1: Correspondance: Aizenberg, Edna.

76 Sosnowski, "El verbo cabalístico en la obra de Borges," 36.

77 Alazraki, *Borges and the Kabbalah*, 58. Emphasis added.

78 Sosnowski, *Borges, la letra y la Cábala*.

Chapter 4   The Trouble with Tradition

1 Jorge Luis Borges, "El escritor argentino y la tradición," *Cursos y Conferencias* 62, no. 250 (1953).

2 We will see how this essay has influenced the articulation of postcolonial literary relations between Latin America and Europe. This same essay has also been used to articulate the position of European literature vis-à-vis modernity as well. For example, see Rancière, "Borges and French Disease."

3 Borges, *Obras completas, 1923–1972*, 270.

4 While the current project will not pay much attention to the Irish component of this analogy, the similarity between Jews and Irish is a point Borges returns to several times in his writings. For a discussion of this pairing, see Fabián Darío Mosquera, "Una leyenda celta ante la zarza ardiente: el dispositivo judaico-irlandés como interpelación nacional en Borges," *Variaciones Borges*, no. 48 (2019).

5 T. S. Eliot, *Selected Essays* (London: Faber and Faber, 1934), 13–22.

6 Thorstein Veblen, "The Intellectual Pre-Eminence of Jews in Modern Europe," *Political Science Quarterly* 34, no. 1 (March 1919).

7 For a discussion of Borges's intellectual circle and activity from the twenties to the Peronist Era, see Louis, *Borges ante el fascismo*.

8 Eduardo Mallea, *El sayal y la purpura* (Buenos Aires, Argentina: Editorial Losada, 1947).

9 Sarlo, *Borges, un escritor en las orillas*, 4.

10 Sarlo, *Borges, un escritor en las orillas*, 20.

11 Borges declares such intentions as early as his first book of essays, *El tamaño de mi esperanza*.

12 Siskind, *Cosmopolitan Desires*, 6.

13 These two are mentioned in many texts, but perhaps most importantly in the context of their belonging to the Judaic, he mentions Heine in Borges, "Yo, Judío."

And Spinoza in two poems—"Spinoza" and "Baruch Spinoza"—published respectively in 1964 and 1976. See Borges, *Obras completas, 1923–1972*, 930; and Borges, *Obras completas, 1975–1985*, 151.

14 An example of the adoption of this frame, and of the centrality of "The Argentine Writer and Tradition," in Latin American studies can be found in Luce López-Baralt, "Escribiendo desde las ínsulas extrañas: Reflexiones de una hispano-arabista puertorriqueña," *Historia y Fuente Oral* 7 (1992). An example of the way this frame and this lecture have been useful in articulating a connection between postcolonial and Jewish studies can be found in Edmund Chapman, "Jewishness and Postcoloniality in Borges and Derrida: The Singular and the Specific," *Textual Practice* 36, no. 8 (2022). For a critique of this frame in discourse on the Western canon, see Daniel Balderston, "Borges: The Argentine Writer and the 'Western' Tradition," in *Borges and Europe Revisited*, ed. Evelyn Fishburn (London: Institute of Latin American Studies, University of London, 1998).

15 The exception to this statement, which has greatly inspired the present study, is Edna Aizenberg's persistent understanding of Jewish marginality as a literary-aesthetic principle in Borges's writing, and not as a sociohistorical statement, even when Borges seems to be making a statement of the latter kind. See Edna Aizenberg, *Books and Bombs in Buenos Aires: Borges, Gerchunoff, and Argentine-Jewish Writing* (Hanover, NH: University Press of New England, 2002), ch. 7.

16 Evelyn Fishburn, "Reflections on the Jewish Imaginary in the Fictions of Borges," *Variaciones Borges* 5 (1998): 152.

17 Graff Zivin, *The Wandering Signifier*, 11.

18 For a discussion of Jewish literature in the context of opening the limit between Jews and non-Jews in Europe into an "in-between" space, see Lewis, *A Permanent Beginning*.

19 Originally published as Borges, "Yo, Judío." Translated as "I, a Jew" in Borges, *Selected Non-fictions*, 110–111.

20 *Crisol*, "Carácter de estas notas," *Editorial*, January 30, 1934, 4.

21 Borges, *Selected Non-fictions*, 110.

22 Borges, *Selected Non-fictions*, 110–111.

23 Borges, *Selected Non-fictions*, 110.

24 *Crisol*, "Otro 'poroto' nuestro," Editorial, May 2, 1934, 4.

25 Judith Podlubne, "Lecturas cruzadas en la revista Sur: Mallea y Borges sobre Kafka y Chesterton," *Anclajes* 9 (2005): 120.

26 Podlubne, "Lecturas cruzadas en la revista Sur," 120.

27 Mallea, *Historia de una pasión Argentina*. Translated as Eduardo Mallea, *History of an Argentine Passion*, trans. Myron Lichtblau (Pittsburgh, PA: Latin American Literary Review Press, 1983).

28 Borges, *Selected Non-fictions*, 210.

29 Mallea, *El sayal y la purpura*.

30 Mallea, *El sayal y la purpura*, 23.

31 Mallea, *El sayal y la purpura*, 22.

32 Mallea, *El sayal y la purpura*, 64.

33 See Jean-Paul Sartre, "Retrato del antisemita," *Sur*, no. 138 (1946). Translated as Jean-Paul Sartre, *Portrait of the Anti-Semite*, trans. Mary Guggenheim (New York: Partisan Review, 1946). The conference proceedings were published as "Literatura gratuita y literatura comprometida," *Sur* 138 (1946).

34 *Sur*, "Literatura gratuita y literatura comprometida," 108.

35 Daniel Fitzgerald, "'El escritor en nuestro tiempo': la conferencia, Entre Ríos 1952," *Variaciones Borges*, no. 42 (2016).

36 Cited in Fitzgerald, "'El escritor en nuestro tiempo': la conferencia, Entre Ríos 1952," 68.

37 Cited in Fitzgerald, "'El escritor en nuestro tiempo': la conferencia, Entre Ríos 1952," 68.

38 Cited in Fitzgerald, "'El escritor en nuestro tiempo': la conferencia, Entre Ríos 1952," 68.

39 Eliot, *Selected Essays*, 13.

40 Eliot, *Selected Essays*, 14.

41 Eliot, *Selected Essays*, 14.

42 This idea is also expressed by Martin Buber in *I and Thou*, trans. Ronald Gregor Smith (New York: Charles Scribner's Sons, 1937). For Buber, the simultaneousness of past and present exists in moments of dialogue. We will see Borges mention Buber's notion of dialogue as a form of writing when we discuss his readings of Buber in chapter 7.

43 Eliot, *Selected Essays*, 14.

44 Eliot, *Selected Essays*, 15.

45 Eliot, *Selected Essays*, 14.

46 Sarlo, *Borges, un escritor en las orillas*, 4.

47 Borges's efforts changed over the course of the late 1930s and early 1940s. His early efforts were to invent a tradition, while his efforts following World War II were to think about the relation of his invented tradition to the European one. For a discussion of Borges's response to World War II, see Aizenberg, "Postmodern or Post-Auschwitz, Borges and the Limits of Representation."

48 Borges, *El tamaño de mi esperanza*. The essay for which the book was named was translated in Jorge Luis Borges, *On Argentina*, ed. Alfred Mac Adam and Suzanne Jill Levine (New York: Penguin Books, 2010), 45–48. Previous to this essay collection of 1926, Borges had published two books of poetry. This was his first book of essays. It was not included in his complete works. In fact, it was not reprinted again until 1994.

49 Borges, *On Argentina*, 47.

50 Borges, *On Argentina*, 47. Borges alludes here to his first book of poetry. See Jorge Luis Borges, *Fervor de Buenos Aires: poemas* (Buenos Aires, Argentina: Impr. Serrantes, 1923).

51 Borges, *Selected Non-fictions*, 425.

52 Borges, *Selected Non-fictions*, 420.

53 Jorge Luis Borges, *Evaristo Carriego* (Buenos Aires, Argentina: M. Gleizer, 1930). Translated as Jorge Luis Borges, *Evaristo Carriego: A Book about Old-Time Buenos Aires*, trans. Norman Thomas di Giovanni (New York: E. P. Dutton, 1984).

54 Borges, *Evaristo Carriego: A Book about Old-Time Buenos Aires*, 42 ff.2.

55 Borges, *Evaristo Carriego: A Book about Old-Time Buenos Aires*, 42 ff.2.

56 Borges, *Obras completas, 1923–1972*, 101. Emphasis added. I offer my own translation here in order to preserve the subjunctive counterfactual tense: "what would it have been nice if it had been." This is an awkward tense in English, which the English translation revised as "What was Palermo like then, and how beautiful would it really have been?" See Borges, *Evaristo Carriego: A Book about Old-Time Buenos Aires*, 33.

57 For further discussion of Borges's early works, see Sarlo, *Borges, un escritor en las orillas*; Montaldo, "Borges: una vanguardia criolla"; Sylvia Molloy, *Signs of Borges*, trans. Oscar Montero (Durham, NC: Duke University Press, 1994).

58 Jorge Luis Borges, *Textos recobrados, 1931–1955* (Buenos Aires, Argentina: Emece Editores, 2001), 50. Originally published as Jorge Luis Borges, "La eternidad y T. S. Eliot," *Poesía* 1, no. 3 (1933).

59 Borges, *Textos recobrados, 1931–1955*, 51.

60 Borges, *Seven Nights*, 76–84.

61 Borges, *Textos recobrados, 1931–1955*, 52.

62 Juan E. de Castro, "De Eliot a Borges: tradición y periferia," *Iberoamericana* 7, no. 26 (2007): 11. Castro suggests this early engagement with Eliot "could be read as a draft of 'Kafka and His Precursors'" (Castro, "De Eliot a Borges," 9), in which Borges will push this thesis to its limits. We will return to this later essay by Borges in chapter 7.

63 Castro, "De Eliot a Borges," 13.

64 Louis, *Borges ante el fascismo*, 21. For more on Argentine intellectual circles in the 1930s, as well as Borges's public intellectual activity in the thirties and forties, see Maria Teresa Gramuglio, *Nacionalismo y cosmopolitismo en la literatura argentina*, ed. Judith Podlubne (Rosario, Argentina: Editorial municipal de Rosario, 2013).

65 Aizenberg goes as far as to argue: "without the confluence of Hitler, the collapse of the Western order as he knew it, the national-fascist revolution in his own Argentina, and the torture, sodomy, rape, and mass executions, the so-so poet and sharp-tongued essayist would not have become 'Borges.'" (Aizenberg, "'I, a Jew': Borges, Nazism and the Shoah," 339.) We have already seen Borges's anti-Nazi activity and its bearing on his literature in the previous part. We will return to the topic of historicizing World War II in Borges's intellectual career in the next chapter as well. However, much of what has been written on this topic is beyond the scope of this book. For further discussion, see Aizenberg, *Books and Bombs in Buenos Aires*, especially chapters 7, 8, and 9. For more on Borges and World War II, see Louis, "La adhesión a la realidad"; Louis, "Borges y el nazismo." For a general account of the effects of World War II on Latin American letters, see Aizenberg, *On the Edge of the Holocaust*.

66 Borges, *Selected Non-fictions*, 425.

67 Borges, *Selected Non-fictions*, 423.

68 See Aizenberg, "Postmodern or Post-Auschwitz, Borges and the Limits of Representation"; and Aizenberg, "'I, a Jew': Borges, Nazism and the Shoah." For a broader discussion of the Holocaust in Latin America, see Aizenberg, *On the Edge of the Holocaust*.

69 Borges, *Selected Non-fictions*, 420.

70 Borges, *Selected Non-fictions*, 420.

71 Eliot, *Selected Essays*, 14.

72 Borges, *Selected Non-fictions*, 211.

73 Borges, *Selected Non-fictions*, 420.

74 Eliot, *Selected Essays*, 14.

75 Borges, *Selected Non-fictions*, 425.

76 Borges, *Selected Non-fictions*, 426.

77 Eliot, *Selected Essays*, 21.

78 Borges, *Selected Non-fictions*, 426.

79 Borges, *Selected Non-fictions*, 426.

80 Borges, *Selected Non-fictions*, 426.
81 This essay by Eliot is also central to the argument in another of Borges's 1951 texts, "Kafka and His Precursors," where the appearance of Kafka on the literary scene alters the past, casting the literary history of a random group of past authors as Kafka's "precursors." We will read this essay carefully in chapter 7 and see the influence of both T. S. Eliot and Martin Buber on this idea. Jorge Luis Borges, "Kafka y sus precursores," *La Nación* (Buenos Aires, Argentina), August 19, 1951, 2.
82 Veblen, "The Intellectual Pre-Eminence of Jews in Modern Europe." Veblen is also well known for his work in economics. In his present article, a great deal of sociological thought goes into defining the place of Jews in modern European society, and no economic thought is involved. I therefore have foregrounded his disciplinary affiliation with sociology. For the reader interested in his contributions to the field of economics, see, for example, Thorstein Veblen, *The Theory of the Leisure Class* (New York: Macmillan, 1899).
83 Aizenberg, *Borges, el tejedor del Aleph y otros ensayos*, 53.

Chapter 5   What Is Jewish Tradition?

 1 Veblen, "The Intellectual Pre-Eminence of Jews in Modern Europe." In this chapter, the discussion about Borges's reading of Veblen is based on and elaborates on my article: Yitzhak Lewis, "Modeling Marginality: Borges, Veblen and the Argentine Writer," *Variaciones Borges* 44 (2017). I thank the editors of *Variaciones Borges* for their permission to reprint excerpts of this article here.
 2 Borges, *Selected Non-fictions*, 246.
 3 Borges, *Selected Non-fictions*, 426.
 4 Veblen, "The Intellectual Pre-Eminence of Jews in Modern Europe," 34.
 5 Veblen, "The Intellectual Pre-Eminence of Jews in Modern Europe," 33.
 6 Veblen, "The Intellectual Pre-Eminence of Jews in Modern Europe," 34.
 7 Veblen, "The Intellectual Pre-Eminence of Jews in Modern Europe," 36.
 8 Veblen, "The Intellectual Pre-Eminence of Jews in Modern Europe," 35.
 9 Veblen, "The Intellectual Pre-Eminence of Jews in Modern Europe," 37.
10 For more on this genre see Josefina Ludmer, *The Gaucho Genre: A Treatise on the Motherland* (Durham, NC: Duke University Press, 2002).
11 Borges, *Selected Non-fictions*, 421.
12 Borges, *Selected Non-fictions*, 423.
13 Borges, *Selected Non-fictions*, 423.
14 For more on Borges and Argentine nationalism during the 1930s and 1940s, see Louis, *Borges ante el fascismo*.
15 For a discussion of the origin of this erroneous idea, see Daniel Balderston, "Detalles circunstanciales: Sobre dos borradores de 'El escritor argentino y la tradición'," *Cuadernos LIRICO*, no. 9 (2013). For a discussion of the Orient as a blind spot in Borges's writing, see Nora Catelli, "La cuestión americana en 'El escritor argentino y la tradición'," in *L'écrivain argentin et la tradition*, ed. Daniel Attala, Sergio Delgado, and Rémi Le Mar'Hadour (Rennes, France: Presses Universitaires de Rennes, 2004). For a discussion of Borges and Orientalism, see Shlomy Mualem, "Imaginative Geography: Dialectical Orientalism in Borges," *TRANSMODERNITY: Journal of Peripheral Cultural Production of the Luso-Hispanic World* 6, no. 1 (2016).
16 Borges, *Selected Non-fictions*, 424.

17 Veblen, "The Intellectual Pre-Eminence of Jews in Modern Europe," 33.

18 Veblen, "The Intellectual Pre-Eminence of Jews in Modern Europe," 40.

19 Veblen, "The Intellectual Pre-Eminence of Jews in Modern Europe," 34.

20 Veblen, "The Intellectual Pre-Eminence of Jews in Modern Europe," 34.

21 Veblen, "The Intellectual Pre-Eminence of Jews in Modern Europe," 40.

22 Borges, *Selected Non-fictions*, 425.

23 Borges, *Selected Non-fictions*, 425.

24 To be clear, Borges's sources on Zionism and, later, his attitude to the State of Israel go well beyond a single article by Veblen. It is not my intention to suggest that Borges simply embraces Veblen's by then outdated views on Jewish nationalism. But to the extent that I am here interested in the representation of the Judaic, and the way it illuminates Borges's thoughts on authorship and literary tradition, the recurrence of Veblen as a point of reference for Borges's articulation of his notion of tradition is noteworthy. As I continue to track Borges's engagement with Veblen's article in "The Argentine Writer and Tradition" and beyond, I will continue to bracket questions of accuracy and maintain my focus on questions of representation and literary expression. For a sense of Borges's many sources on Zionism and Israel, see Cohen, *Borges, el judaísmo e israel*. Also noteworthy in this regard is the impact of Martin Buber on Borges's understanding of Zionism, which will be discussed in the coming chapters. Elsewhere I have discussed Borges's attitude to Zionism and its relation to Jewish tradition. See Yitzhak Lewis, "Borges, Zionism and the Politics of Reality," *Variaciones Borges* 35 (2013). For an historicization of the view I ascribe Borges on Jewish attitudes towards tradition, see Humberto Núñez-Faraco, "Dialogue and Existence in Jorge Luis Borges's 'The Secret Miracle': A Buberian Reading," *Comparative Critical Studies* 20, no. 1 (2023).

25 Veblen, "The Intellectual Pre-Eminence of Jews in Modern Europe," 37. Emphasis added.

26 Borges, *Selected Non-fictions*, 425.

27 Veblen, "The Intellectual Pre-Eminence of Jews in Modern Europe," 33.

28 Borges, *Selected Non-fictions*, 425.

29 This is not the place for a social history of Argentina. Suffice it to say that the large waves of German and Italian immigration that had been arriving for decades before the war, as well as the antagonism between Britain and Argentina, which later culminated in the Falklands War, suggest that Argentina's cultural allegiance was anything but "natural" to either side. For more on Borges and Nazism in Argentina, see Aizenberg, *The Aleph Weaver*; López-Quiñones, *Borges y el nazismo: Sur (1937–1946)*.

30 Borges, *Selected Non-fictions*, 426.

31 Veblen, "The Intellectual Pre-Eminence of Jews in Modern Europe," 37.

32 Veblen, "The Intellectual Pre-Eminence of Jews in Modern Europe," 37.

33 Veblen, "The Intellectual Pre-Eminence of Jews in Modern Europe," 38.

34 Veblen, "The Intellectual Pre-Eminence of Jews in Modern Europe," 39.

35 Veblen, "The Intellectual Pre-Eminence of Jews in Modern Europe," 39.

36 Veblen, "The Intellectual Pre-Eminence of Jews in Modern Europe," 39.

37 Veblen, "The Intellectual Pre-Eminence of Jews in Modern Europe," 39.

38 Veblen, "The Intellectual Pre-Eminence of Jews in Modern Europe," 39.

39 Veblen, "The Intellectual Pre-Eminence of Jews in Modern Europe," 38.

40 Borges, *Selected Non-fictions*, 426.

41 Aizenberg, *Borges, el tejedor del Aleph y otros ensayos*, 112.

42 *Crisol*, "Carácter de estas notas."

43 Borges, *Selected Non-fictions*, 110–111.

44 Borges, *Selected Non-fictions*, 426.

45 Veblen, "The Intellectual Pre-Eminence of Jews in Modern Europe," 35.

46 Veblen, "The Intellectual Pre-Eminence of Jews in Modern Europe," 34.

47 Veblen, "The Intellectual Pre-Eminence of Jews in Modern Europe," 34.

48 Veblen, "The Intellectual Pre-Eminence of Jews in Modern Europe," 38.

49 Veblen, "The Intellectual Pre-Eminence of Jews in Modern Europe," 42.

50 Veblen, "The Intellectual Pre-Eminence of Jews in Modern Europe," 34.

51 Veblen, "The Intellectual Pre-Eminence of Jews in Modern Europe," 42.

52 Veblen, "The Intellectual Pre-Eminence of Jews in Modern Europe," 42. The pun is on the word "interned." The most amiable share may be a guild internship or an internment camp.

53 Veblen, "The Intellectual Pre-Eminence of Jews in Modern Europe," 39.

54 Veblen, "The Intellectual Pre-Eminence of Jews in Modern Europe," 39.

55 On a side note, the question of whether the mere memory of a departure from tradition can suffice to form the basis of group recognition had already been taken up by Nachman of Braslav in his "Parable of the Maddening Wheat" and "Parable of the Turkey Prince." See Lewis, *A Permanent Beginning*, ch. 7.

56 For more on Borges's understanding of the relation between Jewish Diaspora and the State of Israel, see Ilan Stavans, "Borges's Zionist Bent: Newly Translated Poems," *The Jewish Daily Forward*, January 2, 2009; Lewis, "Borges, Zionism and the Politics of Reality."

57 Borges, *Selected Non-fictions*, 426.

58 The lecture was chronicled by Borges's friend and collaborator Adolfo Bioy Casares in *Borges*, ed. Daniel Martino (Barcelona, Spain: BackList, 2010), 40. The text of the lecture was first published in 1951 as Borges's contribution to Max Simon Nordau, *Inicial del nuevo siglo* (Buenos Aires, Argentina: Fundación Max Nordau, 1951). It was reprinted as "Nordau" in Borges, *Textos recobrados, 1931–1955*, 267–271. For a discussion of representations of Max Nordau in Latin American writing at the time, see Graff Zivin, *The Wandering Signifier*, 45–61.

59 Borges, *Selected Non-fictions*, 426.

60 Borges, *Textos recobrados, 1931–1955*, 267. Emphasis added.

61 Borges, *Textos recobrados, 1931–1955*, 267.

62 Borges, *Textos recobrados, 1931–1955*, 267.

63 For a discussion of culture and politics in this period of Latin American history, see Hilda Sábato, *Republics of the New World: The Revolutionary Political Experiment in Nineteenth-Century Latin America* (Princeton, NJ: Princeton University Press, 2018).

64 Borges, *Textos recobrados, 1931–1955*, 267.

65 Edna Aizenberg has worked on this topic extensively: see Aizenberg, "Postmodern or Post-Auschwitz, Borges and the Limits of Representation"; Aizenberg, "'I, a Jew': Borges, Nazism and the Shoah." See also Louis, "Borges y el nazismo"; Senkman, "Borges y el mal del nazismo." For a general discussion of the effects of the Holocaust on Latin American letters, see Aizenberg, *On the Edge of the Holocaust*.

66 In this observation, I echo Edna Aizenberg in her article "Borges, Postcolonial Precursor." However, given that this analogy first "occurs" to Borges in the early

postwar years, I read it as contemporaneous with broader postcolonial thought that emerges at the same period. I would thus read Borges's 1951 understanding of Argentine tradition not as a precursor to but rather as a participant in the development of postcolonial literary thought.

67 For more on the effect of World War II and the Holocaust on Latin American letters, see Aizenberg, *On the Edge of the Holocaust.*

68 Borges, *Selected Non-fictions*, 425.

69 Borges, *Textos recobrados, 1931–1955,* 269.

70 Borges, *Textos recobrados, 1931–1955,* 271.

71 Veblen, "The Intellectual Pre-Eminence of Jews in Modern Europe," 39.

72 Borges, *Selected Non-fictions*, 425.

73 Jorge Luis Borges, "Alfonso Reyes," *Sur* No. 264 (1960): 1.

74 Borges, "Alfonso Reyes." Veblen does not talk about premodern social conditions.

75 Mario Diamant, "Una conversación con Jorge L. Borges," *Plural* 3, no. 19 (Nov. 1978): 6. I have translated as "important" Borges's "importante" in Spanish, which has several meanings: important, valuable, and significant.

76 Veblen, "The Intellectual Pre-Eminence of Jews in Modern Europe," 37.

77 In chapter 7, we will discuss Martin Buber's view of Jews as "middle-folk" and his existentialist notion of "between." The influence these ideas had on Borges's understanding of the Judaic help explain this slippage from in-between as a wedge to in-between as a bridge.

78 I have discussed these poems elsewhere, in Lewis, "Borges, Zionism and the Politics of Reality."

79 Núñez-Faraco, "Dialogue and Existence in Jorge Luis Borges's 'The Secret Miracle'," 29.

80 Diamant, "Una conversación con Jorge L. Borges," 6.

81 Quoted in *Boletin S.H.A.* 20, no. 338 (1951).

82 Balderston, "Detalles circunstanciales," 3.

83 Block de Behar, "Antecedents of an Unexpected Poetic Affinity," 188.

Chapter 6 Tradition and Local Color

1 Quoted in *Boletin S.H.A.* 20, no. 338 (1951).

2 Borges does not name the writers he met in 1969 in this interview. He met Israeli writers again in 1971, when he returned to receive the Jerusalem Prize. In a later interview from 1977, he names Amos Oz as an author that he met in Israel in 1971. See Cohen, *Borges, el judaísmo e Israel,* 177.

3 From an interview published in *Raíces,* 1971. Quoted in Cohen, *Borges, el judaísmo e Israel,* 168–169.

4 Eliot, *Selected Essays,* 14.

5 For more on the confrontation between Jewish Diaspora and Zionism in Borges's thought see Lewis, "Borges, Zionism and the Politics of Reality."

6 Aizenberg, *Borges, el tejedor del Aleph y otros ensayos,* 54.

7 *Crisol,* "Carácter de estas notas," 4.

8 Borges's assumptions about modern psalmic writing should also be read in the context of his early engagement with modern Spanish avant-garde poetry. The genre of modern Spanish psalms began as an avant-garde practice in the circle of Rafael Cansinos-Asséns, whom Borges met in Spain in the early 1920s. Borges himself experimented with writing modern psalms at the time. In his 1964 commemorative poem "Rafael Cansinos–Asséns," written the year Cansinos-Asséns died, Borges

associates him with the Psalms. See Borges, *Obras completas, 1923–1972*, 915. I thank Adam Cohn for drawing my attention to this context and the role of Cansinos-Asséns in the development of Borges's understanding of the psalms.

9   Other authors included Chaim Hazaz, Rachel, S. Yizhar, Yehuda Amichai, Avraham Shlonsky, T. Carmi, and others.

10   Yehoushua Bar-Yosef, "Cuarenta años de literatura israelí," *Sur* No. 254 (1958); Joseph Lichtenbaum, "La nueva prosa hebrea," *Sur* No. 254 (1958).

11   Jorge Luis Borges, "Israel," *Sur* No. 254 (1958): 1.

12   Borges, "Israel," 2.

13   *Boletin S.H.A.* 20, no. 338 (1951).

14   Borges, "Israel," 2.

15   I translate the Spanish "patético" as pathetic, but in this context, it could mean both full of emotional pathos and full of suffering.

16   Borges, "Israel," 2.

17   Borges, *Selected Non-fictions*, 110–111.

18   In "The Sect of the Phoenix," Borges writes, "Martin Buber declares that the Jews are essentially pathetic." See Borges, *Obras completas, 1923–1972*, 522. Here too, my translation of "patético" is the English "pathetic." Andrew Hurley has translated this line as "Jews are essentially sufferers," in Borges, *Collected Fictions*, 171–172.

The reference to Buber's notion of dialogue is from two books Borges read and annotated in the late 1940s and early 1950s. Martin Buber, *Between Man and Man*, trans. Ronald Gregor Smith (London: Kegan Paul, 1947). And Martin Buber, *Dialogisches Leben: gesammelte philosophische und pädagogische Schriften* (Zürich, Switzerland: Gregor Müller Verlag, 1947). Borges found the reference to Jewish pathos in another book he read in those same years: Buber, *Vom Geist des Judentums*. Buber will be the main topic of the next chapter.

19   Borges, *Collected Fictions*, 352–357.

20   Borges, *Obras completas, 1923–1972*, 1029.

21   Diamant, "Una conversación con Jorge L. Borges," 6. I have translated "importante," the word Borges uses in Spanish, as "important." In Spanish this word has several meanings: important, valuable, and significant.

22   The complete remarks of all speakers were transcribed and printed in 1967. See Marcelo Cohen, ed., *Conferencias* (Instituto de Intercambio Cultural Argentino Israeli, 1967). While Borges's comments were printed untitled in this and subsequent publications of the Instituto de Intercambio Cultural Argentino Israelí, they were posthumously titled "Agnon: The Living Memory of this Admirable People" and reprinted in various edited volumes of his writing, including Cohen, *Borges, el judaísmo e Israel*.

23   Borges was a finalist for the prize both in 1965 and in 1967. See Alison Flood, "Nabokov, Neruda and Borges Revealed as Losers of 1965 Nobel Prize," *The Guardian*, January 6, 2016, https://www.theguardian.com/books/2016/jan/06/borges-auden-nabokov-neruda-nobel-prize-literature-1965; Alison Flood, "Nobel Archives Show Graham Greene Might Have Won 1967 Prize," *The Guardian*, Jauary 8, 2018, https://www.theguardian.com/books/2018/jan/08/nobel-archives-show-graham-greene-might-have-won-1967-prize.

24   Both lectures appear in Cohen, *Conferencias*.

25   There are certainly tensions that Agnon works through in his writing. The confrontation between tradition and modernity, the erotic and the sacred, religious language and mundane language, to name a few examples. But there is no

significant confrontation between Judaism and Zionism in his writing. Agnon was both an observant Jew and a Jewish nationalist who spent most of his life living in Jerusalem. For an introduction to Agnon's life and work, see the introduction chapter in Shmuel Yosef Agnon, *A Book that Was Lost: Thirty-Five Stories*, ed. Alan L. Mintz and Anne Golomb Hoffman (New Milford, CT: The Toby Press, 2008).

26 Cohen, *Borges, el judaísmo e Israel*, 201.

27 Cohen, *Borges, el judaísmo e Israel*, 201.

28 Cohen, *Borges, el judaísmo e Israel*, 201.

29 Cohen, *Borges, el judaísmo e Israel*, 202.

30 Cohen, *Borges, el judaísmo e Israel*, 202.

31 Borges, *Evaristo Carriego*. Translated as Borges, *Evaristo Carriego: A Book about Old-Time Buenos Aires*.

32 Borges, *Evaristo Carriego: A Book about Old-Time Buenos Aires*, 42 ff.2.

33 Borges, *The Aleph and Other Stories 1933–1969*, 257.

34 This is a line from Borges's poem titled "Israel 1969." See Jorge Luis Borges, *In Praise of Darkness*, trans. Norman Thomas di Giovanni (New York: Dutton, 1974), 95. For more on Borges's poems to the State of Israel and a discussion of this paradox, see Lewis, "Borges, Zionism and the Politics of Reality." For a more recent study of the connection between paradox and Jewish tradition in Borges's literary expression, see Corinna Deppner, ed., *La paradoja como forma literaria de la innovación: Jorge Luis Borges entre la tradición judía y el hipertexto* (Hildesheim, Germany: Ediciones de Olms, 2018); as well as the review of this collection in Daniel Nahson, "Corinna Deppner (ed.): La paradoja como forma literaria de la innovación," *Iberoamericana* 20, no. 75 (2020).

35 See Aizenberg, *Borges, el tejedor del Aleph y otros ensayos*, ch. 7; and Stavans, "Borges's Zionist Bent: Newly Translated Poems."

36 Murray Baumgarten, *City Scriptures: Modern Jewish Writing* (Cambridge, MA: Harvard University Press, 1982), 94.

37 Baumgarten, *City Scriptures*, 101.

38 See, for example, Agnon's story "The Tale of the Scribe," where the religious rituals surrounding the writing of a Torah scroll are juxtaposed with the practices of marital intimacy in the life of Raphael the scribe. One reading of this story suggests that upon completing the erotically charged task of writing the Torah scroll, Raphael experiences spontaneous ejaculation. It is hard to imagine a more irreverent engagement with the Jewish textual tradition. And yet the juxtaposition in Agnon's story is so invested in the minutia of Jewish scribal practices that it is hard to imagine this metaphor outside of its relation to the Jewish tradition. See Agnon, *A Book that Was Lost: Thirty-Five Stories*, 177–194.

39 Baumgarten, *City Scriptures*, 94–95.

40 Cohen, *Borges, el judaísmo e Israel*, 202.

41 Cohen, *Borges, el judaísmo e Israel*, 203.

42 Baumgarten, *City Scriptures*, 94.

43 Estela Canto, "Entrevista con Jorge Luis Borges," in *Textos recobrados (1931–1955)*, ed. Sara Luisa del Carril and Mercedes Rubio de Socchi (Buenos Aires, Argentina: Emecé Editores, 2007). Emphasis in the original.

44 *Crisol*, "Carácter de estas notas," 4.

45 Borges, *Selected Non-fictions*, 426–427.

46 The other side of this cosmopolitan recognition is the reception of Borges as not Argentine enough by his contemporary and subsequent readers. Fabián Darío Mosquera argues that it was in response to the ideology expressed in such lectures as "The Argentine Writer and Tradition," that Borges came to be seen as not Argentine enough. In our own reading, we have seen that this attitude has a longer reception history, going back at least to the *Crisol* editors who doubt Borges's Argentineity as well, albeit in the nationalist language of hidden or dual allegiance that was more prevalent in Argentina before World War II. See Mosquera, "Una leyenda celta ante la zarza ardiente." For more on Borges and cosmopolitan circles in Argentina, see Louis, *Borges ante el fascismo*. For a discussion of Latin American cosmopolitanism more generally, see Siskind, *Cosmopolitan Desires*.

47 Borges, *Selected Non-fictions*, 427.

48 Veblen, "The Intellectual Pre-Eminence of Jews in Modern Europe," 40.

49 From an interview published in *Raíces*, 1971. Quoted in Cohen, *Borges, el judaísmo e Israel*, 168–169.

50 Borges, *Collected Fictions*, 324.

51 For a related reading of "The Theme of the Traitor and the Hero" see Robin Fiddian, "Borges on Location: Duplicitous Narration and Historical Truths in 'Tema del traidor y del heroe'," *The Modern Language Review* 105, no. 3 (2010). For related readings of "The Aleph," see Lisa Block de Behar, "Rereading Borges' 'The Aleph': On the Name of a Place, a Word, and a Letter," *CR: The New Centennial Review* 4, no. 1 (2004); Edna Aizenberg, "On Borges' Pesky Aleph."

52 Borges, *Selected Non-fictions*, 423.

53 Borges, *Selected Non-fictions*, 423–424.

54 For more on this confabulation and its place in Borges's thoughts on Latin American cosmopolitanism, see Catelli, "La cuestión americana en 'El escritor argentino y la tradición'."

55 For more on Borges's attitude toward "the Orient," see Mualem, "Imaginative Geography" and the works cited therein.

56 Borges, *Selected Non-fictions*, 423.

57 H. G. Wells, *Guide to the New World: A Handbook of Constructive World Revolution* (London: Victor Gollancz, 1941); Bertrand Russell, *Let the People Think: A Selection of Essays* (London: Watts and Company, 1941).

58 Borges, *Selected Non-fictions*, 207–208.

59 Borges, *Selected Non-fictions*, 208.

60 Borges, *Selected Non-fictions*, 208.

61 Veblen, "The Intellectual Pre-Eminence of Jews in Modern Europe," 37.

62 Psalms 33:12

63 And perhaps engaging what is quintessentially Argentine will make Israeli authors Jewish. Borges's lecture suggests an interesting view of the role of Argentina, and Latin America more generally, in contemporary Israeli fiction. Novels such as *Bishvilah Giborim Afim* (2008) by Amir Gutfroind and *Neuland* (2011) by Eshkol Nevo project questions of Jewish and Israeli identity, and the complex entanglement of the two, onto a canvas of Argentine and Latin American local color.

64 Aizenberg, *The Aleph Weaver*, 58.

65 Balderston, "Detalles circunstanciales," 10.

66 In Borges's thought and writing, the State of Israel thus becomes representative of the antithesis of his program for Argentina, in that it offered the opposite outcome to that of Veblen's desired integration, and also in that it negated the

Diaspora existence upon which the Jewish model he had adopted from Veblen was based in the first place. For more on the antithesis of the Argentine and Israeli national projects in Borges's thought and writing, see Lewis, "Borges, Zionism and the Politics of Reality."

67 Borges, *Selected Non-fictions*, 423–424.

68 Diamant, "Una conversación con Jorge L. Borges," 6. I have translated as "important" Borges's "importante" in Spanish, which has several meanings: important, valuable, and significant.

Chapter 7   Authorship and Its Metaphors

1 The book is titled *Otras Inquisiciones* [Other Inquiries] in reference to Borges's 1925 book titled *Inquisitions* [Inquiries]. See Jorge Luis Borges, *Inquisiciones* (Buenos Aires, Argentina: Editorial Proa, 1925).

2 Originally published as Borges, "Kafka y sus precursores."

3 Block de Behar, "Antecedents of an Unexpected Poetic Affinity," 184.

4 It is possible that Buber had influenced Borges's writing before this period as well. Humberto Núñez-Faraco, for example, offers a Buberian reading of Borges's 1943 story "The Secret Miracle." I am here focused on the broader influences of the Judaic on Borges and the central role of this imaginary in constructing his understanding of authorship. I therefore focus my attention on the period in which the specific yet significant influence of Buber on Borges's concept of authorship is notable. See Núñez-Faraco, "Dialogue and Existence in Jorge Luis Borges's 'The Secret Miracle'."

5 "In 1916 … in Geneva a young Borges, seventeen years of age, translated from German into Spanish, the story 'Jerusalem' which Buber had included in the book *Die Legende des Baalschem*." See Block de Behar, "Antecedents of an Unexpected Poetic Affinity," 185.

6 Borges, *Selected Non-fictions*, 200. Vilmar's history of German literature was published in the nineteenth century and subsequently updated from time to time. Borges is referring to the 1936 edition, edited (and censored) by Johannes Rohr. See August Friedrich Christian Vilmar, *Geschichte der deutschen Nationalliteratur*, ed. Johannes Rohr (Berlin: Safari-Verlag, 1936).

7 Borges, *Selected Non-fictions*, 201.

8 In chapter 4, we have already contextualized Borges's interest in questions of tradition in the postcolonial moment following World War II. Borges was certainly not unique in his concern with these questions, and it is not my intention to imply that Buber was significantly implicated in postcolonial questions of tradition anywhere beyond Borges's own thought. At the same time, Borges's engagement with the Judaic as part of his thought about postcolonial literature has been demonstrated in the previous chapters. My argument is that Borges's engagement with postcolonial questions cannot be separated from his Judaic imaginary.

9 These ideas appear in several books by Buber. Over the coming pages, I will offer an account of the timeline of Borges's encounter with these ideas. Between 1946 and 1951, Borges read many books by Buber, including Buber, *Vom Geist des Judentums*; Martin Buber, *Tales of the Hasidim: The Early Masters* (New York: Schocken Books, 1947); Buber, *Between Man and Man*; Buber, *Dialogisches Leben*; Martin Buber, *Hasidism* (New York: Philosophical Library, 1948).

10   It is evident that Borges encountered Buber well before Scholem. I believe that, beyond the dates in which Borges read Buber and Scholem, it is also the case that Buber was the frame of reference for what Borges later discovered in Scholem, which is similar to the dynamic I have presented in part I, where Borges largely finds in Scholem the repetition of what he already knew from his readings on Kabbalah in Bischoff and others. So too with reading Scholem after Buber, Borges reads Scholem against the backdrop of his familiarity with Buber, searching for corroboration of his own views in the alignment between them.

I am disinclined to offer footnotes that go on endlessly. The reader who is satisfied with this framing of Borges's reading process and the place of Scholem within it is encouraged to return to the text of the chapter at this point. The reader who would like to follow a detailed demonstration of how this process can be observed in Borges's marginalia practices will find such a demonstration in the rest of this footnote.

A practical demonstration of this reading process can be found in Borges's marginalia practices, for example, in his annotation of Buber's *Tales of the Hasidim* (1947). (This volume is located at the Fundación Internacional Jorge Luis Borges in Buenos Aires. Scans of these marginalia are in my possession.) In the back pages of the book, Borges left a note about the story titled "To Say Torah and to Be Torah." The story reads: "Rabbi Leib, son of Sarah, the hidden zaddik who wandered over the earth, following the course of rivers, in order to redeem the souls of the living and the dead, said this: 'I did not go to the maggid in order to hear Torah from him, but to see how he unlaces his felt shoes and laces them up again'" (Buber, *Tales of the Hasidim*, p. 107).

Borges's note on this story reads: "To be torah—169. cf. Scholem 344." This is a reference to page 344 of *Major Trends in Jewish Mysticism* (1941), in which Scholem writes: "A tale is told of a famous saint who said: 'I did not go to the 'Maggid' of Meseritz to learn Torah from him but to watch him tie his boot-laces.' . . . The new ideal of the religious leader, the Zaddik, differs from the traditional ideal of rabbinical Judaism . . . , mainly in that he himself 'has become Torah'" (Scholem, *Major Trends in Jewish Mysticism*, p. 344). Scholem himself cites a Hebrew source for the tale, "Cf. *Seder HaDorot HaChadash* p.35." The words "has become Torah" are also in quotation marks but no reference is provided. Regardless of the source of this tale, the similarity between Buber's and Scholem's stories, as well as their proximity to the phrase about becoming or being Torah, is noticeable. And was indeed noticed by Borges.

Although this note was obviously made some time after 1947, it is difficult to determine the order in which Borges read these books. It is possible that Borges was reading the book by Buber when he came across a story that reminded him of a page in Scholem. However, while the reference to page 344 in Scholem's work is correct, the page reference to Buber's book is not accurately recorded in Borges's note. The note erroneously places the corresponding story by Buber on page 169 of *Tales of the Hasidim*, while the story in fact appears on page 107.

It seems odd that Borges would misidentify the page number of the book in his hands at that moment. The explanation for this error is likely that Borges did not in fact open Buber's book to the story. He opened it to the backmatter, where endnote number 9 reads: "*Rabbi Leib, son of Sarah*: see 'If,' p. 86; 'From the Circle of the Baal Shem Tov,' p. 169; '*To Say Torah and to Be Torah*,' p. 107. It is told that on his wanderings he met with influential lords, among them the emperor in

Vienna, who were unfriendly to Jews. In a miraculous way he is said to have caused them to change their opinion" (Buber, *Tales of the Hasidim*, p. 322, emphasis added).

The possibility of accidentally reading "p.169" as the page number for the story "to Be Torah" is clear. This leads me to believe that it was in fact Scholem's book that was open to page 344 and accurately recorded, while Borges only opened to the back pages of Buber's book in order to make a quick note indicating he had encountered a similar story in Scholem. I have not been able to locate Borges's copy of *Major Trends in Jewish Mysticism*. Without access to this copy, it is impossible to know whether a corresponding note was also made in the back pages of Scholem's book.

There is a methodological lesson to be highlighted here as well, which goes back to my intervention into the study of Borges and the Kabbalah in chapter 1. It is not my aim to assess the accuracy of Borges's understanding of what he reads, nor do I believe such assessment should be taken for a methodology that is able to confirm or to demonstrate influence in the first place. However, the alternative is not to ignore questions of accuracy. For the reader who approaches Borges's oeuvre as an evolving corpus, there is methodological value in following Borges's misunderstanding, misremembering, and copying errors. These instances help identify the processes of intellectual development we are here tracking.

11 This lecture was never published and exists only in draft form. See Block de Behar, "Antecedents of an Unexpected Poetic Affinity."

12 See Rosato and Álvarez, *Borges, libros y lecturas*, 74.

13 Buber, *Tales of the Hasidim*. Borges's essay was first published as Borges, "Nota sobre Chesterton." Compiled in Borges, *Otras Inquisiciones* and translated in Borges, *Other Inquisitions 1937–1952*, trans. Ruth Simms (New York, Washington Square Press, 1964).

14 Jorge Luis Borges, "Historia de los ecos de un nombre," *Cuadernos del Congreso por la libertad de la cultura* 15 (1955).

15 Block de Behar, "Antecedents of an Unexpected Poetic Affinity," 184.

16 Franz Kafka, *The Complete Stories*, ed. Nahum Glatzer (New York: Schocken Books, 1971), 22–23.

17 Borges, *Other Inquisitions 1937–1952*, 89. The specific reference to Glatzer is to the line: "For there is door within door, grade behind grade, through which the glory of the Holy One is made known" (Glatzer, *In Time and Eternity*, 31).

18 Buber, *Tales of the Hasidim*, 92.

19 Buber, *Tales of the Hasidim*, 92.

20 Buber, *Hasidism*, 3.

21 Buber, *Vom Geist des Judentums*, 47. Borges's annotations of this book are recorded in Rosato and Álvarez, *Borges, libros y lecturas*, 74.

22 Buber, *Hasidism*, 103.

23 Martina Urban, *Aesthetics of Renewal: Martin Buber's Early Representation of Hasidism as Kulturkritik* (Chicago: University of Chicago Press, 2008), 4.

24 Urban, *Aesthetics of Renewal*, 10.

25 Urban, *Aesthetics of Renewal*, 10.

26 Urban, *Aesthetics of Renewal*, 9.

27 Urban, *Aesthetics of Renewal*, 9.

28 Urban, *Aesthetics of Renewal*, 22.

29 Jorge Luis Borges, *Historia universal de la infamia*, Colección Megáfono (Buenos Aires, Argentina: Editorial Tor, 1935).

30 Borges and Bioy Casares, *Cuentos breves y extraordinarios (antologia)*.

31 Buber, *Tales of the Hasidim*, 258–259.

32 Block de Behar, "Antecedents of an Unexpected Poetic Affinity," 197.

33 Buber, *Tales of the Hasidim*, 258.

34 Buber, *Tales of the Hasidim*, 258.

35 Buber, *Tales of the Hasidim*, 258.

36 Buber, *Tales of the Hasidim*, 259.

37 Buber, *Tales of the Hasidim*, 259.

38 Buber, *Tales of the Hasidim*, 259.

39 Rosato and Álvarez, *Borges, libros y lecturas*, 70.

40 In their catalogue cited above, Rosato and Álvarez leave the reference to Ellmann unidentified. Borges is referencing Richard Ellmann, *Yeats: The Man and the Masks* (New York: Macmillan, 1948). The relevance of this reference will be discussed in the coming pages.

41 Rosato and Álvarez, *Borges, libros y lecturas*, 70.

42 While Borges was using the 1947 edition, in this study I refer to page numbers from the 2002 edition. See Martin Buber, *Between Man and Man*, trans. Ronald Gregor-Smith (London: Routledge, 2002), 241. I emphasize the words Borges quotes in his marginalia.

43 Rosato and Álvarez, *Borges, libros y lecturas*, 70. Emphasis in the original.

44 Buber, *Between Man and Man* (2002), 241.

45 See Buber, *I and Thou*.

46 Buber, *Between Man and Man* (2002), 241–242.

47 Bioy Casares, *Borges*, 32.

48 Podlubne, "Lecturas cruzadas en la revista Sur," 120.

49 Podlubne, "Lecturas cruzadas en la revista Sur," 120.

50 See also Judith Podlubne, "Borges contra Ortega: un episodio en su polémica con Mallea," *Variaciones Borges* 19 (2005); Judith Podlubne, "Sur 1942: El 'desagravio a Borges' o el doble juego del reconocimiento," *Variaciones Borges* 27 (2009).

51 Podlubne, "Lecturas cruzadas en la revista Sur," 121.

52 Borges first published "Kafka and His Precursors" in *La Nación* in August 1951. He delivered the lecture "The Argentine Writer and Tradition" in December of that same year.

53 Borges, *Selected Non-fictions*, 365.

54 Borges, *Selected Non-fictions*, 365.

55 Borges, *Selected Non-fictions*, 365. Emphasis added.

56 Published in Robert Browning, *Pacchiarotto and How He Worked in Distemper: With Other Poems* (London: Smith, Elder & Co., 1876).

57 Borges, *Selected Non-fictions*, 364.

58 Buber, *Between Man and Man* (2002), 197.

59 Rosato and Álvarez, *Borges, libros y lecturas*, 70.

60 Buber, *Between Man and Man* (2002), 195–196.

61 Ellmann, *Yeats: The Man and the Masks*, 198.

62 Borges, *Obras completas, 1923–1972*, 750.

63 Borges, *Obras completas, 1923–1972*, 750.

64 Borges, *Obras completas, 1923–1972*, 751.

65 The line appears in Shakespeare's *All's Well that Ends Well*, Act 4, scene 3. Borges returns to this same coupling of Buber and Shakespeare in a later poem titled

"The Thing I Am," in Jorge Luis Borges, *Historia de la noche* (Buenos Aires, Argentina: Emece, 1977).

66 Borges, *Obras completas, 1923–1972*, 751.

67 Borges, *Obras completas, 1923–1972*, 751.

68 This lecture was delivered in 1928 and reprinted in Martin Buber, *Israel and the World: Essays in a Time of Crisis* (New York: Schocken Books, 1948). The same appears in Martin Buber, *Konigtum Gottes* (Berlin: Schocken, 1932).

69 Martin Buber, *The Writings of Martin Buber*, ed. Will Herberg (New York: Meridian Books, 1956), 261. Emphasis in the original.

70 Martin Buber, *Gog und Magog: eine Chronik* (Heidelberg, Germany: Schneider, 1949).

71 Borges, *Obras completas, 1923–1972*, 751, ff.1.

72 Jorge Luis Borges, *El hacedor* (Buenos Aires, Argentina: Emece, 1960).

73 Borges, *Obras completas, 1923–1972*, 813.

74 Borges, *Obras completas, 1923–1972*, 813.

75 Borges, *Obras completas, 1923–1972*, 751, ff.1.

76 Borges, *Obras completas, 1923–1972*, 813.

77 Borges, *Obras completas, 1923–1972*, 813.

78 Borges uses the Spanish word "trama," which means both plot and conspiracy.

79 Borges, *Obras completas, 1923–1972*, 813.

80 Alazraki, "Borges and the Kabbalah," 255. For a reading of this poem that connects this chain to the metaphor of the mirror in Borges, see Nancy Mandlove, "Chess and Mirrors: Form as Metaphor in Three Sonnets," in *Jorges Luis Borges*, ed. Harold Bloom (New York: Chelsea House Publishers, 1986).

81 Collected in Jorge Luis Borges, *El otro, el mismo* (Buenos Aires, Argentina: Emece, 1969).

82 Borges, *Obras completas, 1923–1972*, 886–887. Italics in the original.

83 Borges, *Obras completas, 1923–1972*, 887.

84 See Jorge Hernandez Martin, "Kabbalistic Borges and Textual Golems," *Variaciones Borges* 10 (2000).

85 The letter to Ben Gurion was discussed in chapter 3. See Cohen, *Borges, el judaísmo e Israel*, 42. The lecture on Agnon was discussed in chapter 6. See Cohen, *Borges, el judaísmo e Israel*, 201–203.

86 Borges, *In Praise of Darkness*, 69.

87 Borges, *Obras completas, 1975–1985*, 196.

Conclusion

1 Borges, *Other Inquisitions 1937–1952*, 8.

2 Borges, *Selected Non-fictions*, 365.

3 Buber, *Between Man and Man*, 195.

4 Borges, *Selected Non-fictions*, 365.

5 Martin Buber, *Die Geschichten des Rabbi Nachman* (Frankfurt am Main, Germany: Rutten und Loening, 1906). Translated as Martin Buber, *The Tales of Rabbi Nachman* (Atlantic Highlands, NJ: Humanities Press International, 1988).

6 Buber, *The Tales of Rabbi Nachman*, 3.

7 Sartre, *Portrait of the Anti-Semite*.

8 Lewis, *A Permanent Beginning*.

9   Yitzhak Lewis, "Writing the Margin: Rabbi Nachman of Braslav, Jorges Luis Borges and the Question of Jewish Writing" (PhD dissertation, Columbia University, 2016).

10 Alberto Gerchunoff is widely seen as the father of Jewish Latin American literature. He was a friend and compatriot of Borges. His most famous work is a collection of vignettes from the Jewish agricultural settlements of Argentina, where he grew up, titled, *The Jewish Gauchos*. See Alberto Gerchunoff, *The Jewish Gauchos of the Pampas*, trans. Prudencio de Pereda (Albuquerque: University of New Mexico Press, 1998). For a recent biography of Gerchunoff, see Monica Szurmuk, *La vocación desmesurada: una vocación de Alberto Gerchunoff* (Buenos Aires, Argentina: Sudamericana, 2018).

Gerchunoff was not the only local Jewish author to rely on "local color" in their work. Argentine Jewish writers in the first decades of the twentieth century made an effort to fit into the new Argentine environment they had recently immigrated to by taking up markedly local themes. For a discussion of Jewish Argentine writing of the period in Spanish, see Naomi Lindstrom, *Jewish Issues in Argentine Literature: From Gerchunoff to Szichman* (Columbia, MO: University of Missouri Press, 1989). For a discussion of Jewish Argentine writing of the period in Yiddish, see Susana Skura, "'A por gauchos in chiripá . . .'. Expresiones criollistas en el teatro ídish argentino (1910–1930)," *Iberoamericana* 7, no. 27 (2007).

11 Gerchunoff's work was serialized in *La Nación* beginning in 1908. It was supplemented and published as a book in 1910. See Alberto Gerchunoff, *Los gauchos judíos* (Buenos Aires, Argentina: Aguilar, 1975).

12 Jorge Luis Borges, "Alberto Gerchunoff, retorno a Don Quixote," in *Prologos con un prologo de prologos* (Buenos Aires, Argentina: Torres Aguero Editor, 1975).

13 Borges, *Obras completas, 1923–1972*, 1029.

Bibliography

Adorno, Theodor W. *Prisms*. Translated by Samuel Weber and Sherry Weber.
Cambridge, MA: MIT Press, 1981.
Adur Nobile, Lucas Martín. "Borges y el Cristianismo: Posiciones, Diálogos y
Polémicas." PhD dissertation, Universidad de Buenos Aires, 2013.
———. "Las biblias de Borges." *Variaciones Borges* 41 (2016): 3–25.
Agnon, Shmuel Yosef. *A Book that Was Lost: Thirty-Five Stories*. Edited by Alan L.
Mintz and Anne Golomb Hoffman. New Milford, CT: The Toby Press, 2008.
Aizenberg, Edna. "A 21st Century Note on Borges's Kabbalism." *Variaciones Borges*
39 (2015): 51–58.
———. *The Aleph Weaver: Biblical, Kabbalistic and Judaic Elements in Borges*.
Potomac, MD: Scripta Humanistica, 1984.
———. *Books and Bombs in Buenos Aires: Borges, Gerchunoff, and Argentine-Jewish
Writing*. Hanover, NH: University Press of New England, 2002.
———. *Borges, el tejedor del Aleph y otros ensayos: del hebraísmo al poscolonialismo*.
Frankfurt am Maim, Germany: Vervuert, Iberoamericana, 1997.
———. "Borges, Postcolonial Precursor." *World Literature Today* 66, no. 1 (1992):
21–26.
———. "'I, a Jew': Borges, Nazism and the Shoah." *Jewish Quarterly Review* 104, no. 3
(2014): 339–353.
———. "On Borges' Pesky Aleph." *Variaciones Borges* 33 (2012): 47–52.
———. *On the Edge of the Holocaust: The Shoah in Latin American Literature and
Culture*. Waltham, MA: Brandeis University Press, 2016.
———. "Postmodern or Post-Auschwitz, Borges and the Limits of Representation."
Variaciones Borges 3 (1997): 141–152.
Alazraki, Jaime. "Borges and the Kabbalah." *TriQuarterly* 25 (1972): 240–267.
———. *Borges and the Kabbalah: And Other Essays on his Fiction and Poetry*.
New York: Cambridge University Press, 1988.
———. "Conversación con Borges sobre la Cábala: Entrevista inédita de 1971."
Variaciones Borges 3 (1997): 163–176.
———. "Kabbalistic Traits in Borges' Narration." *Studies in Short Fiction* 8, no. 1
(1971): 78–92.

Almeida, Iván, and Cristina Parodi, eds. *El fragmento infinito: estudios sobre "Tlön, Uqbar, Orbis Tertius" de J. L. Borges*. 1st ed. Zaragoza, Spain: Prensas Universitarias de Zaragoza, 2006.

Alvarez, Nicolás Emilio. "Borges y Tzinacán." *Revista Iberoamericana* 50, no. 127 (1984): 459–473.

Balderston, Daniel. "Borges: The Argentine Writer and the 'Western' Tradition." In *Borges and Europe Revisited*. Edited by Evelyn Fishburn. London: Institute of Latin American Studies, University of London, 1998.

———. "Detalles circunstanciales: Sobre dos borradores de 'El escritor argentino y la tradición.'" *Cuadernos LIRICO*, no. 9 (2013): 1–12.

———. *How Borges Wrote*. Charlottesville: University of Virginia Press, 2018.

———. *Out of Context: Historical Reference and the Representation of Reality in Borges*. Durham, NC: Duke University Press, 1993.

Bar-Yosef, Yehoushua. "Cuarenta años de literatura israelí." *Sur* 254 (1958): 21–31.

Barrenechea, Ana María. *La expresión de la irrealidad en la obra de Jorge Luis Borges y otros ensayos*. Buenos Aires, Argentina: Ediciones del Cifrado, 1957.

Barthes, Roland. "The Death of the Author." Translated by Stephen Heath. In *Image, Music, Text*. New York: Hill & Wang, 1978.

Baumgarten, Murray. *City Scriptures: Modern Jewish Writing*. Cambridge, MA: Harvard University Press, 1982.

Biale, David. *Gershom Scholem: Kabbalah and Counter-History*. Cambridge, MA: Harvard University Press, 1979.

———. "Gershom Scholem's Ten Unhistorical Aphorisms on Kabbalah: Text and Commentary." *Modern Judaism* 5, no. 1 (1985): 67–93.

Bioy Casares, Adolfo. *Borges*. Edited by Daniel Martino. Barcelona, Spain: BackList, 2010.

Bischoff, Erich. *Die Elemente der Kabbalah*. Berlin: H. Barsdorf, 1913.

Block de Behar, Lisa. "Antecedents of an Unexpected Poetic Affinity: Jorge Luis Borges as Reader of Martin Buber." In *Thinking with Borges*, edited by William Egginton and David E. Johnson, 183–201. Aurora, CO: The Davies Group, 2009.

———. "Rereading Borges' 'The Aleph': On the Name of a Place, a Word, and a Letter." *CR: The New Centennial Review* 4, no. 1 (2004): 169–187.

Bloom, Harold. *Jorge Luis Borges*. New York: Chelsea House Publishers, 1986.

———. *Kabbalah and Criticism*. New York: Seabury, 1975.

Boletin S.H.A. 20, no. 338 (1951).

Borges, Jorge Luis. "1941." *Sur* No. 87 (1941).

———. "Alberto Gerchunoff, retorno a Don Quixote." In *Prologos con un prologo de prologos*, 66–67. Buenos Aires, Argentina: Torres Aguero Editor, 1975.

———. *The Aleph and Other Stories 1933–1969*. Edited and translated by Norman Thomas Di Giovanni. New York: Bantam, 1971.

———. "Alfonso Reyes." *Sur* No. 264 (1960): 1–2.

———. "Anotación al 23 de Agosto de 1944." *Sur* No. 120 (1944).

———. *The Book of Imaginary Beings*. Translated by Andrew Hurley. New York: Penguin Books, 2005.

———. *Collected Fictions*. Translated by Andrew Hurley. New York: Penguin Books, 1998.

———. "Definicion del Germanofilo." *El Hogar*, December 13, 1940.

———. *Discusión*. Buenos Aires, Argentina: M. Gleizer, 1932.

———. *Discusión*. Buenos Aires, Argentina: Emecé Editores, 1957.

———. *El Aleph*. Buenos Aires, Argentina: Editorial Losada, 1949.

———. "El escritor argentino y la tradición." *Cursos y Conferencias* 62, no. 250 (1953).

———. *El hacedor*. Buenos Aires, Argentina: Emece, 1960.

———. *El informe de Brodie*. Buenos Aires, Argentina: Emecé Editores, 1970.

———. *El jardín de senderos que se bifurcan*. Buenos Aires, Argentina: Sur, 1941.

———. *El otro, el mismo*. Buenos Aires, Argentina: Emece, 1969.

———. *El tamaño de mi esperanza*. Buenos Aires, Argentina: Editorial Proa, 1926.

———. "Ensayo de imparcialidad." *Sur* No. 61 (1939).

———. *Evaristo Carriego*. Buenos Aires, Argentina: M. Gleizer, 1930.

———. *Evaristo Carriego: A Book about Old-Time Buenos Aires*. Translated by Norman Thomas di Giovanni. New York: E. P. Dutton, 1984.

———. *Fervor de Buenos Aires: poemas*. Buenos Aires, Argentina: Impr. Serrantes, 1923.

———. *Ficciones, 1935–1944*. Buenos Aires, Argentina: Sur, 1944.

———. "The God's Script." Translated by L. A. Murillo. *Chicago Review* 17, no. 1 (1964): 5–9.

———. *Historia de la noche*. Buenos Aires, Argentina: Emece, 1977.

———. "Historia de los ecos de un nombre." *Cuadernos del Congreso por la libertad de la cultura* 15 (1955): 10–12.

———. *Historia universal de la infamia*. Colección Megáfono. Buenos Aires, Argentina: Editorial Tor, 1935.

———. *In Praise of Darkness*. Translated by Norman Thomas di Giovanni. New York: Dutton, 1974.

———. *Inquisiciones*. Buenos Aires, Argentina: Editorial Proa, 1925.

———. "Israel." *Sur* No. 254 (1958).

———. "Kafka y sus precursores." *La Nación* (Buenos Aires, Argentina), August 19, 1951, 2, 1.

———. "La Cábala." *La Opinión* (Buenos Aires, Argentina), August 17, 1977, 1–3.

———. "La eternidad y T. S. Eliot." *Poesía* 1, no. 3 (1933).

———. *Labyrinths: Selected Stories & Other Writings*. Edited by James East Irby, Andre Maurois, and Donald Yates. New York: New Directions, 1964.

———. "Nota sobre Chesterton." *Los anales de Buenos Aires* 20–22 (1947): 49–52.

———. *Obras completas, 1923–1972*. Buenos Aires, Argentina: Emecé, 1976.

———. *Obras completas, 1975–1985*. Buenos Aires, Argentina: Emecé, 1989.

———. *On Argentina*. Edited by Alfred Mac Adam and Suzanne Jill Levine. New York: Penguin Books, 2010.

———. *Other Inquisitions 1937–1952*. Translated by Ruth Simms. New York: Washington Square Press, 1964.

———. *Otras Inquisiciones*. Buenos Aires, Argentina: Sur, 1952.

———. *A Personal Anthology*. Edited by Anthony Kerrigan. New York: Grove Press, 1967.

———. *Selected Non-fictions*. Translated by Eliot Weinberger. New York: Viking, 1999.

———. *Seven Nights*. Translated by Eliot Weinberger. New York: New Directions, 1984.

———. *Siete noches*. Mexico D.F.: Fondo de Cultura Economica, 1980.

———. *Textos recobrados, 1931–1955*. Edited by Sara Luisa del Carril and Mercedes Rubio de Socchi. Buenos Aires, Argentina: Emece Editores, 2001.

———. *This Craft of Verse*. The Charles Eliot Norton lectures. Edited by Calin-Andrei Mihailescu. Cambridge, MA: Harvard University Press, 2000.

———. "Yo, Judío." *Megáfono*, no. 12 (April 1934).

Borges, Jorge Luis, and Adolfo Bioy Casares. *Cuentos breves y extraordinarios (antologia)*. Buenos Aires, Argentina: Editorial Raigal, 1955.

Borges, Jorge Luis, and Margarita Guerrero. *Manual de zoología fantástica*. Mexico D.F.: Fondo de Cultura Económica, 1957.

Browning, Robert. *Pacchiarotto and How He Worked in Distemper: With Other Poems*. London: Smith, Elder & Co., 1876.

Buber, Martin. *Between Man and Man*. Translated by Ronald Gregor Smith. London: Kegan Paul, 1947.

———. *Between Man and Man*. Translated by Ronald Gregor-Smith. London: Routledge, 2002.

———. *Dialogisches Leben: gesammelte philosophische und pädagogische Schriften*. Zürich, Switzerland: Gregor Müller Verlag, 1947.

———. *Die Geschichten des Rabbi Nachman*. Frankfurt am Main, Germany: Rutten und Loening, 1906.

———. *Gog und Magog: eine Chronik*. Heidelberg, Germany: Schneider, 1949.

———. *Hasidism*. New York: Philosophical Library, 1948.

———. *I and Thou*. Translated by Ronald Gregor Smith. New York: Charles Scribner's Sons, 1937.

———. *Israel and the World: Essays in a Time of Crisis*. New York: Schocken Books, 1948.

———. *Konigtum Gottes*. Berlin: Schocken, 1932.

———. *The Tales of Rabbi Nachman*. Atlantic Highlands, NJ: Humanities Press International, 1988.

———. *Tales of the Hasidim: The Early Masters*. New York: Schocken Books, 1947.

———. *Vom Geist des Judentums*. Munich, Germany: Kurt Wolff Verlag, 1921.

———. *The Writings of Martin Buber*. Edited by Will Herberg. New York: Meridian Books, 1956.

Canto, Estela. "Entrevista con Jorge Luis Borges." In *Textos recobrados (1931–1955)*, edited by Sara Luisa del Carril and Mercedes Rubio de Socchi, 353–356. Buenos Aires, Argentina: Emecé Editores, 2001.

Castro, Juan E. de. "De Eliot a Borges: tradición y periferia." *Iberoamericana* 7, no. 26 (2007): 7–18.

Catelli, Nora. "La cuestión americana en 'El escritor argentino y la tradición.'" In *L'écrivain argentin et la tradition*, edited by Daniel Attala, Sergio Delgado and Rémi Le Mar'Hadour, 25–35. Rennes, France: Presses Universitaires de Rennes, 2004.

Cedrón, José Antonio. "Jorges Luis Borges: Córdoba, invierno del 85, meses antes de su muerte." *Plural* 18–4, no. 208 (1989): 7–19.

Chapman, Edmund. "Jewishness and Postcoloniality in Borges and Derrida: The Singular and the Specific." *Textual Practice* 36, no. 8 (2022): 1226–1243.

Christ, Ronald. "Jorge Luis Borges, The Art of Fiction No. 39." *The Paris Review* 40 (1967): 116–164.

———. *The Narrow Act: Borges' Art of Allusion*. New York: New York University Press, 1969.

Cohen, Marcelo, ed. *Conferencias*. Instituto de Intercambio Cultural Argentino Israeli, 1967.

Cohen, Mario Eduardo, ed. *Borges, el judaísmo e Israel*. 2nd ed., Sefaradica, vol. 6. Buenos Aires, Argentina: Centro de Investigación y Difusión de la Cultura Sefardí, 1999.

Crisol. "Carácter de estas notas." Editorial, January 30, 1934.

———. "Otro 'poroto' nuestro." Editorial, May 2, 1934.

Dan, Joseph. *Al Gershom Shalom: Teresar Ma'amarim*. Jerusalem, Israel: Merkaz Zalman Shazar le-Toldot Yisrael, 2010.

———. "Beyond the Kabbalistic Symbol." *Jerusalem Studies in Jewish Thought* 5 (1986): 363–385.

Dapía, Silvia. "'This Is Not a Universe': An Approach to Borges's 'Tlön, Uqbar, Orbis Tertius.'" *Chasqui: revista de literatura latinoamericana* 26, no. 2 (1997): 94–107.

de Man, Paul. "A Modern Master." *The New York Review of Books* (November 19, 1964): 8–10.

Deppner, Corinna, ed. *La paradoja como forma literaria de la innovación: Jorge Luis Borges entre la tradición judía y el hipertexto*. Hildesheim, Germany: Ediciones de Olms, 2018.

Diamant, Mario. "Una conversación con Jorge L. Borges." *Plural* 3, no. 19 (Nov. 1978): 4–7.

Díaz Pozueta, María. "From Philosophical Idealism to Political Ideology in 'Tlön, Uqbar, Orbis Tertius' and 'Deutsches Requiem.'" *The New Centennial Review* 9, no. 2 (2009): 205–228.

Eisenmenger, Johann Andreas. *Endecktes Judenthum, oder: Grundlicher und wahrhaffter Bericht [. . .]*. 2 vols. Frankfurt am Main, Germany: J. P. Andreae, 1700.

Eliot, T. S. *Selected Essays*. London: Faber and Faber, 1934.

Ellmann, Richard. *Yeats: The Man and the Masks*. New York: Macmillan, 1948.

Fiddian, Robin. "Borges on Location: Duplicitous Narration and Historical Truths in 'Tema del traidor y del heroe.'" *The Modern Language Review* 105, no. 3 (2010): 743–760.

Fishburn, Evelyn. "Borges, Cabbala and 'Creative Misreading.'" *Ibero-Amerikanisches Archiv* 14, no. 4 (1988): 401–418.

———. "Digging for Hrönir: A Second Reading of 'Tlön, Uqbar, Orbis Tertius.'" *Variaciones Borges* 25 (2008): 53–67.

———. "Hidden Pleasures in Borges's Allusions." In *Borges and Europe Revisited*. Edited by Evelyn Fishburn. London: Institute of Latin American Studies, University of London, 1998.

———. "Reflections on the Jewish Imaginary in the Fictions of Borges." *Variaciones Borges* 5 (1998): 145–156.

Fitzgerald, Daniel. "'El escritor en nuestro tiempo': la conferencia, Entre Ríos 1952." *Variaciones Borges* 42 (2016): 59–85.

Flood, Alison. "Nabokov, Neruda and Borges Revealed as Losers of 1965 Nobel Prize." *The Guardian*. January 6, 2016. https://www.theguardian.com/books/2016/jan/06 /borges-auden-nabokov-neruda-nobel-prize-literature-1965.

———. "Nobel Archives Show Graham Greene Might Have Won 1967 Prize." *The Guardian*. Jauary 8, 2018. https://www.theguardian.com/books/2018/jan/08/nobel -archives-show-graham-greene-might-have-won-1967-prize.

Gam-Hakohen, Moran. *Kabbalah Research in Israel: Historiography, Ideology and the Struggle for Cultural Capital*. [In Hebrew]. Tel Aviv, Israel: Resling, 2016.

Gerchunoff, Alberto. *The Jewish Gauchos of the Pampas*. Translated by Prudencio de Pereda. Albuquerque: University of New Mexico Press, 1998.

———. *Los gauchos judíos*. Buenos Aires, Argentina: Aguilar, 1975.

Ginsburg, Christian D. *The Kabbalah: Its Doctrines, Development, and Literature*. London: G. Routledge & Sons, 1920.

Giordano, Jaime. "Forma y sentido de 'La escritura del Dios' de Jorge Luis Borges." *Revista Iberoamericana* 38, no. 78 (1972): 105–115.

Glatzer, Nahum N. *In Time and Eternity: A Jewish Reader*. New York: Schocken Books, 1946.

Gonzalez Echeverria, Roberto. *Myth and Archive: A Theory of Latin American Narrative*. New York: Cambridge University Press, 1990.

Graff Zivin, Erin. *The Wandering Signifier: Rhetoric of Jewishness in the Latin American Imaginary*. Durham, NC: Duke University Press, 2008.

Gramuglio, Maria Teresa. *Nacionalismo y cosmopolitismo en la literatura argentina*. Edited by Judith Podlubne. Rosario, Argentina: Editorial municipal de Rosario, 2013.

Grözinger, Karl-Erich. *Kafka and Kabbalah*. Translated by Susan Hecker Ray. New York: Continuum, 1994.

Gutierrez Berner, Virginia. "Mystical Laws: Borges and Kabbalah." *CR: The New Centennial Review* 9, no. 3 (2010): 137–164.

Hadis, Martín. *Literatos y excéntricos: los ancestros ingleses de Jorge Luis Borges*. Buenos Aires, Argentina: Editorial Sudamericana, 2006.

Harris, Maurice H. *Hebraic Literature: Translations from the Talmud, Midrashim and Kabbala*. New York: Tudor Publishing, 1944.

Hartman, Geoffrey, and Sanford Budick, eds. *Midrash and Literature*. New Haven, CT: Yale University Press, 1986.

Hernández Martin, Jorge. "Kabbalistic Borges and Textual Golems." *Variaciones Borges* 10 (2000): 65–78.

Huss, Boaz. "The Mystification of the Kabbalah and the Myth of Jewish Mysticism." *Pe'amim* 110 (2007): 9–30.

Idel, Moshe. "Hieroglyphs, Keys, Enigmas: On G.G. Scholem's Vision of Kabbalah: Between Franz Molitor and Franz Kafka." In *Arche Noah: die Idee der "Kultur" im deutsch-jüdischen Diskurs*, edited by Bernhard Greiner and Christoph Schmidt, 227–248. Freiburg, Germany: Rombach Verlag, 2002.

———. *The Mystical Experience in Abraham Abulafia*. Albany, NY: SUNY Press, 1988.

Isaacson, José. *El poeta en la sociedad de masas; elementos para una antropología literaria*. Nueva biblioteca de cultura social. Buenos Aires, Argentina: Editorial Américalee, 1969.

Jaén, Didier T. *Borges' Esoteric Library: Metaphysics to Metafiction*. Lanham, MD: University Press of America, 1992.

Kafka, Franz. *The Complete Stories*. Edited by Nahum Glatzer. New York: Schocken Books, 1971.

La Nación (Buenos Aires, Argentina). "Buenos Aires celebró con júbilo la recuperación de la capital francesa." August 24, 1944.

———. "Los aliados desembarcan en Arcachon y han avanzado al sudeste de parís y en provenza." August 23, 1944.

———. "Muchas manifestaciones se improvisaron en la ciudad." August 24, 1944.

———. "Paris fue liberado por las tropas francesas del interior y el alzamiento de su población. Luego entró una división." August 24, 1944.

———. "Una multitud imponente y ferverosa rindió altísimo homenaje a Francia." August 25, 1944.

Lewis, Yitzhak. "Borges, Zionism and the Politics of Reality." *Variaciones Borges* 35 (2013): 163–180.

———. "Modeling Marginality: Borges, Veblen and the Argentine Writer." *Variaciones Borges* 44 (2017): 173–188.

———. *A Permanent Beginning: R. Nachman of Braslav and Jewish Literary Modernity*. Albany: State University of New York Press, 2020.

———. "Writing the Margin: Rabbi Nachman of Braslav, Jorges Luis Borges and the Question of Jewish Writing." PhD dissertation, Columbia University, 2016.

Lichtenbaum, Joseph. "La nueva prosa hebrea." *Sur* No. 254 (1958): 31–48.

Lindstrom, Naomi. *Jewish Issues in Argentine Literature: From Gerchunoff to Szichman*. Columbia: University of Missouri Press, 1989.

López-Baralt, Luce. "Escribiendo desde las ínsulas extrañas: Reflexiones de una hispano-arabista puertorriqueña." *Historia y Fuente Oral* 7 (1992): 113–126.

López-Quiñones, Antonio Gómez. *Borges y el nazismo: Sur (1937–1946)*. Granada, Spain: Universidad de Granada, 2004.

Louis, Annick. *Borges ante el fascismo*. Bern, Switzerland: Peter Lang, 2007.

———. "Borges y el nazismo." *Variaciones Borges* 4 (1997): 117–136.

———. "La adhesión a la realidad: las ficciones de Borges durante la Segunda Guerra Mundial." In *El enigma de lo real: las fronteras del realismo en la narrativa del siglo XX*. Edited by Geneviève Fabry and Claudio Canaparo. Oxford, UK: Peter Lang, 2007.

Ludmer, Josefina. *The Corpus Delicti: A Manual of Argentine Fictions*. Translated by Glen S. Close. Pittsburgh, PA: University of Pittsburgh Press, 2004.

———. *The Gaucho Genre: A Treatise on the Motherland*. Durham, NC: Duke University Press, 2002.

Mallea, Eduardo. *El sayal y la purpura*. Buenos Aires, Argentina: Editorial Losada, 1947.

———. *Historia de una pasión argentina*. Buenos Aires, Argentina: Sur, 1937.

———. *History of an Argentine Passion*. Translated by Myron Lichtblau. Pittsburgh, PA: Latin American Literary Review Press, 1983.

Mandlove, Nancy. "Chess and Mirrors: Form as Metaphor in Three Sonnets." In *Jorges Luis Borges*. Edited by Harold Bloom. New York: Chelsea House Publishers, 1986.

Mathers, S. L. MacGregor. *The Kabbalah Unveiled*. London: Routledge & Kegan Paul, 1957.

Mendes-Flohr, Paul. *Gershom Scholem: The Man and his Work*. Albany, NY: SUNY Press and The Israel Academy of Sciences and Humanities, 1994.

Meyrink, Gustav. *Der Golem*. Leipzig, Germany: Kurt Wolff, 1915.

Miron, Dan. *The Animal in the Synagogue: Franz Kafka's Jewishness*. Translated by Yitzhak Lewis. Lanham, MD: Lexington Books, 2019.

———. *From Continuity to Contiguity: Toward a New Jewish Literary Thinking*. Stanford, CA: Stanford University Press, 2010.

Molloy, Sylvia. *Signs of Borges*. Translated by Oscar Montero. Durham, NC: Duke University Press, 1994.

Montaldo, Graciela. "Borges: una vanguardia criolla." In *Yrigoyen entre Borges y Arlt: 1916–1930*. Edited by Graciela Montaldo. Buenos Aires, Argentina: Contrapunto, 1989.

Moreiras, Alberto. "The Villain at the Center: Infrapolitical Borges." In *Comparative Cultural Studies and Latin America*. Edited by Sophia A. McClennen and Earl E. Fitz. West Lafayette, IN: Purdue University Press, 2002.

Mosquera, Fabián Darío. "Una leyenda celta ante la zarza ardiente: el dispositivo judaico-irlandés como interpelación nacional en Borges." *Variaciones Borges* 48 (2019): 17–37.

Mualem, Shlomy. "Imaginative Geography: Dialectical Orientalism in Borges." *TRANSMODERNITY: Journal of Peripheral Cultural Production of the Luso-Hispanic World* 6, no. 1 (2016): 131–151.

———. *Poets of the Ein-Sof: Borges and the Literature of Kabbalah*. Tel Aviv, Israel: Idra, 2019.

Nahson, Daniel. "Corinna Deppner (ed.): La paradoja como forma literaria de la innovación." *Iberoamericana* 20, no. 75 (2020): 288–300.

———. *La crítica del mito: Borges y la literatura como sueño de vida*. Madrid, Spain: Iberoamericana, Vervuert, 2009.

Nelson, Eric. *The Hebrew Republic: Jewish Sources and the Tranformation of European Political Thought*. Cambridge, MA: Harvard University Press, 2011.

Nordau, Max Simon. *Inicial del nuevo siglo*. Buenos Aires, Argentina: Fundacion Max Nordau, 1951.

Núñez-Faraco, Humberto. "Dialogue and Existence in Jorge Luis Borges's 'The Secret Miracle': A Buberian Reading." *Comparative Critical Studies* 20, no. 1 (2023): 27–46.

Piglia, Ricardo. "Ideología y ficción en Borges." *Punto de Vista* 2, no. 5 (1979): 3–6.

———. "Teoría del complot." *Ramona: revista de artes visuales* 23 (2002): 11.

Pirota, Kleber Roberto. "This is the Universe: David Bohm, Borges and the Wholeness of the World in 'Tlon, Uqbar, Orbis Tertius.'" *Variaciones Borges* 53 (2022): 153–176.

Plato. *Republic, Volume II: Books 6-10*. Edited and translated by Christopher Emlyn-Jones and William Preddy. Cambridge, MA: Harvard University Press, 2013.

Podlubne, Judith. "Borges contra Ortega: un episodio en su polemica con Mallea." *Variaciones Borges* 19 (2005): 169–181.

———. "Lecturas cruzadas en la revista Sur: Mallea y Borges sobre Kafka y Chesterton." *Anclajes* 9 (2005): 119–139.

———. "Sur 1942: El 'desagravio a Borges' o el doble juego del reconocimiento." *Variaciones Borges* 27 (2009): 43–66.

Rabi. "Fascination de la Kabbale." *L'Herne* (1964): 265–271.

Rancière, Jacques. "Borges and French Disease." Translated by Julie Rose. In *The Politics of Literature*. Malden, MA: Polity Press, 2011.

———. *The Ignorant Schoolmaster: Five Lessons in Intellectual Emancipation*. Stanford, CA: Stanford University Press, 1991.

Raz-Krakotzkin, Amnon. *The Censor, the Editor, and the Text: The Catholic Church and the Shaping of the Jewish Canon in the Sixteenth Century*. Jewish Culture and Contexts. Philadelphia: University of Pennsylvania Press, 2007.

Rodríguez Monegal, Emir. "Borges and Derrida: Apothecaries." In *Borges and His Successors: The Borgesian Impact on Literature and the Arts*. Edited by Edna Aizenberg. Columbia: University of Missouri Press, 1990.

———. *Jorge Luis Borges: A Literary Biography*. New York: Dutton, 1978.

Rosato, Laura, and Germán Álvarez, eds. *Borges, libros y lecturas: catálogo de la colección Jorge Luis Borges en la Biblioteca Nacional*. Buenos Aires, Argentina: Ediciones Biblioteca Nacional, 2010.

Russell, Bertrand. *Let the People Think: A Selection of Essays*. London: Watts and Company, 1941.

Sábato, Hilda. *Republics of the New World: The Revolutionary Political Experiment in Nineteenth-Century Latin America*. Princeton, NJ: Princeton University Press, 2018.

Said, Edward W. *Beginnings: Intention and Method*. New York: Basic Books, 1975.

Salvador, Gonzalo. *Borges y la Biblia*. Madrid, Spain: Iberoamericana and Vervuert, 2011.

Sarlo, Beatriz. *Borges, un escritor en las orillas*. Buenos Aires, Argentina: Ariel, 1995.

———. *Jorge Luis Borges: A Writer on the Edge*. London: Verso, 1993.

Sartre, Jean-Paul. *Portrait of the Anti-Semite*. Translated by Mary Guggenheim. New York: Partisan Review, 1946.

———. "Retrato del antisemita." *Sur* No. 138 (1946): 7–41.

Scholem, Gershom. "Das Buch Bahir ein Schriftdenkmal aus der Frühzeit der Kabbala." Aurinia, 1922.

———. "Die Vorstellung des Golem in ihren tellurischen und magischen Beziehungen." *Eranos–Jahrbuch* 22 (1954): 235–289.

———. *Major Trends in Jewish Mysticism.* New York: Schocken Books, 1995.

———. *Major Trends in Jewish Mysticism: Based on the Hilda Strook Lectures Delivered at the Jewish Institute of Religion, New York.* New York: Schocken, 1941.

———. "Martin Buber's Hasidism." *Commentary Magazine*, 1961.

———. "Mi-tokh hirhurim 'al ḥokhmat Yiśra'el." In *Devarim be-go: pirke morashah u-tehiyah*, 385–403. Tel Aviv, Israel: 'Am 'oved, 1976.

———. *On the Kabbalah and Its Symbolism.* New York: Schocken Books, 1965.

———. "Redemption Through Sin." In *Messianic Idea in Judaism and Other Essays on Jewish Spirituality.* New York: Schocken Books, 1971.

———. "The Science of Judaism—Then and Now." In *The Messianic Idea in Judaism.* New York: Schocken Books, 1995.

———. *Zehn unhistorische Sätze über Kabbala.* Zurich, Switzerland: Rhein-Verlag, 1958.

Scholem, Gershom, and Edna Aizenberg. Series 1: Correspondance: Aizenberg, Edna. 1980. ARC.4* 1599 01 0026, Gershom Gerhard Scholem Archive, The National Library of Israel, Jerusalem.

Scholem, Gershom, and John Hollander. Series 1: Correspondance: Hollander, John. 1969. ARC.4* 1599 01 1180, Gershom Gerhard Scholem Archive, The National Library of Israel, Jerusalem.

Senkman, Leonardo. "Borges y el mal del nazismo." In *Borges en Jerusalén*, edited by Myrna Solotorevsky and Ruth Fine, 167–180. Madrid, Spain: Iberoamericana, 2003.

Siskind, Mariano. *Cosmopolitan Desires: Global Modernity and World Literature in Latin America.* Evanston, IL: Northwestern University Press, 2014.

Skura, Susana. "'A por gauchos in chiripá . . .'. Expresiones criollistas en el teatro ídish argentino (1910–1930)." *Iberoamericana* 7, no. 27 (2007): 7–23.

Solotorevsky, Myrna. "The Model of Midrash and Borges' Interpretative Tales and Essays." In *Midrash and Literature*, edited by Geoffrey Hartman and Sanford Budick, 253–264. New Haven, CT: Yale University Press, 1986.

Sosnowski, Saul. *Borges y la cábala: la búsqueda del verbo.* Buenos Aires, Argentina: Editorial Hispamérica, 1976.

———. *Borges, la letra y la cábala.* Madrid, Spain: delCentro Editores, 2016.

———. "El verbo cabalístico en la obra de Borges." *Hispamérica* 3, no. 9 (1975): 35–54.

———. "'The God's Script'–A Kabbalistic Quest." *Modern Fiction Studies* 19, no. 3 (1973): 381–394.

———. "'Tlon, Uqbar, Orbis Tertius': Historia y desplazamientos." In *The Contemporary Latin American Short Story.* Edited by Rose S. Minc. New York: Senda Nueva, 1979.

Stavans, Ilan. "Borges's Zionist Bent: Newly Translated Poems." *The Jewish Daily Forward*, January 2, 2009.

Stehelin, John Peter. *The Traditions of the Jews; With the Expositions and Doctrines of the Rabbins, Contained in the Talmud and other Rabbinical Writings. Translated from the Hight Dutch.* London, 1732.

Steiner, George. *After Babel: Aspects of Language and Translation.* London: Oxford University Press, 1975.

Strauss, Walter A. *On the Threshold of a New Kabbalah: Kafka's Later Tales*. New York: Peter Lang, 1988.

Sufrin, Claire E. "On Myth, History, and the Study of Hasidism: Martin Buber and Gershom Scholem." In *Encountering the Medieval in Modern Jewish Thought*. Edited by James A. Diamond and Aaron W. Hughes. Leiden, the Netherlands: Brill, 2012.

Sur. "Literatura gratuita y literatura comprometida." Editorial. 138 (1946): 105–121.

Szurmuk, Monica. *La vocacion desmesurada: una biografia de Alberto Gerchunoff*. Buenos Aires, Argentina: Sudamericana, 2018.

Trachtenberg, Joshua. *Jewish Magic and Superstition: A Study in Folk Religion*. New York: Behrman's Jewish Book House, 1939.

Urban, Martina. *Aesthetics of Renewal: Martin Buber's Early Representation of Hasidism as Kulturkritik*. Chicago: University of Chicago Press, 2008.

Veblen, Thorstein. "The Intellectual Pre-Eminence of Jews in Modern Europe." *Political Science Quarterly* 34, no. 1 (March 1919): 33–42.

———. *The Theory of the Leisure Class*. New York: Macmillan, 1899.

Vilmar, August Friedrich Christian. *Geschichte der deutschen Nationalliteratur*. Edited by Johannes Rohr. Berlin: Safari-Verlag, 1936.

Wassner, Dalia. "The Salience and Pervasiveness of the Literary Figure of the Jew in Latin America: From Sor Juana Inés de la Cruz to Jorge Luis Borges." *Latin American Research Review* 54, no. 2 (2019): 398–412.

Wells, H. G. *Guide to the New World: A Handbook of Constructive World Revolution*. London: Victor Gollancz, 1941.

Wimsatt, William K., and M. C. Beardsley. "The Intentional Fallacy." *The Sewanee Review* 54, no. 3 (1946): 468–488.

Index

Abulafia, Abraham, 20, 174n5, 176n46
Acevedo family, 1, 3, 60, 79
Adorno, Theodor, 51
Agnon, Shmuel Yosef, 9, 11, 115, 159; *A Book that Was Lost*, 186n25; as Borges's precursor, 156–157; irreverence in, 121–123, 186n38; local color in, 124, 125; memory of Israel in, 118–123; Veblen and, 121–122
Aizenberg, Edna, 4, 6, 17, 30, 121; *The Aleph Weaver*, 66–67, 163n27, 169n5; on Bloom, 169n5; on Jewish marginality, 99, 178n15; on the Judaic, 77–78, 87; on mysticism, 174n8; on Nazism, 99, 180n65; on Veblen, 89; on Zionism, 130–131
Alazraki, Jaime, 11, 15–17, 61; Aizenberg and, 30, 66–67; *Borges and the Kabbalah*, 19, 63; on "The Golem," 25–26, 151; on Kabbalah, 30; Scholem and, 19, 61–63; on "A Vindication of the Kabbalah," 53
aleph: as cosmic sphere, 4, 117, 126, 155; as Hebrew letter, 5, 23, 32. *See also under* Borges, Jorge Luis, works of
Alvarez, Nicolás Emilio, 55
Alvear, Marcelo T., 86
Amézaga, Juan José de, 42
anti-Nazi polemics, 4, 43–48, 80, 173n84; Aizenberg on, 99, 180n65; Buber and, 136; cosmopolitanism and, 128; Kabbalah and, 7, 9, 156; national

literature and, 136. *See also* Germanophiles
antisemitism, 79, 99, 107; national literature and, 136; Sartre on, 81, 157
"The Argentine Writer and Tradition" (Borges), 3, 7, 69, 73–89, 123–124; Agnon and, 119–120; Buber and, 140; Kafka and, 144–148; Veblen and, 91–111
argentinidad, 45, 80–81, 145
author: death of, 170n27; defining of, 33–37; as "divinity," 37–40, 56–58, 137, 156, 170n27; historical sense of, 82–85, 88; Holy Spirit as, 35; ideal, 29–31; intention of, 170n27; vindication of, 31–33. *See also* intellectual author
authorship, 7–8, 69–70, 156; Buber on, 140–141; Kabbalistic allusions to, 31–32, 51, 69, 152; metaphors of, 8, 30, 135–138, 148–153, 155; models of, 62; poetic, 35

Balderston, Daniel, 46–47, 49, 110, 131
Balfour Declaration (1917), 101. *See also* Zionism
Barthes, Roland, 6–7, 170n27
Baumgarten, Murray, 121–122, 123
Ben Gurion, David, 60–61, 152
Bhagavad Gita, 53
Biale, David, 164n3
Bible translations, 163n27. *See also* Scripture
Bioy Casares, Adolfo, 80, 144

About the Author

YITZHAK LEWIS is an assistant professor of humanities at Duke Kunshan University in China. His research interests include comparative literature in Hebrew, Spanish, and Yiddish; literary and cultural theory; transnational writing; and world literature. He is author of *A Permanent Beginning: R. Nachman of Braslav and Jewish Literary Modernity*.